THE FAMILY OF WOMAN

THE FAMILY OF WOMAN

Lesbian Mothers, Their Children,
and the Undoing of Gender

Maureen Sullivan

University of California Press   Berkeley   Los Angeles   London

University of California Press
Berkeley and Los Angeles, California

University of California Press, Ltd.
London, England

© 2004 by the Regents of the University of California

Library of Congress Cataloging-in-Publication Data

Sullivan, Maureen, 1963–.
    The family of woman : lesbian mothers, their children, and the
undoing of gender / Maureen Sullivan.
        p.   cm.
    Includes bibliographical references and index.
    ISBN 0-520-23963-6 (alk. paper)—ISBN 0-520-23964-4 (alk.
paper)
    1. Lesbian mothers—United States—Case studies.   2. Children
of gay parents—United States—Case studies.   3. Sex role—United
States—Case studies.   I. Title.

HQ75.53.S85   2004
306.874'3'08664—dc22   2003070281

Manufactured in the United States of America
13   12   11   10   09   08   07   06   05   04
10   9   8   7   6   5   4   3   2   1

The paper used in this publication meets the minimum requirements of ANSI/NISO Z39.48–1992 (R 1997) (*Permanence of
Paper*).

For the women and children whose
stories are in this book

CONTENTS

Acknowledgments   ix

Introduction   1

1. The Emergence of Lesbian-Coparent Families
   in Postmodern Society   17

2. Becoming Parents: Baby Making in the Age
   of Assisted Procreation   40

3. Being Parents: The End of Oedipus and the Expansion
   of Intimacy   62

4. Undoing the Gender Division of Labor   93

5. Truth and Reconciliation: Families of Origin Come
   Around and Come Out   124

6. Becoming Familiar in the Community
   of Strangers   157

7. The Structure of Donor-Extended Kinship   190

8.   The Theoretical Future of a Conscious
      Feminist Kinship   211

      Appendix: Families by the Bay: The Study Design,
      Method, and Participants   231

      Notes   247

      Bibliography   285

      Index   305

ACKNOWLEDGMENTS

I am indebted to a great number of people whose support, guidance, and critical feedback enabled me to complete this book. The book was first conceived as a doctoral dissertation research project in 1993, and my mentors in the Department of Sociology and Women's Studies Program at the University of California at Davis (UC Davis) generously gave me their unflagging confidence and encouragement throughout the dissertation research and writing process. Judith Stacey, Carole Joffe, Linda Morris, and Diane Wolf gave me critical feedback and gentle prodding at the most crucial moments, enabling me to complete the doctoral requirements and begin to see the book that would emerge. I am especially grateful to Judith Stacey, whose rigorous intellectual tutelage and creativity inspired me to pursue themes I would not have if left to my own devices. At the same time, Carole Joffe tempered my wilder impulses with her consistently sensible counsel. Linda Morris and Diane Wolf provided critical feedback on a later draft of this work.

I am indebted to other colleagues and friends who have shown their support for this project and who have read portions or all of the manuscript at various stages. I am grateful to Erik Olin Wright, whose ongoing engagement with the theoretical concerns of the book encouraged me to think expansively and creatively about them. Ellen Lewin and Arlene Stein served as exceptionally able, insightful reviewers of the manuscript when it was en route to becoming a book. I am also grateful to faculty board readers of the University of California Press for crucial interventions in later drafts of the manuscript and to executive editor Naomi Schneider for her unwavering confidence in the project. Conversations with colleagues and friends at UC Davis over the years—John Hall, Victoria Johnson, Lori Kendall, Melinda Milligan, Estee Neuwirth, Rosemary Powers, and Ellen Scott—were enormously helpful as I struggled to organize the themes of the book to resemble something like their present coherence. My colleagues on the UC Davis–based editorial collective of the journal *Theory and Society*, including executive editor Janet Gouldner, offered an intellectually stimulating collegium of which I am grateful to have been a part, and without which undoubtedly this book would have been deprived of much theoretical substance.

I am also grateful to many other people, including Amy Agigian, Kevin Anderson, Issac Balbus, Mary Bernstein, Barbara Epstein, Carla Goar, E. J. Graff, Mary Holmquist, Loura Howey, Lora Lempert, Lonna Malmsheimer, Laura Mamo, Denise McCoskey, Kathy Miriam, Ilene Phillipson, Renate Reimann, Jack Rhodes, Cathaleen Rich, Beth Schneider, and Etta Worthington, for inspiring me to revise or rethink ideas with which I was struggling at certain times, for listening, and for their supportive intellectual and personal friendship.

Members of the UC Regents' Fellowship Committee in the Department of Sociology at UC Davis awarded me fellowship support that enabled me to complete the research and writing for the dissertation, and my faculty position in the Department of Sociology at Northern Illinois University has provided a welcome financial and institutional base from which to launch the book.

I thank my aunt, Sylvia Schroll, who has demonstrated time and again that wisdom and grace are still possible in these tense and disturbed times. My sister Carol Sullivan has nourished my soul and cared for me in ways that have sustained me, especially during the earlier stages of this research. And to my sister Pat Sullivan, who perhaps more than any other person fostered my feminist intellectual and political development, I give my deepest, warmest thanks.

I continue to be sustained by the love and companionship of John Sanbonmatsu and other members of my family, including those of the feline kind. And as this book has gone to press, the newest addition to my family, my baby son Emmanuel, celebrates his first birthday.

Finally, I wish to thank the women who participated in this research for generously sharing their time, energy, emotional labor, and critical insights. This book is a product of our collaboration. I dedicate it to them, their children, and all our kin.

An earlier version of Chapter 4 was published in *Gender and Society* (Vol. 10, No. 6, December 1996: 747–67) as "Rozzie and Harriet? Gender and Family Patterns of Lesbian Coparents." Portions of Chapter 6 were published in "Alma Mater: Family 'Outings' and the Making of the Modern Other Mother," in *Queer Families, Queer Politics: Challenging Culture and the State,* edited by Mary Bernstein and Renate Reimann (New York: Columbia University Press, 2001).

At the stroke of midnight on January 2003, a baby born to a lesbian couple in Washington, D.C., became, to great media fanfare, the capital's first newborn of the year. At the time of her arrival the baby's mothers were moving their residence to a district where the nonbiological mother could legally adopt the baby she had helped bring into the world, because she was prohibited from doing so in the place she and her partner worked and lived and called home. On June 26 of that same year, the United States Supreme Court overturned an antisodomy law on the books in the state of Texas, ruling, effectively, that the private sexual activity of consenting adults is none of the government's business. And when, during the early summer of 2003, Canada became the third country in the world to recognize same-sex marriage at the national level, streams of gay and lesbian couples made their way to Toronto, Ottawa, and other metropolitan centers to be legally wed.

These three events do more than tell us about the state of social and political acceptance of the rights of same-sex couples in these two regions in North America. They point to social changes in the industrialized world that have been underway since at least the latter part of the twentieth century—changes in which sexuality and procreation have become uncoupled and baby making of all sorts, including the hi-tech and clinical kind, has increasingly occurred outside heterosexual marriage. Governments respond in different ways to these new modes of family formation and intimacy. But the results of these changes must be understood as nothing less than novel kinship formations that depart radically from those of the past and from all convention.

New social formations themselves prompt innovations in other institutional arenas, including those that helped to produce the new formations in the first place. Social relations between women and men, sexuality, concepts of self and identity, knowledge, politics, and culture—all of these and more are affected by the new family formations appearing in North America and throughout the developed world. There is much to be learned from these families that break with convention, not the least of which is how they are doing and the ways they are transforming our culture. The theoretical, political, and social implications for Western society are potentially staggering, particularly the changes that may occur, for example, in the societal gender order, in which men remain dominant, controlling resources and wielding authority, while women gain snippets of status here and there but rarely "freedom" or "emancipation" on a collective level. What may we expect to see within and outside such a significant societal institution as "the family" when a major structural feature of it has been radically altered?

Historically, feminist analysts, from first-wave white, middle-class feminist writers and activists during the mid–nineteenth century in the United States and England to later second-wave radical thinkers (again mostly Euro-American and middle class), have trenchantly criticized what they have seen as a recurrent pattern within families for which heterosexual procreation and parenting supplied the basic familial context: women assume primary responsibility for child care and other unremunerated domestic labor while men develop relationships and maintain status in the extrafamilial public sphere of production, politics, and culture. With women doing more unpaid, socially necessary labor than men, the consequences for them as a subservient class have been predictable and enduring. Women and their children are dependent on unreliable male income providers or the state for their very survival. In the United States, the feminization of poverty, the growing number of children living in poverty, and, more recently, the increase of African American children living in extreme poverty illustrate the net material effect of generations of women doing unpaid domestic labor and low-paid wage labor while husbands and male partners exercise the freedom to determine their own fate and theirs alone.

At the beginning of the twentieth century, Charlotte Perkins Gilman conceptualized this situation as the "sexuo-economic relation," whereby women, put simply, trade sex for their daily bread. Women's bodies, reproductive capacity, sexuality, emotions, and labor are used by men, whose superior social capital has enabled them to own and control these female commodities. Seventy years later, Shulamith Firestone, in her second-wave radical feminist treatise *The Dialectic of Sex,* expressed the belief that the problem lay substantially in the fact that only women were biologically equipped and responsible for the reproduction of the species. As soon as reproductive technology eliminated physiologically based conception, gestation, and birth of new humans, she argued, women would no longer be disproportionately burdened with this task of population replacement and, more important, could no longer be exploited by men on account of it.[1]

At the beginning of the twenty-first century, Western biomedical science is quickly approaching the Firestone moment. But the implementation of ever greater "advances" in reprogenetic technologies points out what other feminist observers have thought for some time: Firestone's apparently "natural" unequal distribution of biological reproductive tasks between the sexes does not in itself give rise to gendered social relations, which merely reflect or accommodate the underlying biological division. Rather, gender conventions—enduring ideas about women's and men's appropriate roles, responsibilities, and conduct—constitute the ground on which men justify their exploitation and subordination of women and extract women's "consent" to this state of affairs. Ideas and assumptions about biological reproduction, about what women's and men's sexed bodies mean, or even that bodies are sexed create the basis for our thinking that reproductive anatomy furnishes important natural clues as to how human society, and more specifically human primary groups such as families, ought to be organized.

Radical socialist contemporaries of Firestone, such as the French philosopher Monique Wittig, following de Beauvoir, along with authors of feminist utopian fiction, such as Marge Piercy and Ursula Le Guin, theorized (and fantasized) that the prospects for societal gender egalitarianism were promising where domestic experiments in conscious, equitable child care and household labor were possible. But for Le Guin and Wittig, the categories of male and female, the "classes" of "women" and "men" themselves, first needed to be abolished. Thus Le Guin populated her utopian society in *Left Hand of Darkness* with androgynous beings, while Wittig emphasized that the categories of "male" and "female" construct the differences that are then attributed to biology and that consequently these metaphysical constructs must be eradicated.[2]

Short of androgyny as the ideal solution, social experiments in conscious sex equity within domestic arrangements seemed desirable to some second-wave feminists. For heterosexual-parent families, such experiments (whether based on communal or dual-parenting arrangements) would involve male partners actively and equally sharing in domestic work and child rearing, perhaps even forgoing occupational achievement and economic security in favor of more flexible jobs enabling them to uphold their egalitarian family practice. For heterosexual-parent families, this would be a solution to the gendered power men exercise over and against women, for in redistributing unremunerated domestic labor equally between adults, partners would discontinue the process whereby men vis-à-vis women accumulate economic advantage, or what the social theorist R. W. Connell calls the "patriarchal dividend."[3] Gilman's sexuo-economic relation would be disabled.

Although some analysts documenting trends from the 1970s to the 1980s viewed changes in the economic and sexual independence of white, middle-class women as movement toward equality, second-wave feminists did not see their vision of equitable domestic arrangements materialize in the United States. Similar efforts to achieve this vision in many northwestern European countries produced few significant results.[4] Although women's aggregate labor force participation and educational opportunities steadily expanded, such ostensibly favorable societal trends actually did little to ameliorate women's subordinated economic and social position. For, as feminist economic analysis points out, women's level of labor force participation is in fact dictated by their family responsibilities, responsibilities that nowadays include not only child care and household work but care of elderly family members as well.[5]

Some second-wave feminist analysts and other women, both during the heady decades of their political writing and social experimentation and later, concluded that egalitarian heterosexual relations and families were not possible. Several women who are the subjects of this book were in their twenties during the late 1960s and 1970s and were exclusively heterosexual then. Now they are coparents to children borne by younger women partners, and they describe poignantly, sometimes angrily, their earlier family situations with indifferent or willfully dominating male spouses and partners. One in particular saw her ex-husband's abusively controlling behavior as stemming from his breadwinner role: at the time, it seemed to her that because her husband earned more money than she did, he could claim the prerogative of demanding her total compliance with his wishes. Others recall their observations over the years of heterosexual-parent families, including their own families of origin, in which the evidence of male domination and often violence so powerfully etched itself in their minds that they view the fatherless families they have now created and live in as blessings.[6] But whether they see male domination within heterosexual-parent families in its brute expression as physical violence or psychological abuse or as a "rational" playing out of men's advantaged economic position compared to women's, women in this book as well as many critical feminist analysts doubt that gendered social power in families is a thing of the past. The institutionalization of the battered women's movement and the feminization of poverty offer sufficient evidence for the persistence of male dominance in families.

More affirmatively, feminist and sociological analyses have indicated what *would* be needed for more egalitarian gender relations both within and outside families. For heterosexual-parent families, the proposition has mostly remained unchanged from the earlier analysis: heterosexual men must consciously resist, must continuously foreswear, their gender privilege, becoming real partners to their wives and lovers and involving themselves fully with their children as caregiving and not just recreational or breadwinning parents. For too many African American families, the denial of these basic family roles to incarcerated male kinfolk creates an impossible burden for women to bear alone—even with assistance from extended family. For black communities all throughout the United States, the institutionalized racism that has prevented scores of African American men from participating in family life more fully and constructively must be eradicated. There must be an ongoing abolition movement to end the slavery of prison and the unjust incarceration of African Americans everywhere—not just those with celebrity status.

Since the possibility of full male participation in family life has yet to be realized on any substantial collective level[7]—a situation that clearly reflects powerful social structural, ideological, and psychological resistance—it is important that we may now have a viable alternative family type from which to learn whether and how gender equality might be achieved. For with the emergence of lesbian- and gay-parent families in recent years comes the promising opportunity to explore how their practices, in principle free of historically produced, socially enforced gender conventions, might point the way toward the disconnection of gender and power, not only in their families, but in other societal arenas and institutions. A primary aim of this book is thus to explore whether, and how, the practices of dual-mother families may challenge the constitutive substance of gendered social power.

UTOPIA NOW?

The family, in most strands of social thought, is intricately bound up with gender, so much so that it is difficult to understand the relationship between them. The most rudimentary (and schematic) expression of the relationship between family and gender is that the family produces gender and is itself structured by gender, where gender is understood broadly as a set of social relations that distributes humans into dimorphic sexes and thereby organizes biological reproduction, emotional cathexis, and erotic desire around those two sexes.

The family's role in the production and reproduction of gender, on the one hand, occurs through the socialization of children. In Freudian terms, children's gender identity consolidates by means of the successful resolution of the oedipal crisis. On the other hand, parents themselves have already been "socialized" by the gender system—which includes the wider cultural meanings and expectations associated with dimorphic sex—and project their own internalized understandings of gender and sexuality in their relations with spouses, lovers, and children. None of these relations or processes is a matter of straightforward reproduction or correspondence; they are extremely complex, with the family itself mediated so much by and through other institutions, including mass media, that it may make sense to begin thinking of the *family-in-representation* as more important than families in actuality in the production of gendered persons.[8] Summarizing the relationship of gender to family, Nancy Chodorow wrote in 1978:

> Psychoanalysis shows us how the family division of labor in which women mother gives socially and historically specific meaning to gender itself. This engendering of men and women with particular personalities, needs, defenses, and capacities creates the condition for and contributes to the reproduction of this same division of labor. The sexual division of labor both produces gender differences and is in turn reproduced by them. [Psychoanalysis] suggests that major features of the social organization of gender are transmitted in and through those personalities produced by the structure of the institution—the family—in which children become gendered members of society.[9]

Sexual orientation (sexual object choice) is predicated on the social constitution of individuals as male and female, so the significance of lesbian- and gay-parent families in relation to gender and power has more to do with the gender of parents than the sexual orientation of parents per se.[10] The significance of same-sex-parent families for the gender order also moves beyond a simple question of whether children will be conventionally gendered, for this question does not speak directly to the issue of the source of gendered power in families. Power is immanent in gender relations as a result of what Connell calls "the creation of a relevance" upon, and the suppression of sameness of, the reproductive biology of human bodies. Like anthropologist Gayle Rubin before him, who conceptualized the sex/gender system as social arrangements by which "the biological raw material of human sex and procreation is shaped," Connell sees the social structure that is gender as a "particular historical response to human reproductive biology." That historical response, the creation of a sexual distinction of and relevance upon human reproductive biology, conveys social power relationally toward those whose sex as defined by the distinction subsequently benefit from that distinction. The power of gender derives from the definition, meaning, and practices of women in relation to the definition, meaning, and practices of men. Men in relation to women have historically benefited from the sexual distinction and relevance made of human reproductive biology, and because this distinction and relevance occur most dramatically and initially within the family, the power of gender and gendered relations is felt perhaps most acutely here.[11]

Within families headed by heterosexual parents, for whom gendered relations of power have been operative—from the overt violence committed by men against women to the subtler forms of male prerogative exercised over and against the wishes of women—the newest members of society see these displays of the power of gender and learn from them. Children see the relational exercise of power, not just the benign "doing" of gender, and parents feel the force of their relative domination and subordination in the myriad ways it is played out between them.

Theoretically, then, if two parents within a family are of the same gender, the power exercised relationally between them will not be attached to gender: that is, it will not be the expression of power immanent to the social construct of sexual distinction. If gender is a particular historical response to human reproductive biology, as I believe with Connell and Rubin and other theorists that it is, and further, if "it is possible to make other collective responses," as Connell asserts,[12] same-sex parenting may represent such an alternative response. If the social arrangements by which sexuality and procreation are organized do not honor the sociohistorical distinction made of reproductive anatomy, and if parents do not in their own relationship represent biological sex distinction, then theoretically the power immanent in gender, and gender relations themselves, will be profoundly disrupted. Casting it in Freudian terms, Rivers asked speculatively:

> If families increasingly exist in American society where children are being socialized in a same-sex environment, does this not alter Freud's famous formulation? Are the law of the father and the castration fear that accompanies it not affected by the fact that both primary caregivers are women? Or by the fact that there are two fathers, and not a mother existing in opposition to a father who represents the social order?[13]

The theoretical implications reach beyond the family, however, since "the law of the father" suffuses practices in virtually all of social life, including the division of labor, the definition and distribution of authority, and relations of emotional attachment and desire. As Connell has argued, these three domains especially—"labor," "power," and "cathexis"—constitute the structures of gender. They are the fields of social practice in which gendered power arises and that concomitantly pervade such social institutions as the family. A change in the gender arrangements within the family, a disconnection of the organization of sexuality and biological reproduction from gendered power, could have ramifications for the gender order in these other fields of social practice. For instance, if the recalcitrance of contemporary gender inequality is linked to a continuing sexual division of labor within families, which in turn reinforces the sexual division of labor within the economy and society, the prospects for destabilizing this system would seem to be located most plausibly in the practices of people living in families where the family structure itself provides an alternative to the heterosexual-parent model.

Theoretically, much would be different in a family in which another woman parented in lieu of a heterosexual father whose position relative to his spouse and children and within society was one of material advantage and cultural dominance. And as distinguished from single-mother families, only the most privileged of which enjoy economic security and social well-being, dual-mother families with their prospects for dual earning theoretically would be more economically viable and thus perhaps less racked by the stress and hardship single-mother families experience in their daily survival. Though less advantaged economically than heterosexual-parent families with the superior male wage, the potential improvement in quality of life for children and women in lesbian-coparent families suggests an important social and economic benefit of this new family form.[14]

At the same time, the possible quality-of-life benefits of these families may redound not only to family members themselves but potentially throughout the culture as mothers and children educate friends and their own extended-family members, make themselves visible to neighbors and work colleagues, and demand recognition from the most public of audiences: state legislatures, schools, and the like. In this light, as lesbian-coparent families in their everyday lives cycle back and forth through the most intimate space of their own families and friendship circles to the more socially distanced world of work and public interaction, the prospects for progressive social change appear dramatic. For the more viable, visible, and institutionalized these families become, the greater are the opportunities for educating people to new, unconventional ways of thinking about the contexts in which children might be raised with an abundance of love, economic security, social well-being, and justice. It is a twenty-first-century utopian fantasy, guilty of the same romanticism as the earlier movements. But there may be reason for the optimism: if other "collective responses to human reproductive biology," such as same-sex procreation and parenting, became viable, "what would be lost," as Connell writes, would be "the necessary connection of the elements of gender relations to institutionalized inequality on one side and biological difference on the other. The depth of this change should not be underestimated. It would be a fundamental departure from a key condition of our present culture, which might be summarized as the sense that gender is fatality."[15]

As an ethnographic study of lesbian-coparent families living in the San Francisco Bay Area in the late-twentieth-century United States, this book offers an in-depth, theoretically informed analysis of the everyday life-world of families who, until now, have mostly appeared in fantasy and fiction. Lesbian couples all over the world, in the United States, and in the San Francisco Bay Area are creating families by bearing and adopting children and parenting them together. The families who are the subjects of this book are headed by lesbian couples who intentionally incorporated biologically related children into their lives by means of donor insemination.

As one of several so-called assisted-reproduction procedures employed to bring about human conception, donor insemination, like other procedures, does not just assist with biological procreation. It facilitates the generation of new types of families, such as lesbian-coparent families, but it also creates conditions for even more elaborate kinship networks to develop, a topic I address specifically in Chapter 7. The point, for now, is that the "new" reproductive technologies facilitate the creation of "new" families that, in their multiplicity of forms, their definitional fluidity, and, quite simply, their unconventionality, at once reflect a postmodern kinship situation and offer the possibility of substantial, self-conscious social change in family practice. New reprogenetic technologies also threaten to alter, permanently, the nature of human and nonhuman life as we and history have known it, as Margaret Atwood's 2003 dystopian novel *Oryx and Crake* envisions so vividly. It depends on who controls the technology and who is permitted access to it. Families of the two-mother kind where at least one mother is biologically related to the child due to mothers' access to certain procreative technologies represent, for some, an unambiguously beneficial application of the new technologies. In fact, some would argue that gay and lesbian couples present the most socially and politically defensible case for the need for procreative technologies because without them no gay person would be able to exercise biological kinship or reproduction rights, which are increasingly defined legally and culturally as human rights. (This is why the right to—and in the United Kingdom state support of—infertility "treatment" for heterosexual people is considered inviolate, despite the moral injunctions of theologians with a stake in preserving the opposition between God and science.) Procreative technologies and developments in reproductive medicine are central to the contemporary formation of new and alternative families such as lesbian-coparent families; they thus form part of both the larger and the more local context in which these families come into being and live their lives.

Ongoing legal developments also contribute to social context here. Families with two mothers and no father push family law beyond its twentieth-century limits. Actually existing families with two mothers who may not legally marry each other must be reckoned with doctrinally and pragmatically by the legal system. Pragmatically, the mechanism favored by judges and legal scholars interested in promoting the welfare of these families is second-parent adoption, by which judges grant nonbirth mothers legal standing as equal parents vis-à-vis their birth-parent partners. But within the larger political arena, neoconservative politicians and right-wing operatives (as well as more than a few liberal academics) have no interest in seeing the state promote families intentionally formed without fathers. Lesbian-coparent families have thus been born into a society that facilitates their creation through assisted-reproduction technology and enterprise but then politically, legally, and culturally contests their right to exist.

Setting aside for the moment the question of how mainstream culture and legal and political institutions in the United States are processing the latest kinship innovation (which I take up in the final chapter), I want to indicate, in the outline of chapter contents that follows, the ways in which lesbian-coparent families may be understood as agents of social change at the "grass roots" and are thus potentially capable of destabilizing the ground upon which gendered power historically has been founded. If, as so many feminist observers over the years have argued, the reproduction of the social organization of gender—in which men and masculinist values dominate—has depended in part upon the gender hierarchy precipitated and perpetuated within heterosexual-parent families, the larger cycle may be partially broken by a historically new familial formation whose structure and practice represents a substantial break with convention. Lesbian coparents, their children, and their practice, I argue, may very well constitute this break.

ORGANIZATION OF THE BOOK

One of my primary objectives with this work has been to describe and interpret these families' everyday practices and patterns of experience as they narrated them in intensive interviews and as I observed some of them in action. The subjects of this book are thirty-four San Francisco Bay Area families made up of lesbian couples and their children, in which the children were planned and conceived in the context of the couple relationship, and one partner gave birth. In the methodological appendix I offer a complete description of my research design and method, the sociodemographic features of the families, and the social and economic context within which they go about their business.

This group of families is not especially diverse in racial-ethnic or social class composition. No African American families responded to my recruitment efforts, and many families who participated earned comfortable levels of income in the Bay Area of the mid-1990s. The absence of black lesbian mothers in this group is deeply problematic insofar as their experience is also absent from these pages. The degree to which racism shapes, organizes, and colors their experience as partners in lesbian-coparent families goes unrepresented. Throughout the book, but especially in the appendix, I remark on the role these absences play in what counts as knowledge about lesbian-coparent families.

Beyond what may be claimed about this group of Bay Area families, the larger political and cultural context for lesbian and gay parents everywhere has become, in one sense, clarified, especially with the 2003 Supreme Court *Lawrence* decision. In the United States today, gay and lesbian existence, civil rights, visibility, and cultural politics are more substantially asserted within mainstream public discourse and media than ever before. At the same time, homophobic, fundamentalist, antifeminist, and more moderate conservative discourses and groups collectively compose a back-lash force that serves to check the progress of gay and lesbian liberation. In turn, the backlash incites new rounds of gay/lesbian political organiz-ing, reinvigorated educational efforts, and campaigns for social justice. The women and families who are the subjects of this book are part of this much larger story and discourse about gay identity and politics. The story involves strategic policy making and politics at the national (and interna-tional level); the changing values of a culture that has been slow to ac-knowledge that it ceded the moral high ground on matters sexual some time ago and thus repeatedly finds itself in hypocritical stances toward gay and lesbian existence; and liberal academic positions that echo the con-servative family values line about the need to repair "broken" families and to "get back" to a more "traditional" (read: neopatriarchal) family struc-ture and ethos.

Chapter 1 describes some of the features of this larger national cultural context as a way to highlight some of the political stakes and practical con-cerns for lesbian- and gay-parent families in the United States more gen-erally. This chapter also outlines a sociohistorical account of the relation-ship between the formation of gay identities and families, arguing that the relationship has been marked by definitional practices that earlier con-structed gay identity and families as incompatible but later turned to gay family creation as an affirmative act of political and cultural affirmation.

Chapters 2 through 7 present an ethnographic account of the lives of the families who generously shared their thoughts, experiences, memories, and opinions with me. As the interpreter and teller of one of many stories that may be derived from those of my subjects, I've chosen to present this account in a format that focuses first on the couple relationship before children came along. The story then gradually moves from "inside" the family to "outside," from internal family dynamics to relations with moth-ers' families of origin and finally to relations with social others and insti-tutions. Though tracing the contours of their lives in this way imposes an ordering upon their lifeworld that is entirely my invention,[16] it does offer, I think, a helpful structure for apprehending the complexity and depth, the texture and rhythms of discrete life arenas starting with the most inti-mate and ending with the most public. The connections between the per-sonal and political, and between biography and history, come to life.

Chapter 2 thus introduces some of the families and begins the ethnographic journey at the moment of these women's transition from being a couple to becoming parents, exploring the decisions, from the most mundane to the most philosophically vexing, that the women made in starting their families. In this chapter they recollect their family planning process and their experience of conceiving their children by medically managed donor insemination.

Following Chapter 2's account of their experience of becoming parents, Chapter 3 looks at their narrated experience of being parents. In particular, it raises questions about whether and how the psychodynamic mechanisms that reproduce gendered parenting practices in heterosexual-parent families are operative in these families. Here I draw upon feminist psychoanalytic social theory to analyze mothers' parenting practices and their likely effects for children's development—including children's "acquisition" of gender identity.

Chapter 4 continues the analysis of parents' practices within their immediate domestic context, taking up, this time, their division of labor. It considers the total complex of work-and-family labor and thus also takes into account parents' paid work practices that, strictly speaking, do not occur within the household. But whereas in the analysis of heterosexual-parent families one speaks of household work and child care as the "second shift"[17]—what heterosexual wives working in the paid labor force do after putting in full days on the job—there is no "women's second shift" in the analysis of lesbian-coparent work-family labor. One does not begin with an assumption of a gendered and therefore unequal division of labor that has created the second shift. We see how these mothers' division of paid and unpaid labor, like their parenting practices examined in Chapter 3, fails to replicate the unequal, gendered arrangements that most contemporary heterosexual-parent families are still unable to avoid even when they strenuously attempt to do so.

Chapter 5 takes the first look at lesbian-coparent families' relationships with people who are not immediate members of the families they have created, relationships that are consequently somewhat less intimate. But they are not exactly distant, either, since the focus of this chapter is on mothers' accounts of their relationships with members of their own families of origin. Specifically, this chapter attempts to understand whether and in what ways mothers' relations with their natal kin change with the arrival of their own children. It examines differences between the depictions of biological and nonbiological mothers' relations with their families of origin to understand the role that beliefs about biological relatedness might play in these extended kin relations.

Chapter 6 examines families' interactions with people who are nonintimates: strangers in public places, casual acquaintances, co-workers, members of parenting support groups, medical and health professionals, counselors, teachers and principals, and other individuals with whom mothers necessarily interact in the course of their daily rounds. This social interaction plays out differently for partners who are nonbiological parents. Since families "obviously" cannot have two mothers, and birth mothers have the status of biogenetic relatedness going for them, nonbiological mothers find themselves in the position of explaining who they are in relation to their children, thereby creating a new social identity as comother in dual-mother families. In proving that families need not issue from heterosexual-parent couples, they deploy various information management strategies that revolve around the disclosure of sexual identity. Nonbiological lesbian mothers are thus peculiarly positioned (vis-à-vis their birth-parent partners) to educate and foster understanding about a two-parent family form that is not supposed to exist.

This analysis of the interactional accomplishment of a new category of kinship extends to the presentation and representation of the entire family in public places. In becoming visible and recognized, lesbian-coparent families interactionally signify themselves as "family." Their constitutive performances of family occur at their children's schools (with principals and teachers), in doctors' offices, at day care, and at parents' places of work. Chapter 6 thus also describes how families inscribe their existence into the public and institutional realms where they conduct their lives and, in so doing, transform the expectations and normative categories of kinship.

Chapter 7 examines how lesbian mothers may choose to constitute their families in another way: by recognizing members of the sperm donor's family (when he is known) as their family and by recognizing as family other lesbian-coparent families whose children share a donor with theirs, mothers may extend the borders of their kin to include elaborate sets of relationships. I refer to both these ways in which lesbian-coparent families can extend their kinship via the donor as a type of latent donor-extended kinship network. This donor-extended kinship structure becomes manifest only to the extent that mothers choose to act upon knowledge of their children's biological relatedness to others via the donor. This variation of new kinship formation is the result of mothers' use of assisted-procreation procedures.

This situation raises questions about how families and kinship will be defined more generally as a result of expanding First World use of increasingly sophisticated and expensive reproductive technologies. By considering the relationship among reproductive technologies and commerce, the law, and family definition and practice, Chapter 8 returns to the larger societal context. This chapter attempts to account for the ways in which lesbian-coparent families fit into the developing Western family and kinship system and contribute to the undoing of the gender order from which they, and it, have emerged.

Chapter 1 | THE EMERGENCE OF LESBIAN-COPARENT FAMILIES IN POSTMODERN SOCIETY

The trend toward economic globalization in the last three decades of the twentieth century created social conditions in the industrialized world variously referred to as postmodernity, radicalized modernity, postindustrial society, media or spectacle society, and the information age. These terms try to capture the idea that the international order is changing so rapidly, with the breathless rate of technological innovation and the global movement of capital, that the West is in transition from one epoch to another.[1]

Globalizing capitalist forces produce different effects on national, regional, and local cultures. In the United States the effects often register and resonate within public discourse as crises of moral leadership and cultural values. The United States' late-century "culture wars" in particular have persistently revolved around sexuality, family, and reproduction, issues that necessarily involve gender relations more broadly.[2] In the context of the culture wars, in which, for some social and political conservatives, nothing less than the "moral bedrock" of American society is at stake, real American families and real communities of diverse sexualities, desires, and politics have pioneered new forms of intimacy. Openly lesbian- and gay-parent families constitute one of these recent formations. Specific to First World consumer societies in the postmodern era, these new families represent a distinct departure from modern conventional families and present a unique opportunity to assess how a substantive change in a social institution such as the family is likely to affect social relations and practices both within these new kin groupings and in the surrounding culture.

One specific variant among these alternative family formations is the lesbian-coparent family in which the partners of a lesbian couple have planned and conceived children through donor insemination and are currently raising them in a nuclear-type family. A plethora of social institutions, norms, practices, and generations of people stand to be affected by the emergence and viability of families headed by two mothers. In particular, the implications of dual-mother families for the social organization of gender and gendered power are significant, since so many facets of gendered power and gender inequality, not to mention historically influential schools of thought such as psychoanalysis and even political liberalism, are founded in assumptions about the immutability of heterosexual-parent families or are constituted by them in connection with other components of social structure, such as occupational sex segregation within the societal division of labor, or institutions, such as schools or the mass media as agents of enculturation.[3]

To illuminate the specific ways in which such a new, perhaps even avant-garde, form of kinship might be effecting social change, the analysis must necessarily consider the social, political, and cultural context within which it has arisen. This chapter thus traces the historical emergence over the last three decades or so—the beginning of the postmodern era by some accounts—of gay-parent families as alternative families to the modern, nuclear, heterosexual-parent family. Since the politics of "family values" in the United States constitutes the most immediate and contested arena in which alternative families have negotiated the terms of their existence, I turn first to examining how it has played out over the last three decades.

THE POLITICS OF FAMILY VALUES

Some years before the 1992 Democratic presidential campaign soundbite "It's the economy, stupid" temporarily, and successfully, instructed voters that Americans' "family values" were not the problem, right-wing groups in the mid-1970s mobilized to oppose the values of the counterculture, the gains won by second-wave feminists, and the increasing visibility of gay existence and relationships. What we now think of as various permutations of contemporary family values ideology began as a backlash movement in the immediate wake of such landmark victories for women's reproductive freedom as *Roe v. Wade* and other catalyzing emancipatory events such as the 1969 Stonewall Riot.

In the 1970s and early 1980s in the United States, members of the New Right and so-called profamily movements mobilized antifeminist and antigay sentiment, building a mass ideological base, financial infrastructure, and organization at the national level around sexual, reproductive, and family issues. Whether it was Anita Bryant's antigay crusade, Phyllis Schlafly's stop-ERA campaign, or New Right and profamily movement leaders' aggressive organizing of a mass base of "Middle Americans" around "traditional" values, the conservative politics of backlash then, like the family values campaigns and their cavalries of Promise Keepers and Million Man Marchers in the 1990s, worked to reassert patriarchal forms of family structure and male dominance.[4] In her 1982 pamphlet "The New Traditional Woman," profamily movement leader and spokesperson Connie Marshner enjoined the American woman to adhere to traditional values and moral absolutes but also recognized the social and economic tugs of late modernity on her apron strings. The New Traditional Woman, she wrote, "is new because she is of the current era, with all its pressures and fast pace and rapid change. She is traditional because, in the face of unremitting cultural changes, she is oriented around the eternal truths of faith and family. Her values are timeless and true to human nature."[5]

Family values politics in the 1990s conveyed effectively the same message as the backlash to feminism, gay liberation, the counterculture, and sexual revolution in the 1970s and early 1980s in the United States (and in the United Kingdom), which mobilized around reinstating the "traditional" family, resisting the values of secular humanism, and reasserting the legitimacy of male authority and female deference. But in the 1990s, the players expanded to include individuals and groups from across the ideological spectrum and were joined by self-identified "objective" social scientists and academics. The 1990s message emphasized, variously, the pathology of all families not adhering to the structure of the nuclear, heterosexual-parents-and-children family; the specific deviance and pathological effects of single-mother families; the extreme dysfunction of black families headed by women reprehensibly demonized as welfare cheats; and, most recently, the myriad social problems caused by a category of family referred to simply as "fatherless families." In other words, the family values ideology of the 1990s still pronounced as normative a family structure consisting of a heterosexually married couple with children in which the father maintained—or, as some of the rhetoric had it, "reclaimed"—a position of authority and responsibility as the head of household.[6]

Given the almost hysterical moral-panic quality subtending much of the right-wing discourse on family values, it is striking that real, nonconformist families of every imaginable type and practice continue to live in ways that simply do not reflect the story being told about them. Even when political and academic liberals tone down family values rhetoric by offering amelioration rather than condemnation, the story about the moral and social superiority of two-parent, heterosexual nuclear families does not change. Here we see an interesting dynamic that signals a postmodern state of affairs. The French philosopher Jean-François Lyotard claimed that the postmodern condition may be characterized as a moment when the legitimation of the existing order—achieved through historical metanarratives—breaks down and grand stories whose function is to keep people believing in the goodness of the social order lose their credibility.[7] Despite the grand stories being told in family values rhetoric and campaigns, real American families are more diverse than ever; they borrow some elements from the past in configuring their domestic arrangements at the same time that they introduce new practices, especially where procreative methods are concerned; they are fluid, mobile, recombinant, unresolved. In short, they reflect all the features of a postmodern reality that cannot possibly be contained or controlled by the family values mythology.

INTERNATIONAL PATTERNS OF SEXUAL-FAMILIAL CHANGE

If "alternative" families such as those headed by lesbian and gay parents or unmarried single mothers have negotiated their family creation within a turbulent national context of family values politics, larger-scale demographic patterns of sexual-familial change in the United States and other postindustrial countries constitute the broader context.[8] In the second volume of his sweeping three-volume treatise on the contemporary era as "the information age," social theorist Manuel Castells boldly asserts in a chapter titled "The End of Patriarchalism: Social Movements, Family, and

Sexuality in the Information Age" that "[i]f the patriarchal family crumbles, the whole system of patriarchalism gradually but surely, and the whole of our lives, will be transformed." For Castells, the destruction of the patriarchal family is key to "the end of patriarchalism" because without this critical stronghold, "patriarchalism would be exposed as sheer domination."[9] This apparently simple idea is controversial, for it posits the family both structurally and ideologically as the sine qua non of patriarchy, such that ideologically the discourse of "the family" veils the brute social facts of male domination and female subjugation.

Many feminists and scholars disagree with the assertion that the (patriarchal) family is the key to the entire heteropatriarchal system. These objections notwithstanding, Castells argues that indeed the patriarchal family is crumbling, and he outlines major demographic trends that signal a "crisis of previously stable patriarchal patterns," patterns that have been replaced by a growing acceptance of divorce and of sexual relationships outside marriage; an increasing variety of household structures that effectively dilute the prevalence of the heterosexual-parent family, including single-person households and single-parent households; and, perhaps most important, the rise of woman-headed families in which children have been born out of wedlock or in which divorced mothers have not engaged in "successive patriarchalism, the reproduction of the same model with different (male) partners."[10]

Castells presents statistical data from a wide range of studies reflecting increases in divorce rates, percentages of women who have never married, and nonmarital births, as well as changes in family and household formation, fertility, and women's labor force participation for various developed (and some "developing") countries over a period of fifteen years beginning in 1970. The period of change is important for his argument in that he ties the changes directly to the social movements of the 1960s and particularly to the trend toward sexual liberalization and women's increased consciousness of oppression.[11]

The statistical and demographic portrait of change that Castells presents is not in itself especially disputed, as most scholars agree about the basic "facts."[12] They concur that the widespread separation of sex from marriage, the reconstruction of marriage as a terminable arrangement, and the separation of childbearing and child rearing from marriage are well established[13] and that the household with a breadwinner-father, housewife-mother, and biological children under the age of eighteen—the apotheosis of patriarchalism in Castells's view—represents a statistical minority amidst the complex diversity of living arrangements and family forms that now characterizes kinship conditions in North America and most developed countries of northern Europe.

But researchers interpret these demographic trends differently. Whereas Castells sees traditional patriarchal ways of ordering sexuality and reproduction as giving way to markedly different, enduring patterns of intimate association, others "see" in the data a much less dramatic scenario. Arguing, among other things, that the institutionalization of divorce is less significant than the persistent popularity of marriage and that women's apparently permanent presence in the workforce does little to reconfigure the nuclear family, Robert Chester suggests that contemporary trends point to the rise of the "neo-conventional family," a different but not radically altered version of the heteropatriarchal conjugal model. In contrast, John Scanzoni and his colleagues argue that the values associated with lifetime monogamy have been replaced, in practice if not necessarily in public discourse, with nonbinding commitments and the serialization of relationships. Cycles of cohabitation, marriage, and divorce characterize the way people live today in multiple family arrangements, and the fact that (heterosexual) couples continue to have children at relatively stable (though dipping below population replacement) rates is less important than that they increasingly do so outside marriage. Thus, they argue, contemporary sexual and parental relations are based on principles radically different from those of the past, signaling a diversity in kinship arrangements and a greater liberalization of sexual relations that could not, with any credibility, be said to accurately characterize familial relations before the 1960s. These two perspectives emphasize a more "traditional" (Chester) versus a more "liberal" (Scanzoni) interpretation of values and behavior that have changed little, in the first view, and so substantially, in the second view, that they represent an identifiable qualitative shift in late-century kinship arrangements.[14]

Other analysts acknowledge a coexistence of traditional and liberalized forms of intimate association in the contemporary period. They suggest that the ambiguity, ambivalence, and contradiction created by, for example, the disconnection between declared values and actual practices best describe sexual-familial relations today. Jeffrey Weeks has argued that "the permissive moment" heralded by the 1960s did represent a historic shift in the regulation of sexuality and family life from public to individual determination and from moral absolutism to a pluralism increasingly sanctioned by law. Yet because our culture is so suffused by heteronormative familial values, images, and language, most people still aspire to create families of this type, however unsuccessful they will be in achieving them. Pluralism and diversity may thus be the watchwords, but a sociocognitive dissonance seems more the presiding effect of this clash between the forces of past and present, of nostalgia and utopia.[15]

While Castells heralds the end of patriarchalism with an optimistic interpretation of changes in practice, the analysis of attitudes and ideals—especially as they resonate with family values talk—points to a much shakier, uncertain quality of life for single-mother and gay-parent families, particularly because policy is considerably informed by public opinion. And if the public still views "traditional" modes of family life as ideal even while the majority cannot attain them, those who appear willfully deviant or noncompliant will continue to be vilified.[16] Depending on how the politics of backlash continues to play out, the public denunciation of "deviant" families may quietly fade away, especially as same-sex relationships and gay-parent families gain greater visibility. That openly gay-parent families have come into social existence at all is evidence of yet another process that has intersected with these others but is distinguishable from them. The cultural history of the relationship between gay identity and family constitutes the remaining part of the sociohistorical dynamic that has produced gay-parent families in the contemporary era.

GAY IDENTITY AND FAMILY: A TALE OF
TWO PATTERNS AS HISTORICAL PROCESS

No single or coherent path has led to the collective rise of lesbian- and gay-parent families today, but different paths have shared some basic elements: awareness of affective and erotic desire for people of the same gender, intimate practice based on that awareness, and personal and collective definitions of family. I see two patterns that encompass these elements. From historical texts, theoretical and empirical descriptions, and various discourses about the relationship between being gay, on one hand, and living in, growing up in, or wanting families of one's own, on the other, I see a dialectical struggle for self-determination occurring in slightly different, but related, historically contingent patterns. The first pattern involves the separation of sexuality from procreation throughout the larger culture and its correspondence with the formation of gay identity. I characterize this a "revolving-door" pattern, for reasons I clarify in what follows. The second pattern has to do with the politics of gay assimilation versus separation from (or resistance to) mainstream culture. Depending on one's political perspective, either "the gay family" is an undesirable instrument of assimilation into heteronormative culture, or it is desirable precisely because it transgresses heteronormativity.

The Revolving Door of Family and Gay Identity

While several historiographic projects have examined the social processes and events that have been implicated in the "making of the modern homosexual,"[17] John D'Emilio's *Sexual Politics, Sexual Communities* stands out for the role he attributes to capitalism and the family in the separation of sexuality from procreation.[18] Building on other sociohistorical accounts of the relationship between families and industrialization,[19] D'Emilio argues that within industrializing regions, the rise of waged labor and the movement of production from household to factory meant that family life became less and less organized around domestic production. Increasingly, as households became primarily agents of consumption rather than production, children became a "liability," since instead of contributing their labor to the domestic economy they now became burdens, depending on the "family wage" earned by breadwinning fathers. The shift in the family away from production focused it more intensively as a site of affective relations such that the meaning of sexual relations between men and women came under greater scrutiny and reflection. "It became possible," writes D'Emilio, "to release sexuality from the 'imperative' to procreate," since the need for large families had begun to disappear with the family farm.[20]

According to D'Emilio, the overall effect of the shift was that heterosexual intimacy began to be conceived of more in terms of personal pleasure and happiness than in terms of strictly procreative activity. In promoting this disconnection of (hetero)sexuality from reproduction, capitalism allowed for "some men and women to organize a personal life around their erotic/emotional attraction to their own sex" and to discover a way to "survive beyond the confines of the family."[21]

D'Emilio's account of capitalism's liberating effect upon the reproductive function of the family (which had the secondary effect of liberating some individuals to pursue nonheterosexual experiences) complements accounts of modernity that credit urbanization with luring individuals away from traditional, patriarchal rural communities. Cities offered the promise of anonymity and escape from "the surveillance of family, neighbors, priests, . . . all the suffocating pressures of the closed small-town world."[22] Thus the emergence of gay and lesbian subcultures, in these explanations, is a by-product of the growth of industrial capitalism and urbanization, but the relationship to family is what is important here for present purposes.

Taken together, these accounts point to something like a *flight from the family*, an exodus, as a condition of the emergence of gay identity, even though the family itself as an institution had seen dramatic changes, with the gradual reduction of family size being the most important such change for D'Emilio's argument. But even though heterosexual relations within families were no longer oriented toward reproduction as a primary concern, the separation of (hetero)sexuality from prolific procreation and childbearing did not alter the basic heterosexual character or definition of families: the paradigm of family still consisted in heterosexual parenting, intimacy, and sexuality. The shift was more quantitative than qualitative.

For many people facing the emotional and psychological complexities of apprehending their same-sex desire within a larger heterosexually organized family culture, a popular response involved the practice of living in "front" (heterosexual) families and marriages while surreptitiously conducting same-sex erotic and emotional relationships. The historian Lillian Faderman has documented the practice of lesbians and gay men marrying each other and maintaining "heterosexual" households while conducting sexual affairs within their respective gay circles, especially during the 1950s.[23] Other lesbians, Faderman noted, married heterosexual men and conducted a bisexual lifestyle, some in order to live under the protective cover of respectable heterosexuality, others because they were "genuinely" bisexual.[24] A 1983 study summarizing the findings of seven studies of gay men and four studies of lesbians found that 20 percent of the former and about one-third of the latter had been heterosexually married.[25] These studies and Faderman's observations, in combination with the above notion of a flight or exodus from the family, suggest a kind of revolving-door dynamic, where some gay people have *exited* heterosexual family life (having come round to understanding their homoerotic desire), while others have *entered* heterosexual marriages and front families for security and protection (and continue to do so).

This dynamic of establishing the gay self in the act of either fleeing or joining the family seemed to take a decisive turn toward the former in the politics and struggle for gay liberation during the late 1960s and 1970s. For lesbians and gay men organizing around liberation and separatism, families clearly embodied some of the most oppressive values from which they sought emancipation. In much the same way that 1960s and 1970s radical feminism, and to a certain extent white liberal feminism, had vigorously criticized the patriarchal family, identifying it as the primary site of women's oppression, theorists of gay liberation did this but took the critique one step further. According to R. W. Connell, gay liberation theorists viewed the family essentially as a "factory" of heterosexuality that served to meet "capital's need for a labour supply and the state's need for subordination."[26] Marriage and family would always be the products and agents of compulsory heterosexuality, as Adrienne Rich famously conceptualized it, since their main function was the repression of homosexual desire. In this view, the family's historical reproduction has depended on the repression of nonheterosexual sexualities. Dennis Altman perhaps made the point most succinctly: "The homosexual represents the most clear-cut rejection of the nuclear family that exists, and hence is persecuted because of the need to maintain the hegemony of that concept."[27]

Gay and lesbian liberation politics thus coalesced around the separation of sexuality from procreation, asserting the primacy of pleasure, desire, and intimacy over marital love and reproductive duty in sexual practices. This more explicitly antifamily "exodus" stance, of course, would be used against gay liberatory politics by the Supreme Court in its 1986 decision in *Bowers v. Hardwick,* upholding Georgia's antisodomy statute. In the majority opinion, which denied the applicability of privacy laws established in the *Griswold v. Connecticut* case involving marital contraception, the language directly referred to the separation of (gay) sexuality from family, marriage, and procreation: "Accepting the decisions in these cases and the above description of them, we think it evident that none of the rights announced in those cases bears any resemblance to the claimed constitutional right of homosexuals to engage in sodomy that is asserted in this case. No connection between family, marriage, or procreation on the one hand, and homosexual activity has been demonstrated."[28] But as Connell and others noted, gay emancipatory politics also asserted more generally a critical theory of sexuality, echoing Marcuse's thought in *Eros and Civilization* and to a certain extent reframed by Audre Lorde in her essay "Uses of the Erotic: Erotic as Power."[29] According to gay liberation theory and politics, then, the heterosexual family was a primary tool not only of homosexual repression but of oppressive sexual regulation and social control more generally.

At the same time that gay liberation theorists held the heterosexual family in such contempt, some lesbians and gay men in the 1970s had been quietly negotiating the revolving door of gay identity and family: they maintained front families, they entered into heterosexual marriages only to exit them later as they exited the closet, and they struggled to maintain custody of the children from those marriages, as the earliest custody cases starting in the late 1960s attest.[30] And importantly, they began to consider bringing children into their lives as openly gay persons.

In one of the first attempts to grasp the emerging reality of "open" gay and lesbian parenting, Frederick Bozett compiled a collection of writings that presented a number of voices and views on the experience of living as both a self-affirmed gay person and a parent. Most of the writings speak to the experience of parenting children from former heterosexual marriages and relationships. Another work, published in 1993, was one of the first book-length studies of lesbian mothering to document the experiences of women in the 1970s who either had been heterosexually married or were consciously incorporating children into their lives as self-affirmed lesbians. Though published fifteen years after she conducted the first interviews, the study, by the anthropologist Ellen Lewin, reflects the ambivalence of some lesbians negotiating not only the dilemma of how to resolve the apparently contradictory need for gay identity affirmation with the desire for children and family of one's own but also the political dilemma of having family in "contra-indication" of the antifamily stance of liberation politics.[31]

Lewin interpreted the mothers' narratives as highly self-conscious, reflexive negotiations of two identities, "lesbian" and "mother"—identities that liberation politics had constructed as incompatible. In Lewin's account, mothers often felt torn between their loyalties to their children and to the lesbian communities from which they had become increasingly estranged, but ultimately their experience as lesbian mothers served positively (and importantly) to reaffirm their gender identity: motherhood reaffirmed their womanhood. As one-time exiles from normative gender identity, lesbians could, by virtue of their motherhood, "claim membership in the group known as 'women.' "[32]

Resistance versus Assimilation

This "redomestication" of lesbian experience and politics fueled concerns about gay parenting and family formation as assimilationist, moving the discourse of gay identity, politics, and family to a framework of resistance versus assimilation, as Lewin herself observed.[33] This framework, which I see as a new pattern succeeding the revolving-door pattern, reflects the experiences and decisions of the first postliberation generation of gay men and lesbians, who came out (perhaps by means of rejecting and being rejected by their families of origin) and have since wanted to create families of their own. The problem for many in this period, which spanned the 1980s and early 1990s, became one of reconciling the desire for (and actual creation of) families with the unsavory prospect of replicating the heterosexual (and patriarchal) model of family and compromising gay politics through assimilation into heteronormative culture *via* the family.

It should be noted that this resistance-assimilation tension as mediated by the family would not have arisen had openly gay persons not pursued family formation in the first place, marking an important shift in practice from the antifamily political position toward a profamily one. For some of the women now understood as being responsible for the lesbian baby boom of the late 1970s through the 1980s, "choosing children" proved personally empowering but politically challenging, as the essays in the first anthology on lesbian parenting suggest.[34] Lesbian parents' experiences challenged the opposition of gayness to parenthood, while their writings reflected the tensions of forging some way through the resistance-assimilation dilemma. Family legal theorist and practitioner Nancy Polikoff summed up the concerns of many lesbian parents faced with this dilemma: "Having a child is a principal indicator of heterosexuality. [Lesbian mothering] . . . does not negate or transform the institution of motherhood. Motherhood, like marriage, is too loaded with this patriarchal history and function to be an entirely different phenomenon just because lesbians are doing it."[35]

At the same time that thousands of gay people across the country became parents, the worry continued—on both the radical (straight) right and radical (gay) left—that these gay profamily practices would "normalize" same-sex parenting and families. The putative concern on the (straight) right was and always has been that gay parenting would morally corrupt and contaminate the sacredness of heterosexual procreation, marriage, and family. The concern on the (gay) left was that gay parenting would siphon much-needed energy and resources from liberation politics; would "redomesticate" lesbians; and, in line with Polikoff's views above, would serve to replicate existing social relations by means of adherence to and uncritical mimicry of the white, middle-class, heterosexual (patriarchal) family model.

By the early to mid-1990s, the resistance-assimilation problem had crystallized around the issue of legal same-sex marriage. Viewing same-sex marriage as a matter of equal civil rights—like equal protection and nondiscrimination—legal practitioners and political activists had generated political momentum and interest in the case *Baehr v. Lewin,* brought before the state Supreme Court in Hawaii in 1993.[36] The prospect of legal same-sex marriage generated a swift and decisive reaction from the political and religious right, as well as the Clinton administration, which signed into law in 1996 the Defense of Marriage Act (DOMA)—a law that, among other things, defined marriage as a union between one man and one woman. The strong reaction from liberals and conservatives alike signaled that gay marriage was supremely threatening to the heterosexual political establishment. In gay community discourse and politics, however, worries were mounting concerning assimilation into and reproduction of inherently unequal, conservative, and repressive institutions, of which legal marriage is crucially emblematic. Nancy Polikoff, again, articulated these concerns in a 1993 article in the *Virginia Law Review.* In that article she wrote: "Advocating lesbian and gay marriage will detract from, and even contradict, efforts to unhook economic benefits from marriage and make basic health care and other necessities available to all. It will also require a rhetorical strategy that emphasizes similarities between our relationships and heterosexual marriages, and denies the potential of lesbian and gay marriage to transform the gendered nature of marriage for all people."[37]

Some of the most compelling arguments in favor of legalized same-sex marriage draw on a social de/constructionist view of social process and provisionally suggest a way out of the problem of resistance-assimilation as it concerns marriage. Legal scholar Nan Hunter has argued that gay marriage, as an institution that would necessarily consist in the practices of the same-sex partners involved, holds the promise of deconstructing the gendered, patriarchal character of marriage for all. Echoing Hunter, Evan Wolfson asserted that the institution of marriage is intrinsically neither equal nor unequal but is greatly contingent upon macro-sociological changes in culture and politics. Both Richard Mohr and Morris Kaplan have made similar arguments in favor of legalized same-sex marriage, both pointing to a socially radicalizing or democratizing effect upon marriage as an institution. Mohr claims legalized gay marriage could help to socialize the meaning of marriage, providing "a nurturing ground for social marriage," while Kaplan suggests that it offers a "site of deliberate and democratic transformation of social norms."[38]

In most of these accounts, the view seems to be that the definition and meaning of marriage, while showing some remarkably stable features historically—features that have appeared inexorably to reinforce male authority and control while at the same time repressing alternative forms of marriage and sexuality—are also subject to transformation through concerted, viable social practice and political action. Further, the meaning of marriage thus transformed stands to have some progressive impact on wider societal norms.

Beyond the Resistance-Assimilation Dilemma

In her influential 1991 book, *Families We Choose*, the anthropologist Kath Weston argued that lesbian and gay definitions of family need not be derived from a single position relative to the heterosexual norm. That is, they need not base notions of family in opposition to or agreement with biological or legal definitions of family produced by and serving the interests of a heteropatriarchal order.[39] Instead, Weston proposed that gay and lesbian families be understood as "chosen" families. By incorporating the element of choice, gay and lesbian families may be unbounded, fluid, and permeable groupings based on any combination of a range of intimate, erotic, social, economic, and biological relations. Weston's account of gay families shifts the focus from legal and institutional definitions to a more conceptual and practical level, concentrating on the experiences and practice of gay families as members define them.

Weston's project was and is extremely important for its acute, even prescient, observation that gay families are inherently pluralistic or, more importantly, that they must be understood as such lest the gay community make the same mistakes in creating families as heterosexual society has done with its hierarchies and preferences for unequal authority, its almost fetishistic emphasis on the sexual-conjugal parent unit[40] and putative monogamy, and its formal, instrumentalist treatment of children as the necessary accoutrements of proper bourgeois existence. A fluid, pluralistic notion of gay family life circumvents the resistance-assimilation problem altogether, offering a model of family-defining practices and procedures that is affirmatively non-normative.[41]

Apart from the patterns of the revolving door and resistance-assimilation, which continue today, the sociohistorical emergence of "open" lesbian- and gay-parent families on a collective level over the last two decades in North America and Europe has been facilitated by more mundane activities such as the dissemination of practical information, outreach, education, and support provided within lesbian/gay communities and networks.[42] In the San Francisco Bay Area in the mid- to late 1980s, "considering parenthood" groups formed and met regularly to guide women through the complex of practical, emotional, and legal issues involved in creating families in the absence of greater societal support and sanction. Educational "how-to" films such as *Choosing Children* began circulating at the same time that parenting support groups formed—many of them organized and sponsored by the beloved Lyon-Martin organization in San Francisco. Out of these earlier pioneering efforts the 1990s witnessed a veritable growth industry explosion of popular and thoughtful advice books, legal aid services, formal gay-parent organizations, and summer camps for children. In short, gay and lesbian communities mobilized to help engineer the gay family revolution that has now secured for gay families an irrevocable, perhaps vanguard position in the increasingly diverse and as yet unsettled array of postmodern kinship arrangements.

MIDWIVES TO THE GAY FAMILY REVOLUTION: ASSISTED REPRODUCTION AND THE LAW

While profamily gay/lesbian communities, by their own activism, helped to achieve recognition for gay families worldwide,[43] they were assisted by changes occurring within other institutional domains: the domain of medical, technoscientific knowledge and practice often referred to as "assisted reproduction," as well as that complex of jurisprudence and practice known as family law.

If Weston's idiom of "choice" applies to today's gay- and lesbian-parent families, it does so significantly in the area of family planning. When prospective parents choose to incorporate children into their lives, they make decisions and undertake planning and preparation with considerable deliberateness and self-reflexivity. The formation of gay families with children throughout the 1990s and up to the present has revolved around careful consideration of, and involvement with, institutions and organizations that facilitate the planning and (pro)creation of children and contribute to families' social functioning and legal protection. The historical emergence of lesbian-coparent families as a particular variant of the gay family revolution is thus crucially linked to the evolution of organized reproductive assistance services and to changing juridical attitudes and principles in family law.

Alternative Insemination as a Form of Assisted Reproduction

For lesbian parents who chose or who continue to choose donor insemination, often referred to as alternative or artificial insemination by donor (AID), this path to parenthood was facilitated and made attractive by the increased availability of organized "assisted-reproduction" services to lesbians—namely donor insemination programs. Nonmedicalized donor insemination has always been available to lesbians and single heterosexual women interested in creating families without men, as the insemination procedure itself is relatively straightforward and does not require "expert" medical intervention. Indeed, self-insemination groups like the London-based Feminist Self-Insemination Group, formed in 1978, pioneered the practices (and ideology) involved in woman-controlled alternative insemination that would later become incorporated in feminist health centers throughout the United States and northern Europe.[44]

Today, many of the feminist principles informing these earlier efforts may be found in the organizational philosophy and practices of procreative service organizations that cater specifically to lesbians, gay men, and women who desire biological children outside heterosexual marital and nonmarital relationships.[45] What has changed significantly from the earlier self-insemination movement to the present arrangement of procreative service provision to alternative families is the increased need for organized procurement and "dissemination" of "clean product" and the management of information and risk. Lesbians will continue to self-inseminate "the underground way," as one of my informants put it, and even though there is no way of knowing how many lesbians are opting to self-inseminate versus using a donor insemination program, the need for, at a minimum, the screening of donor semen for transmissible pathogens including HIV makes the coordination and organization of other tasks under one roof attractive. For, ultimately, among a vast array of "enhancements" like sperm washing, treatment, and centrifuging, sperm recipients pay for semen that has been screened, for the task of locating a donor, and, perhaps most important, for the management of information about the donor's identity. Whether prospective parents want a known or anonymous donor, these alternative insemination organizations sell the service of suppressing or releasing—managing—information about the donor, which is of vital importance to the self-determination and sovereignty of alternative families.[46]

Feminist, lesbian, and gay-oriented assisted-reproduction facilities are thus in many ways less techno-medical organizations than procreative service organizations. But unlike impersonal and rationalized financial service or legal service firms, these procreative service organizations aspire to provide more humanistic, socially progressive services than a strictly profit-driven model would suggest.[47] Still, the potential for increased commercialization and the trend toward providing extra services evokes images, as Amy Agigian has noted, not of "sperm-banking but of a speciality goods model, with product innovation and enhancement, niche marketing, and entrepreneurial middlemen selling their product at a brisk mark-up."[48] Part procreative brokerage firm, part cryo-bank, and part retail outlet, the alternative insemination organization that sees its mission as helping women have children rather than as "treating" a medical condition (infertility) would seem to stand outside male-controlled medical establishment protocols that both assume and dictate heterosexual marital norms among those seeking procreative assistance.

That these services are widely available to lesbians and single heterosexual women throughout the United States—independent of geographic residence, since frozen sperm may be shipped anywhere via overnight delivery—speaks to the growing autonomy of woman-centered family creation. This trend in procreative service provision to lesbians and other women not attached to men thus contributed to the lesbian baby boom(s) in the 1980s and throughout the 1990s, and it clearly arose in response to the discrimination women experienced when attempting to use (male-controlled) medicalized insemination services.[49]

Now well-established, alternative procreative service organizations facilitate the creation of all types of alternative families, matching gay men longing to become fathers with women who will provide gestational services, matching prospective lesbian mothers with gay sperm donors, and generally offering a wide range of family "brokerage" services.

The Law

Family law powerfully defines which forms of intimate association shall count and which, because they remain outside the dominant conceptual system underlying judicial decision making, remain socially and legally denigrated. In the current complex of federal, state, and local statutes and rulings composing family law in the United States, male-headed, heterosexual-parent families are privileged and protected at the expense of all other family forms, especially single-mother families and gay- and lesbian-parent families.

The very definition of family that most state courts recognize and use in their rulings—persons related by marriage, biology, or adoption—was reinforced most recently at the federal level by the 1996 passage of the Defense of Marriage Act (DOMA), which defined marriage as a union between one man and one woman and exempted states from recognizing marriages granted in other states.[50] Because family law is generally carried out within state and local jurisdictions, DOMA's primary legal effect has been to reinforce the autonomy of states in defining familial rights and responsibilities and granting legal status, as legal scholar Nan Hunter has written:

Family law has always been a province primarily of state rather than federal regulation, and often has varied from state to state; grounds for divorce, for example, used to differ dramatically depending on geography. What seems likely to occur in the next wave of family cases is the same kind of variability in the legal definition of the family itself. Those very discrepancies may help to denaturalize concepts like "marriage" and "parent," and to expose the utter contingency of the sexual conventions that, in part, construct the family.[51]

Hunter's optimistic view of the potential for variations in the legal definition of family occurring at the state level reflects the complex and contradictory field in which alternative families in general, and lesbian couples with children in particular, have used family law to negotiate some measure of legal protection and legitimacy for their families. However, this same variability that ought to enhance gay couples' chances at winning legal recognition of their familial status has been just as likely to play out more in accordance with the general conservative tendencies of the law, as feminist family law scholars Katherine Bartlett and Rosanne Kennedy have noted:

> As an institution, law has both helped to implement and constrained feminist agendas. . . . One such constraint is the law's respect for precedent. Law may be changed, but because law purports to preserve institutional stability and continuity, reform must build from existing legal precedents and doctrines. For feminists, this requirement presents two problems. First, existing precedents are often decidedly androcentric, taking for granted and reinforcing a status quo that is more favorable to male interests than to female ones. Second, arguments that deviate significantly from precedent or accepted doctrine are often considered extreme and thus are less likely to be successful than moderate proposals.[52]

With respect to gay marriage, these conservative ideological tendencies in the law appear to have superseded the progressive potential alluded to in Hunter's assessment of state-level variability and discretion: by midyear 2003, thirty-seven states had enacted laws specifically banning same-sex marriage; in November 1998, both Hawaii and Alaska, two of the states in which the marriage restriction stood some chance of being overturned, had passed constitutional amendments banning same-sex marriage. Currently Vermont is the only state to have passed a law permitting a marriagelike registration of domestic partnerships called civil unions.[53]

To compare the United States with other postindustrial countries, those with legal same-sex marriage include Canada, the Netherlands, and Belgium. Those with registered partnership provisions include Denmark, Finland, Germany, Greenland, Iceland, Norway, and Sweden. The Czech Republic and Spain, as of summer 2003, were considering similar laws. France offers "civil solidarity pacts" that provide for tax, welfare, and inheritance rights. In other parts of the world, the South African government formally endorses same-sex marriage; Hungary has a common-law marriage that includes same-sex couples; and the most populous state in Australia, New South Wales, amended its version of common-law marriage to include same-sex relationships. Finally, other countries or regions with some same-sex partnership recognitions include England, Israel, Brazil, and New Zealand.[54]

In the United States, the systematic denial of legal recognition of the partnerships of lesbian and gay couples affects real, living families in profoundly pernicious ways, in areas concerning housing, insurance, intestate succession, and, increasingly important as it concerns residence and citizenship, immigration. For example, because couples may not become legal spouses, foreign-born partners who have lived and made their homes with U.S. citizens but whose temporary visas expire are denied the automatic citizenship rights granted to the foreign-born legal spouses of heterosexual people. In a revealing response to one New Jersey couple's plight to avoid the deportation of the foreign-born partner, an immigration judge asked, "Isn't there some state where you two can get married?"[55] This seemingly innocent question speaks to the core of the problem: even in Vermont, which has legalized a version of same-sex marriage, immigration falls within the purview of federal law, and under DOMA, judges still may not grant spousal rights to same-sex couples for immigration purposes.

The immigration judge deciding the fate of the New Jersey couple was remarkably ignorant concerning the degree to which her decision depended on state and federal laws pertaining to gay relationships and concerning the state of family law itself: same-sex marriage at the state level would gain for couples some measure of parity with heterosexual spouses, but DOMA stands waiting in the wings to deny other freedoms and rights.[56] The contingent, nonuniform patchwork of local, state, and federal statutes and laws pertaining to gay partnerships and families makes it nearly impossible for families easily to do the most ordinary of activities that nongay families and couples take for granted, including the expectation that, when things go wrong in their relationships, they can count on the state to play intermediary with enforcement authority.

How, then, do we understand "the law" as playing midwife to the birthing of lesbian-coparent families? If, despite DOMA, the state-level definitions of family are widely variable, contingent, and prone to promoting an excess of idiosyncratic, judicial discretion, then this contingency may be (and has been) exploited favorably in various cases so as to gradually substitute new precedents for old ones. For instance, functional definitions of family may be used instrumentally for select purposes, as in the ruling by a New York City judge who determined that the surviving partner in a gay couple (who had lived "as spouses" for years before the partner who legally held the couple's long-term tenancy died) could hold onto the tenancy on the grounds that the couple, for all intents and purposes, had lived as and were family.

The same functional arguments provide for the establishment of legal parental status for nonbiological mothers through second-parent adoptions.[57] The creation of families through contractual and technologically assisted procreation has given rise to a crisis of meaning concerning parenthood.[58] Courts are increasingly called upon to determine parental status and rights in such situations as the now legendary Baby M. surrogacy case. Lesbian-comother families constitute another case in which the meaning and definition of parenthood must be revised to account for the social fact of dual motherhood. On a highly idiosyncratic, discretionary basis, then, select county and state judges have recognized nonbiological mothers by granting them second-parent adoptions, and thus lesbian-coparent families have exploited the contingent nature of family law.

Lesbian-parent couples often strategically reside in (or have relocated to) areas where the local jurisdiction has shown a liberal attitude toward gay parenting, granting second-parent adoptions to nonbiological mothers.[59] As of September 2002, nine states, including California, had granted second-parent adoptions at the statewide level, while select counties in these and another fifteen states, including the most populous counties in northern California, had established such precedents.[60] All of the mothers I talked with for this book either had contemplated, had completed, or were taking steps in preparation for the second-parent adoption. (Couples who could not relocate to jurisdictions where second-parent adoption precedents had been set—a circumstance that in itself draws attention to the socioeconomic discrimination lesbian parents face—resorted to other legal steps such as having the nonbiological mother sue the biological mother for uncontested joint custody.)

This second-parent adoption mechanism for securing parental status under the law for comothers is critical for protecting the rights of mothers and their children, who, in the event of parental separation or death, potentially face conflicting custody claims between parents themselves (in the case of separation), from extended-family members, and from donors.[61] With respect to sperm donors, lesbian mothers are denied explicit legal protection from paternity claims because state statutes governing alternative insemination apply to married women and their ("infertile") husbands whose paternity is created legally through the invalidation of that of the donor.[62] Only by physician insemination can a donor's paternity be invalidated, and thus the law compels lesbian mothers, like married heterosexual couples, to use physicians. But even with this medically provided protection—a protection that is not medical at all except in that a medical doctor's authority is invoked as legal authority—a nonbiological lesbian mother's parental status is not automatically established like that of the nonbiological father-husband.[63]

In sum, the second-parent adoption mechanism for nonbiological parents establishes state sanction and societal recognition of families headed by same-sex parents in a way that is more oblique and therefore less politically inflammatory than legal marriage. Moreover, it is a legal fiction that compensates for the procreative asymmetry between partners in a family system where historically the contributors of genetic material through the (heterosexual) procreative act become, by some other socio-juridical fiction or unexamined cultural axiom, The Parents. Second-parent adoptions have thus provided a way for lesbian-coparent families to achieve some margin of legal protection and familial sovereignty, though these achievements may prove to be Pyrrhic, as the same excess of judicial discretion that engendered them may just as easily overturn them. For now and into the foreseeable future, they remain the best option these families have, a state of affairs pointing to the profound ambivalence, if not outright hypocrisy, of a society that claims to want to strengthen families.

Chapter 2 | BECOMING PARENTS

Baby Making in the Age of Assisted Procreation

On a clear day from midway up Mount Tamalpais, with its popular hiking trails and fragrant eucalyptus trees, one can usually see three of the five bridges connecting the various landforms that make up the larger San Francisco Bay Area. Most days the City of Lights itself is nestled in a bed of fog and is known for its chilly summers requiring several layers of cotton, heavy sweaters, and often leather. Many of the denizens of the San Francisco metropolis, however, require neither weather conditions nor fashion trends to display, proudly, their membership in a community that sports and supports an affinity for leather. For here, in the Gay Capital of the United States, as *Life* magazine famously dubbed it in 1964, reside hundreds of thousands of people who have something in common but also diverse racial-ethnic identifications, nationalities, masculinities and femininities, ages, religious affiliations, class statuses, and cultural styles—including those who are in fact quite indifferent to leather. What they have in common concerns the people they choose to love, those they desire, and now, those with whom they choose to raise children.

The San Francisco Bay Area, along with its surrounding counties, is by all accounts one of the regions of the United States most densely populated by citizens who identify with or claim membership in communities of gay, lesbian, bisexual, and transgender people. The city is home to the Gay and Lesbian Historical Society of Northern California, which holds one of the nation's most comprehensive archives of material related to the "history of homosexuality."[1] Over the years the Bay Area has been home to some of the most significant figures and organizations not only in regional gay culture and politics but in national and international literary circles and political, economic, and social movements. The modernist literary figure Gertrude Stein and her life partner, Alice B. Toklas, both had roots in the Bay Area. Harry Hay, radicalized by his participation in the massive San Francisco General Strike of 1934, extended his Marxist analysis to the oppression suffered by gay people and founded the country's first "homophile" organization, the Mattachine Society.[2]

Like the rest of California and the nation, the Bay Area has had cycles of economic boom and bust with continuous movement toward deindustrialization—marked importantly by the 1998 announced departure from San Francisco to Third World production sites of Levi-Strauss & Co., one of the last holdouts of domestic brand-name clothing fabrication and rated by gay employees as one of the best companies to work for. The Silicon Valley still operates some electronics assembly facilities, but more common are the corporate complexes that function as brain trusts for research and development. Like most dense urban centers in the United States and elsewhere in the early to mid-1990s, the Bay Area went digital, and gay groups with names like Digital Queers have assisted various political and service organizations with their conversions to cyberspace.[3] Today, despite the collapse of the dot-com "new" economy, service and information organizations still make up important economic sectors that both serve and employ members of gay and lesbian communities in the Bay Area, including organizations that facilitate gay family creation.

The thirty-four families who are the subjects of this book reside in the larger Bay Area corridor. In the city itself, they live in the gritty Mission District with its savory tacquerias; Bernal Heights, a well-known lesbian neighborhood; and the upscale Twin Peaks area with its panoramic views. In the South Bay they live in Daly City, Palo Alto, and even Felton, a small community nestled in the mountains just east of Santa Cruz. They live in the heart of Silicon Valley—San Jose and its suburbs. To the east they live in Oakland, Berkeley, and Richmond; to the north they have put down roots in the more sedate Sonoma and Napa Counties, the lush coastal region known simply as wine country.

In mid-January of 1994, I drove my aging Honda to the East Bay home of Eliza Cohen, Gretchen Zindosa, and their eleven-month-old daughter, Rayna.[4] As I approached the house, which I was later to learn they rented, I saw a stroller parked at the bottom of the steps and some of Rayna's toys at the top, and it occurred to me that, in meeting these families, I was going to be around young children again for the first time in about twenty years—a long hiatus from my babysitting days. I realized I had forgotten completely what it was like to be with children. When I rang the doorbell, a tall, slim woman with large brown eyes and dark hair pulled back in a ponytail greeted me with "Hi, I'm Eliza," and, pointing to a strawberry-blond-haired toddler, said, "and this is Rayna. Come on in." Rayna was dressed in a one-piece outfit that looked like pajamas. She held a blue plastic block in one hand and then suddenly, letting out a couple of squeals, started waving it. Eliza introduced me to Gretchen, who also had long, thick dark hair. When I saw the two mothers together with their child, the thought crossed my mind that the way in which Rayna had been brought into the world, and the family in which she was being raised, were profoundly unique.

It seems fitting to begin an exploration of a relatively new family form "at the beginning," the point at which a desire for children and family of one's own becomes a practical plan and consequent reality. Like other prospective parents using assisted-procreation services, lesbian would-be mothers such as Eliza and Gretchen may justifiably claim that every child brought into the world under their auspices is not just wanted but wanted in a big way. Prospective lesbian parents want children so much that they undertake even more than the considerable financial, emotional, and practical planning that many prospective parents do when they start families. Just to get to the starting gate of family planning, they must decide how they are going to get pregnant and whose sperm will be used to do it.

Their problem is the opposite of that of millions of women using contraceptives to avoid pregnancy and is at once similar to and different from that of the growing numbers of heterosexual women and couples seeking infertility "treatment" and medically assisted procreation. For lesbian couples seeking to become parents using procreative assistance, their process differs in that their first task is to locate a sperm donor (or broker); they must procure what neither partner is able to supply from her own body. The lesbian mothers I spoke with had different names for it, like "baby juice" and "liquid gold." But for many of the Bay Area couples, even before the gold rush began, there was some deliberation about adopting versus birthing a child. Their rationales for having biological children are revealing of their views about biogenetic relatedness and kinship and the demands of assisted-procreation procedures.

Most of the Bay Area mothers said that they decided not to adopt because it was their impression that getting pregnant was easier. Nina Taringetti, a labor lawyer and birth mother, reasoned: "The concept of adopting is fine except that it takes a lot of time and you have to go through lots of hoops and so on, and it just seemed a lot faster to just get pregnant and do it, you know." This assumption was borne out for some couples, like Nina and her partner Emily Trindall, who got pregnant on the first try, but for others, difficulty in becoming pregnant proved emotionally and economically draining, especially as anxiety set in after months of trying, months of hopes dashed as pregnancy tests reported negative results and menstruation cycles continued uninterrupted.[5]

Most other rationales offered for getting pregnant rather than adopting had to do with the desirability of biogenetic relatedness. But this assumption led to a different set of concerns for many couples. Perhaps one of the most interesting and culturally revealing versions of the biogenetic rationale was provided by Cathy Lotti and Katrina Smith. Cathy and Katrina were one of the most methodical, planning-oriented couples of those with whom I became acquainted. At thirty-four, with a master's degree in health services, Cathy was well on her way to realizing her career goals as a hospital administrator, with a roomy $80K salary to match. Earning roughly a third less than Cathy, thirty-six-year-old Katrina Smith worked for the same university hospital as a budget analyst, though at one time during their relationship she had seriously toyed with the idea of returning to school and doing art restoration, a divergent path from her undergraduate business degree and budget work. Their thinking on the subject of adopting versus birthing a child revealed them to be not only "goal oriented" and "planners," as they declared to me with some pride, but also quite sensitive to discourses of biological determinism and the ways in which biogenetic connection with a child would automatically trump other forms of relationship and attachment. The concept of a self-evident correspondence between biogenetic and ontological relatedness—that is, a correspondence by which relatedness by blood and genes defines human connection—permeated their thought as their considerations moved from adoption, to one partner giving birth, to acceptance by families of origin, to determining a donor, as illustrated in the following dialogue:

KATRINA: We thought first that the only way to feel like equal parents was to adopt, do an independent adoption. I think we were completely convinced of that and that was what we planned on doing.

M: Why would adopting help you feel like equal parents?

KATRINA: Well, now we don't see it that way, but I think it was just sort of, it would be hard not to be the birth parent.

CATHY: But I think another part of it was our families, that we were thinking, like, Katrina's family might not be able to give *equal credence* to the child I bore and my family might not, you know . . . like somehow they might not *buy in* as much as they would if there were a totally *neutral* baby that was adopted. I don't know, this is how we felt then. It's hard to remember why.

KATRINA: Right. We came a long way from there so it's kind of hard to even think about it.

CATHY: So we started there and then went to . . .

KATRINA: Then we realized, wait a minute, why don't we, we could at least have *one of us in our children, rather than have none of us in our children.*

CATHY: And at that point we were focused on, *let's get the other half* from somebody on the other side of the family. You know, like one of Katrina's brothers. We talked about that, we never approached anybody and decided that that was really weird.

KATRINA: We just thought that it would never work. Thanksgiving dinner would be . . .

CATHY: Right. You know, "Here's your uncle and your father!" It was just too weird. Plus we were worried about somebody wanting to have custody in some way. So we [had] made this shift [from adoption] to we were going to have the baby. And then, that we, there was nobody in our lives that we would use as a donor. I mean it would have to be an exceptional situation to even think of it, because of our not wanting interference. 'Cause we didn't want to do a third-party arrangement. We wanted to be the parents, period. We didn't want anybody potentially to have custody.

Cathy and Katrina's conceptualization of biogenetic relatedness as an agent of legitimation providing "credence" winds its way through their thinking in the preceding sequence. They implicitly recognize the social and cultural power of biogenetic connection as a credential of ontological connection. In their earlier thinking, an adopted child would be "neutral" because it would lack the cachet of shared DNA, the genealogical assurance of a shared bloodline with either parent's family. And a baby "neutralized" by virtue of having no DNA or blood in common with either parent would provide the basis for their being equal parents. Despite this, the possibility of a biogenetic connection was alluring, so that they could next speak of "having one of us" rather than "none of us in our children," and "getting the other half" from the nonbirth parent's "side of the family." Remarkably, although these thought experiments assign primacy to biogenetic relatedness over and above other ways of construing human being and relationship, by envisioning how they might play out in concrete social situations (the Thanksgiving scenario resulting from having gotten "the other half" from "the other side") Cathy and Katrina inadvertently reveal the social constructedness of a putative biogenetic relationship. Finally, and somewhat paradoxically, the biogenetic credential that would play so well with the family of whoever became the birth mother could in fact be turned against them should a donor wish to pursue a custody claim. Thus it would be better to "get the other half" from an anonymous donor and to secure the nonbirth mother's parental status through legal means.

Cathy and Katrina's reflections shed some light on how resilient and protean the power of biogenetic determinism is. It never loses its grip on their thinking, and it exerts its influence in a way that requires them to employ the kind of strategic thinking one uses in chess, projecting scenarios or moves into the future.

For lesbian couples, starting families via pregnancy launches them into the world of techno-procreation and its metaphysical ramifications, where even the most seemingly practical considerations require contemplation of questions, such as the nature of being, that would ordinarily be the province of philosophers. They must grapple with conceptions of being and relationship, ontological status and connection, that arise from both the unconventional, technologically assisted method of procreation and the social fact of their being same-sex parents. One could argue that these concerns are present for heterosexual couples using procreative technologies as well, but in practice, the metaphysical issues are already resolved by the structural requirements of heteropatriarchy. That is, to sustain its dominance, heteropatriarchy requires a mystified reproductive process that starts with (hetero)sexual intercourse (although this is less and less the case), creates a sexual differentiation of bodies, and leads to a division of parenting based on the presumed naturalness of that sexual differentiation. Thus, even for heterosexual prospective parents who do not contribute genetic material "equally," or who engage a gestational surrogate, the couple, because they are heterosexual, almost always retain parental rights in contested custody cases and play out their gendered mother/father roles accordingly.[6]

The Biological/Nonbiological Mother Decision

When lesbian couples thinking of starting families have ruled out adoption for their first child, as did all the Bay Area couples, the next decision they face is who will become pregnant if they plan on having only one child, or who will become pregnant first if they plan on having more than one and both partners wish to be birth mothers.[7] Among the group of thirty-four Bay Area couples, only one, Kelly Kronenberg and Diane Chaucer, had biological children borne by each partner. For Kelly and Diane and other couples, the decisions concerning who would become pregnant, or who would become pregnant first, almost always revolved around three primary factors: age, desire, and work; extended-family considerations such as those discussed by Cathy and Katrina were cited less often, but with some frequency, as an important consideration.

Since couples in which only one partner wished to be a birth parent represented half of all the couples, those seventeen whose decisions about maternity concerned both partners cited age or work (or unpreparedness) as reasons why one partner tried to become pregnant first. For the four couples citing age considerations, there existed an age gap between partners that they perceived as significant enough to warrant the older partner's trying first. About thirteen couples—three-quarters of the couples in which both partners wished to be biological mothers—cited as a reason the nonbirth parent's work or career situation, stating that it seemed incompatible with the demands of pregnancy and childbirth at the time. These work and career issues also seemed to involve feelings of "not being ready" for maternity.

But since nonbiological mothers in half of the couples did not wish to become pregnant or give birth, desire played the most substantial role in couples' decisions concerning maternity. Jill Collins, whose partner, Nora Duncan, gave birth to their son Danny, had never wanted to give birth to a child but had always wanted to parent, a typical explanation given by these nonbirth mothers. Jill expressed this preference in her inimitable jovial style: "I'm not opposed to getting pregnant, it's just that I don't . . . You know when people talk about their biological clocks ticking and stuff, I don't have any feelings like that. Like I wanted to have a kid, but I'd be perfectly happy to get it from someplace else (laughs). Find it on the street! A knock on the front door, 'Oh, here's your little package.' That would be fine!"

Decisions concerning which partner becomes pregnant and in what order once again highlight the amount of planning, reflection, research, and rehearsal that lesbian prospective parents undertake in making their desire for families materialize. After deciding whose body will bear the challenges and joys of pregnancy and childbirth, whose ovaries will provide the DNA, whose blood will nourish the child in the womb, couples must locate a sperm donor, a task made considerably easier by the increased prevalence of sperm banks and fertility and insemination clinics that serve lesbians.[8] But the logistics of locating a sperm donor flow from the type of donor couples want, and this decision, as we learned from Cathi Lotti and Katrina Smith's protracted deliberations, involves careful consideration of the social relationships that shape and are shaped by it.

The Donor Decision

In the Bay Area in the late 1980s, the open adoption movement began in an atmosphere of heated dispute. Public debates and forums in San Francisco and the East Bay, especially among lesbians considering parenthood, took up the issue of whether it was better for adopted children to know or have access to biological parents. The discussions grew strident, and, according to mothers I spoke with, a "correct" recommendation emerged for lesbian prospective parents: choose a known donor so that your children will be spared the pain of a potentially protracted or unsuccessful search later in life and the insecurity of not knowing "where they came from." Kelly Kronenberg and Diane Chaucer described the tense, emotionally charged atmosphere at the time:

KELLY: There was this whole big controversy in the lesbian community about women who had been adopted. [They] felt very strongly that lesbians should not use anonymous donors because it would deprive the child of its biological roots. I mean it was this very, I mean, emotional issue to people. I had thought that that was . . . that it had sort of turned people away from the anonymous donor, to some extent.

DIANE: People were really being harassed. People were, I mean, you know, I just felt sorry for everybody I knew who had kids with an anonymous donor. I mean people were just saying it's criminal, it's horrible. There was really this vitriol.

KELLY: And you kind of felt like, "Oh I'm really glad I did this with a known donor."

DIANE: You know, it was scary. I mean, there were like big community forums and it was a big deal. I feel really strongly that women should be able to have, do what they think is best for their families, but um, I don't know . . .

As is clear from Diane's and Kelly's recollections of these debates, and from Cathy's and Katrina's worries about where they would "get the other half," the donor decision is fraught with emotional, social, political, and philosophical concerns. What has changed for many lesbian parents and couples considering parenthood since the late 1980s, however, is that now numerous "how to" books, support groups, and parenting classes organize the variables that must be reckoned with when couples begin thinking about creating families.

For example, in her popular 1993 resource book, *The Lesbian and Gay Parenting Handbook,* the psychologist April Martin combines practical advice with anecdotes from both her own experience in forming a lesbian-coparent family and the experience of the gay male and lesbian families she interviewed. Her work typifies the practical assistance and information gay and lesbian parents seek and use in making decisions about creating and sustaining families. As such, it has become part of the common stock of knowledge and has taken on the authority and normative character of rules. Martin's advice concerning the donor selection recognizes the continuing importance of this decision for the lives of children and parents. She writes that couples "must decide who the sperm donor or biological father will be, whether he will be known to the child, and whether he will assume a parenting role. In short, they have to define the family. The family unit has to be defined."[9] Whereas an infertile heterosexual couple may choose a sperm donor with the knowledge that the husband's social paternity will stand in for his lack of biological paternity, so that there is little in the way of actively "defining the family unit," prospective lesbian parents cannot avoid making these decisions: each step of the way, they engage in definitional acts involving biological elements that they must reckon with.

Among the Bay Area couples, only five had selected known donors; the remaining twenty-nine had anonymous donors, selected from the offerings of the bank or clinic whose services they had employed for this purpose. Of the twenty-nine anonymous donors, twenty-eight were "yes" donors, meaning that they had agreed to release their identity to a child when that child would reach majority age. The twenty-ninth donor would remain anonymous permanently. In an already logistically challenging method of procreation, the "yes" donor option offered by the fertility and insemination organizations has provided a welcome solution to a vexing decision. The Bay Area mothers' recollections of their donor decision are instructive for illustrating how the known and anonymous options can play out.

The Known-Donor Choice

When a couple opt for a donor who will be known to them and to their children, they transform a hidden, socially insignificant biological event—a conveyance of genetic material—into a durable social relationship. This is a moment in which culture organizes and shapes nature. From the decision to select a known donor stems another decision about the character of the donor's relationship to the couple and the children. Three different types of relationship appear to result: the donor may be a symbolic father; a flexibly defined male figure with whom the child has a relationship but to whom no parental status is imputed; or, finally, an active, practicing parent with all the rights and responsibilities implied by that co-parent status but without legal custody.

In the first type of relationship, that of symbolic father, the child will have a live human being to whom the sign "father" is attached but of whom no one has parental expectations. The sign may be something else, like "daddy," or even "seed daddy," to indicate the procreative rather than the parental function of the donor. A known donor who is a symbolic father is simply someone the family can hang the label "dad" on—an embodied human referent that the child may identify as his or her progenitor. But it is a purely sign-driven, semiotic arrangement, because the sign *pater* pervades our culture as an entity independent of embodied referents, thus compelling the need for flesh-and-blood daddies even in cases in which they were not part of the original plan. Known donors who function as symbolic fathers are fathers in name only but in the person of the donor.

Kelly Kronenberg told a story of how this worked for her six-year-old, Noam, and Noam's friend Jake, who also has two mothers. Noam and Jake were having a disagreement about family structures, and Kelly overheard Noam saying, "I don't have a dad and neither do you, Jake, so don't talk about that." Jake said, "I do too, I have a seed daddy," to which Noam replied, "Well, I have that too."

It appears to be important for the mothers and children with these known donors who are primarily if not exclusively symbolic fathers that *daddy, dad, father,* or some other conventional signifier of paternity be included in the term they use to refer to him. The term *donor* or *sperm donor* defeats the purpose of having a symbolic father, as Cathy Lotti indicated:

> We went to family night and one of the other guests who came, a woman with her daughter, told a funny story about her daughter on the playground. I think the story went like: one little girl was upset because her parents were getting divorced, and the daughter of the lesbian came over and said, "Oh, don't feel sad, I don't have a father either, I just have a sperm." Which was very funny but which was also like, "Oh my God!" That's not quite what we would want our children to have in their mind, that they don't have a father, first of all, 'cause they do. But . . . "I have a sperm," I mean, that was just bizarre.

The advantages of having a symbolic father in the embodied person of the known donor are that children can have a living human referent whom they may regard as a real figure in their lives in a society that still views heterosexually created kinship as the rule, even though increasing numbers of children are actually raised in mother-only families. It should be noted here that there is no necessary or "naturally" logical relationship between donating sperm and fulfilling the role of symbolic father. The relationship is brought about entirely by a couple's having chosen a sperm donor who, in addition to providing genetic material, agreed to this symbolic role. In other words, the choice of a known donor fuses, in one individual, a biological event and a semiotic function that could have been fulfilled by two different individuals.

Some couples with known donors want their children to know and have a relationship with the donor but do not emphasize the symbolic role. Parents with this second type of arrangement refer to the donor by his first name, as do their children. They downplay his semiotic function as *pater* unless children ask. The point of his being known to them is purely pragmatic: children can know him as being related to them, connected to them. Though they do not relate to him as "Dad," they can know that they have *a* dad with whom they may pursue a relationship at any time as they mature and as their understanding of their family structure changes. Mothers themselves can contact him at any time should the need arise, for example, in the event they want a second child by him. There is a built-in flexibility when the known-donor relationship is defined in this way. Indeed the very definition can evolve according to the needs and desires of all parties. Olena Porzak and Resa Frank recalled a situation in which this flexibility proved helpful:

RESA: We have been very careful to never ever say [to daughter Sarah], "You don't have a dad," because we felt like, well, she does. We didn't use a[n unknown] donor, we purposely picked a friend. We wanted them to be able to have a relationship. But she doesn't call him Dad; she calls him Rick. Ricky.

OLENA: So, a while ago, Sarah started saying, "I don't have a dad." But Resa said, "Yeah, you do have a dad, Rick." And Sarah said, "Rick? He's not my dad, he helped make me grow as a little tiny baby." So she had a way of making sense of where he fit into our family. She has once since actually called him "Dad." It was just so out of the ordinary that it struck us. She was sitting here and looked up and said, "Can I call my dad, Mom?" [on the telephone]. So we said "Sure." And then she got distracted and never called him.

RESA: She was just trying it out.

OLENA: Yeah, I think she was just trying it out.

Of the five families who chose known donors, all but one have donors who are either symbolic fathers or nonfather figures whose relationship with the family is continually and flexibly defined.

The remaining couple with a known donor has a quasi-multiparenting arrangement with the donor. Donors involved in this type of relationship fulfill a symbolic role as "father" and, in practice, become active, involved parents. This construction of the donor thus fuses the biological, semiotic, and social or parental elements in one person. The only aspect missing is de jure paternity, or legal custody, which is where mothers draw a very important line in their family definitions. I know of no families with two mothers in which the donor is also a legal parent, guardian, or custodian.

In general, a known-donor choice represents a decisive moment in the path to family formation for lesbian couples insofar as it sets one of the boundaries signifying immediate family status beyond the couple-child unit to include at least one additional adult, usually as a symbolic father or flexibly defined father/male figure but occasionally as a fully active, involved one. There is no disavowing this relationship once it has been established, most importantly because the act of establishment institutes and socially legitimates a biological occurrence that itself, as a cultural symbol, wields great authority. At a more practical level, lesbian couples who choose the known-donor option and wish to retain the status of primary parents generally do so confidently—that is, with the foreknowledge that they can (and do) successfully negotiate the donor's nonactive role as a function of choosing a particular donor. Thus most lesbian couples whose children have known donors who are also fathers in name are still regarded by all involved as the parents.[10]

The alternative to a known donor is an anonymous one. Anonymity may be achieved through the use of an intermediary, or someone known to the couple and entrusted with the task of finding them a donor and the duty of keeping secret his identity from them and theirs from him. Because this method is precarious in terms of the intermediary's capacity both for suppressing information and for screening the donor, the most secure, most depersonalized, and thus most preferred avenue for transacting with an anonymous donor is by way of a sperm bank or physician. Eighty-five percent or twenty-nine of the Bay Area couples chose this option, even those who were not recruited from the clinic database.[11]

More important than the means of achieving anonymity is the question of what is achieved with anonymity. The choice of an anonymous donor means that couples trade knowledge of biological connection for protection from claims of kinship. Their not knowing is exchanged for protection from potential kinship claims and from the very basis of such claims: paternity. Kinship claims, such as those involving custody of children, are rarely pursued without evidence of biological consanguinity. When a third party such as a sperm bank controls the evidence, bilateral ignorance of paternity among donors and recipients prohibits any pursuit of such claims. The whole configuration is a social mechanism for suppressing the symbolic power of biology. In one sense, ignorance, or not knowing, trumps and therefore gains greater value than knowledge in this social game that gets played around biology.[12] For lesbian couples who choose anonymous donors, this protection from kinship claims—and coincidental erasure of paternity—is manifested pragmatically on the child's initial birth certificate where "the father" is listed as unknown. (Later, when a second-parent adoption is successfully undertaken by the nonbirth mother, her name is listed as a second, legal parent.)

Lesbian parents who choose an anonymous donor via a sperm bank or fertility facility have yet another option when choosing anonymity. They may choose lifetime anonymity, or they may choose a "yes" donor, as mentioned earlier, where the "yes" indicates the donor's agreement to allow children to learn of his identity when they reach eighteen and to contact him if they desire. Of the twenty-nine couples who chose anonymity, all but one opted for a "yes" donor. Indeed, this provision was the most frequently cited criterion for donor selection. This provision in a sense offers the best of both worlds: couples are protected during the child-raising years from external threats to their family sovereignty, and once they reach majority, children may pursue the officially suppressed knowledge of the identity of their progenitor if they so desire.

GETTING PREGNANT, PART II:
THE VICISSITUDES OF SPERM
MANAGEMENT AND THE COMOTHER'S ROLE

Sperm Management

The mothers I spoke with talked about the trials and tribulations of getting pregnant when careful charting of ovulation patterns and coordination with the insemination clinic often failed to produce a pregnancy or, perhaps worse, began to take over their lives to the extent that the emotional stakes became very high indeed.[13] A primary reproductive task becomes sperm management: the prospective parents must decide whether to use frozen or fresh sperm (fresh is highly desirable but far more difficult to coordinate with the donor at the right time) and whether to inseminate at home, where partners can make insemination attempts ceremonial and thereby satisfy the social need of creating meaning and memory of a life-changing event, or in the clinic, where partners can meet the practical need of ensuring that the procedure is most efficient.

Mothers spoke variedly and candidly about how mundane and "clinical" the procedure was; about the economic exploitation they experienced as lesbian couples who needed medically screened, potent, and anonymous-donor sperm in order to conceive; and about their attitudes toward creating meaning from the procedure versus ensuring efficiency. Birth mother Shannon Cavner, whose working-class background may account for some of the cynicism with which she viewed both the procedure and the institutional arrangements necessary for her to become pregnant, described the process, with her partner Marian Gould-Whitmer, as at once mundane and manipulative:

SHANNON: Well, I mean, it's just very clinical. I mean, you go in, you
             know, you lay there, they put sperm in you, you lay there some

more. A lot of people [inseminate] at home. I'm glad that I didn't do it that way the first time because the donor actually had a sperm problem, a low sperm count problem. Which is not something you would obviously be able to detect if you were doing it at home. And because they were doing it in the office, when they unfroze it they saw [the problem] so they double dosed it in the office. So, but it's a lot of money to pay for a problem like that because I know there are a lot of people, there were other people using the donor who didn't get pregnant, or who had a hard time getting pregnant. You certainly have to wonder if that's the reason for it, or if they were just having . . . you can't ever say for sure. But in this particular case I was glad that I did it that way. When you get inseminated you really have to sort of lay there, you know, upside down more or less, you know, while the sperm works its way up and you know that wasn't an option necessarily because they had all these people coming in and out [of the clinic]. That actually really irritated me. The second time I did it I told them I wasn't leaving. (Marian laughing). Forget it, "I'm staying here, upside down," you know? It's too much money, it really is, and to them it's a business. It's not really, it's not that they're mean or anything like that, but it's still a business and they treat it like a business. We're just people to make money off of. No matter how nice anybody is or what their best of intentions are, you are still someone to be made money off of. And that's really how I feel about it after going through it. I mean it's like, heterosexual people boink and they get a baby. All right. It costs nothing, they do nothing. No, to me, I see that and I see the whole [second-parent] adoption process too, and I mean it's just a way to make money off of gay people. Really it is, because it's a lot of money for not a lot. But, that aside, it's still just a clinical procedure. That's how I feel about it. You know, if you do it at home, it's still a clinical procedure but at least you're at home. (Marian laughing). It's just something . . . I mean it's just the means to the end. That's sort of how I look at it.

MARIAN: There's nothing really romantic about it; I mean, you can make something romantic out of it.

SHANNON: Even if you do it at home, I mean, you know, you're still shoving sperm up there and you know, to me that's not overly romantic (laughs). It's like I said, it's just the means to the end. The faster, the sooner, the better.

The average cost to recipients of donor semen, just the semen, runs about $100 per vial, and this is not covered by insurance. When couples inseminate at home using frozen semen that they have thawed, that is their cost per insemination attempt. Costs begin to increase if the insemination is done in the clinic, if couples do "double dosing" as Shannon mentioned, if intrauterine insemination is done, and especially when unsuccessful attempts begin to add up. The average length of time it takes to conceive has been widely cited at six months. Thus most couples can expect that, at a minimum, their semen costs alone will amount to $600. The costs involved with second-parent adoptions, depending on the county in which they are undertaken, can run anywhere from $500 to $3,000, which mostly covers the cost of the home study, in which a social service worker comes into the home and effectively collects and reports data on the home environment and on the nonbirth mother's background and perceived fitness to be a parent. In terms of the second-parent adoption expense, since this money flows into local government treasuries, Shannon's perception of the economic exploitation involved is not unfounded, as the state is effectively extorting money from a class of citizens whom it denies the right to marry, which would automatically confer parental status on the non-birth-giving spouse.

Shannon and Marian were fortunate in that Shannon became pregnant on the second attempt, which makes her observations of the process even more remarkable for the sense of antigay, economic injustice they reveal, as though she had been involved in the process much longer. Like Shannon and Marian, Belinda Tarpin and Caitlin Simonds expressed unsentimental views about the logistics and meaning of becoming pregnant via alternative insemination:

BELINDA: I don't know. We didn't really have a need to do a whole ritual. I mean, I have a spiritual perspective and that, but my perspective was not that this little soul was waiting to come in and it was ready. And it didn't matter really if the candles and, you know, all that stuff.

CAITLIN: (chuckling) We just split the cost of the sperm 50–50, half of it went on my credit card and half of it went on hers!

Shannon and Marian and Belinda and Caitlin were not the only mothers to express concern over the costs involved in becoming pregnant via donor insemination. Other low-income couples expressed their frustration with the expenses, often with a weariness or even matter-of-factness that betrays a lifetime of struggling to make ends meet, as Clara Mueller, the comother of eight-year-old Andrea and three-year-old Ethan, complained: "It's expensive. Each kid cost about a thousand dollars each. We wanted the donor to be anonymous so that there could be no legal claims made in the future. We paid about a thousand dollars for the vials of sperm per kid. And that is not covered by insurance." Clara explained that it took six months for her partner Madeline Lovadas to become pregnant with each child, making their monthly conception costs about $165 per attempt. Jill Collins and Nora Duncan mentioned the expense as well:

NORA: If you hold onto the sperm and do it [inseminate] yourself, it's cheaper; when they do it for you, it's really expensive. One hundred sixty-five dollars each time.

JILL: No insurance will pay for this. They'll cover some of the other tests, but they won't cover this.

And Pat Keating proclaimed about the expense of conceiving the son her partner Sarah Alton had given birth to: "This was not a cheap child! To hell with his college, he wasn't cheap getting here!"

But it wasn't just lower-income couples who complained of the cost, as Cathy Lotti, the hospital administrator, attested:

But buying the sperm is not covered, or any of the procedures. Now had I gotten to an infertility point, then it would have been covered by my insurance, the infertility part of it, but not the artificial insemination part of it. Yeah, it adds up. I mean every month, it's probably, it was probably $375 between purchasing the ovulation kits and buying the stuff and the pregnancy tests and, I mean it's an interesting thing that lesbians have to go through just to get pregnant. The cost is tremendous. Now, even the fact that we've purchased some sperm that's in deep freeze, we have to pay rent! We have to pay storage fees on the sperm that's reserved for future attempts!

Nor was it strictly lower-income prospective parents who took an unromantic view of the procedure. Marilyn Weiss also described her partner Brenda Jacobsen's and her perspective in terms of means and ends and money: "Oh yeah, I could have inseminated [at home] for the weekend, but we sort of felt for that kind of money maybe we should have a professional do it, you know, we don't need to light candles and be all romantic and everything." One professional, socially active couple, Serena Walby and Carrie Johnson, described the logistical hazards of sperm management in a story about packing and transporting their frozen "baby juice" on a trip that happened to overlap with Serena's peak time to inseminate:

SERENA: It's comical now. One time, the fourth time [insemination attempt], we dragged this stuff [frozen semen] all over Vancouver. I was in the Gay Olympics. We dragged it to Seattle and then to Vancouver for two weeks and kept it perfectly, with the dry ice. And then one day we found a dry ice company in Vancouver and Carrie said . . .

CARRIE: He said, "Shall I fill it up?" I said, "Great." So he took it [cooler] into the back and came back with it all filled and I thought it was fine but then two days later when I started looking for it realized the specimen was gone! Apparently he had just dumped out the old ice. Put in the new!

SERENA: So there's $254 when you think of all the costs.

Despite the costs and logistical difficulties of inseminating, some couples were quite interested in the romantic or ceremonial aspect, as Angeline Bowen and Dana Engels described:

ANGELINE: It felt really important [for me] to be inseminating her, to really be having a role from the very beginning. I mean, I'm real glad that I did, even though that feels like maybe it shouldn't be that important, it felt really good.

DANA: Yeah, we know people who weren't able to have that [partner inseminating at home], who needed to be inseminated at the clinic. But it was nice . . .

ANGELINE: Yeah, it was, it felt important that I inseminated her.

Angeline related the importance of inseminating Dana in the comfort and privacy of their home to how it would make her feel more involved, more included from the very beginning, as a coparent to a child with whom she would not share the culturally defined, all-important bio-genetic link. For many comothers lacking the bio-ontological credential, other means of creating the meaning and feeling of connection to the child become paramount. At what point prospective parents undertake this social-symbolic work varies depending upon how they view their needs in relation to economic exigency, logistical convenience, and philosophical outlook.

"Tying in" the Nonbirth Mother

Angeline and Dana's approach to the insemination process and pregnancy as equally involved prospective parents illustrates that becoming a parent is a social process, or rather, the result of social practice. In Angeline's words, "I'll be a coparent as much as I feel that I am one." Implicit here and in the views presented by most of the Bay Area couples is the understanding that the degree to which one feels and acts like a parent (or prospective parent) is related to what one does to make that happen. Partners recognized both implicitly and explicitly the power of the bio-ontological credential the birth mother would possess, a type of unfair advantage in the construction of parental status, so, paradoxically, they both compensated for this while simultaneously acknowledging that it—the biological credential—is itself socially, culturally, and legally determined and not given by the biological facts of pregnancy, parturition, and breastfeeding. Thus all of the prospective-parent couples actively thought about or pursued opportunities for "tying in" the nonbirth parent, to use a popular expression of the mothers.

Tying in the nonbirth mother can take many forms: giving the child her last name exclusively or in hyphenated form with the birth mother's; putting the child on her health insurance policy if possible; securing the second-parent adoption, perhaps the most socially and legally important step lesbian parents attempt toward ratifying the parental status of the nonbirth mother; and providing for the total and equal involvement of nonbirth mothers from the very beginning, as Angeline and Dana endeavored to do.

The equal involvement of both prospective parents among the Bay Area couples over the course of the birth mother's becoming and being pregnant reached levels mostly unheard of among heterosexual couples. Cathy Lotti and Katrina Smith had this to say about their equal involvement and those "unfortunate" women who do not have this level of support during their pregnancies:

KATRINA: I actually wanted to be part of everything, absolutely everything. I went to every appointment. I may have missed one, but I really felt part of things by being at every appointment and hearing every question, hearing every response and every decision along the way.

CATHY: Well you had to be there. We wouldn't have done it any other way. I mean the first time you hear the heartbeat and all those things. I mean how could you . . . I don't know how women, so many women, do all that part alone. I don't know how they do it. I couldn't stand it.

If the insemination process reflects the inequities of being gay in heteronormative society and exacts economic and social penalties, the penalties appear to be mitigated somewhat by the potential rewards from not following the identity rules that straight society has created for heterosexual couples. Without overstating the case, since a great many heterosexual men have consciously or unconsciously begun to think of themselves more as their wives' and girlfriends' partners, and to support them more than have previous generations,[14] it is still striking that nonbirth partners in lesbian-parent couples, unlike heterosexual male partners, not only earnestly and enthusiastically engage in a personal and interpersonal process of becoming parents but do so with both a sense of matter-of-factness and self-conscious practice. Their level of attentiveness simultaneously betrays a kind of "but of course" attitude *and* an intentional praxis involving "tying in" the nonbirth mother, as Pat Keating described, comparing her earlier experiences of being an unsupported heterosexual wife and mother and her current situation as lesbian comother to baby Seth, to whom her partner Sarah Alton had given birth:

PAT: This has been a team thing that we work together at raising him. I always felt terribly alone before [as a heterosexual mother]. Like this childbirth thing. You know it's supposed to be this wonderful pride thing for the fathers, but for me it wasn't. That's not what I saw from them [former husbands]. You know, this was something that was my job, my responsibility, and I was supposed to take care of the baby and go out to work and still take care of the house and do all this crap. And it was like, bullshit! That's not right. So a lot of what I come into this [lesbian family] with was, I want to make it different. I want to do it the way I thought it should have been done. And that's that you're supported.

SARAH: I think that that's why my pregnancy was so, was so positive, is because she was always there. She was there to say, "Did you take your vitamins? Why not?" Or "Don't eat that, don't take that." Or "This is good for you, take this." And just really, really supportive.

Pat and Sarah attributed this supportive mutuality in their expectations and experience of Sarah's pregnancy to the fact that they were "two women doing this," an argument in line with the thesis (and primary subject of the following chapter) that gender socialization both prepares women for mothering and orients their behavior toward relationality. But as Pat's account of her decision to support Sarah attests, along with the accounts of all the nonbirth mothers in this book who made clear they had no desire to physically bear a child, it is not given in nature or in some primary, socially acquired gender identity that women *as* women will automatically or necessarily mother, nurture, or support loved ones who do. Rather, mothering and gender are reproduced (or not) in a particular interpersonal and sociohistorical context.

Chapter 3 | BEING PARENTS

The End of Oedipus and the Expansion of Intimacy

The San Francisco neighborhood called Noe Valley is known to locals as, among other things, a place where lesbians, their friends, and increasingly their children can reside relatively comfortably with likeminded folk. Like the rest of San Francisco and its suburbs, affordable housing for the middle class has all but disappeared here, but some lesbian couples have managed to acquire modest homes, packed in alongside other homes strung together like necklaces lining the hilly streets. There's almost no space between houses, with the outer walls providing the only real boundaries where one home ends and the next one begins.

The interior layouts of these dwellings, by physical necessity, run long and narrow, with two sequences of paired rooms paralleling each other from front to back, opening, finally, into back porch spaces and small patches of yard, the only greenery or unpaved earth to be found. With the upward pressure on housing prices in the Silicon Valley–Bay Area corridor continuing unabated despite the dot-com collapse, the value of these homes has increased dramatically since I first set foot in some of them to speak with mothers and their children in 1994. But even in the early 1990s, couples buying homes here generally relied on financial assistance from family and friends.

Such was the case for Marjorie Rawlins and Sophie Mesner when they bought their place with the "great southern exposure" at the rear. They had a lot of work to do yet to make it the home that they wanted for the two of them and their infant son, Zeke. When I first arrived to visit with Marjorie and Sophie, upon walking up the path leading to their front door, which was open, I spotted Sophie with paint roller in hand and her thick dark hair peeking out from under a scarf. It was a beautiful weekend day in late summer, a time of year when San Francisco actually feels as if it might warm up and stay warm. Taking advantage of this prime opportunity, when doors and windows could be kept open to allow fumes to escape, Sophie and Marjorie were painting the interior of the front hallway.

Our interview appointment let them take a needed break from this home improvement project, and after Sophie introduced me to Marjorie, we assembled in a comfortable TV room and began to talk. Before settling down for what would be a two-hour interview, however, both women, separately, mentioned to me that Zeke was napping. I was coming to recognize this among the couples I was meeting: both mothers in many of the couples knew exactly the disposition of their child at any given time or could recite the child's activities, discoveries, moods, and so forth in great detail and demonstrated this informed attentiveness spontaneously and frequently during our sessions together.

My routine upon first meeting couples had been to try to guess from their behavior and comments which partner had given birth to the child when I did not know this before meeting with them. But I was discovering that I could not ascertain this from the initial in-person introductions and conversation, and this implied several important possibilities about how these mothers perceived their status as parents and their parenting objectives.[1] It appeared to affirm that, aside from the physiological exigencies of pregnancy and childbirth, individuals wanting to fulfill culturally defined parental duties and responsibilities are not prohibited from doing so by biological incapacities related to being a nonparturient parent—the argument most often invoked to justify men's lack of interest or involvement in a new infant son or daughter's care. Nonbirth parents, these mothers were showing, can be fully involved, aware, and proactive given sufficient motivation.

But there was something else intriguing besides this demonstration of the fallacy of the biological sex determinist argument. The Bay Area parents also seemed to be demonstrating something important about the gendered social arrangements that historically have resulted in mothers' bear-

ing far more responsibility for child care and primary parenting than fathers—even when there is no biological basis, as when children are
adopted. However one wants to view heterosexual mothers' near-exclusive
primary parenting—that is, as biologically or socially determined or
both—lesbian coparents' obvious display of equal involvement in the care
of their infant and older children appeared to demonstrate that gendered,
unequal parenting is optional.

In heterosexual-parent families, women's and men's differing levels of
involvement in the care and lives of their children might be said to be a
matter of conscious and unconscious gender production on the part of
parents: relative to mothers, fathers who remain distant from their children's lives reserve for themselves a certain amount of autonomy from the
emotional labor of caring for children's day-to-day needs, thereby exercis-
ing their prerogatives as men. For many men emotional distance from
their children under ordinary circumstances enables them to absent themselves altogether from their children's lives in the event of divorce from the
mother. In short, parenting in which mothers, more than fathers, assume
primary care of children reinforces male privilege by enabling men to divest themselves of relationships that pose real or imagined threats to their
self-interest and autonomy.

So the question of whether two women coparents, like Marjorie and Sophie and all the Bay Area mothers, create a genderlike distinction or hierarchy in their parenting practices, based upon the birth/nonbirth parent
difference or some other difference, and the theoretical implications of
their practice, becomes important. What would it mean for children and
parents if some of the familial mechanisms theorized as initiating early
gender identification and differentiation were, in fact, disrupted? Those
mechanisms, theorized first by Freud and later reformulated by various
schools of thought in psychoanalysis, are described by the object relations
perspective, of which feminist and sociologically informed approaches
provide especially useful accounts.

FEMINIST OBJECT-RELATIONAL
REVISIONS OF FREUD

Freud used the term *cathexis* to refer to the attachment of psychic charges
or instinctual energies to a mental object, where mental objects represent

introjected, or internalized, external objects—people. The gender theorist R. W. Connell has used the phrase "the structure of cathexis" to refer to "the construction of emotionally charged social relations with 'objects' (i.e. other people) in the real world."[2] Together these statements essentially describe the main principles of the object relations school of thought within psychoanalysis, whose sociologically oriented feminist thinkers include Nancy Chodorow, Dorothy Dinnerstein, and Jessica Benjamin. Those thinkers' revisions of Freud attempted to account for the ways in which women's mothering is consequential for social gender inequality by means of complex object relations resulting in the formation of the psyche—in particular, gender identity.

In her 1978 book *The Reproduction of Mothering*, Nancy Chodorow argued that heterosexual-parent families in which women do primary parenting reproduce the basic psychic contours of gendered personalities. The main issue for Chodorow (and for Dinnerstein, Benjamin, and to a certain extent, Juliet Mitchell)[3] is the apparent monopoly women exercise over primary caregiving—mothering—relative to their male partners. This monopoly produces lasting psychic effects in daughters and sons that in turn help to reproduce the sexual division of labor both in families and in society. In subsequent essays, while reaffirming her basic argument, Chodorow did respond to critics by distancing herself from the more universalizing and essentializing aspects of her theory. Critics charged Chodorow with assuming a homogeneity among heterosexual-parent families, both in the United States and cross-culturally, that was unsupported by empirical evidence. In the United States, for example, African American families with extensive kinship ties based on both "blood" and affiliation are not represented by the conjugal-nuclear family model of either Freudian or object relations theory. Chodorow's theory has been described as a "character typology" or even tautology, where the outcomes of definite masculine and feminine personalities are fixed and inevitable. Her claims in *The Reproduction of Mothering* were also criticized for the legitimacy they lent to the idea of essential differences between men and women, even though her analysis thoroughly discredited biological determinist accounts. The lesbian feminist poet Adrienne Rich questioned Chodorow's focus on heterosexual outcomes when, by Chodorow's own analysis, heterosexuality "fragments the erotic from the emotional in a way that women find impoverishing and painful." Rich also observed that if "the search for love and tenderness in both sexes" originally leads toward women, "why in fact women would ever redirect that search" was a question Chodorow did not address.[4] Chodorow did not, in fact, attempt to account for same-sex desire in *Mothering,* since her aim was to theorize the socioaffective and intrapsychic processes by which generations of women come to engage in exclusive primary caregiving of children in societies where heterosexuality is strictly enforced.

Since Chodorow's argument *does* apply to conjugal-nuclear families, especially of the white, Euro-American kind, her analysis of biological determinist claims is helpful for understanding how the Bay Area lesbian mothers address the birth parent/nonbirth parent asymmetry in their parenting practices. The biological basis for women's primary parenting in heterosexual-parent families, Chodorow concluded in an early chapter of *The Reproduction of Mothering,* is indefensible theoretically because

> [b]eyond the possible hormonal components of a woman's early mothering of her own newborn, there is nothing in parturient women's physiology which makes them particularly suited to later child care, nor is there any instinctual reason why they should be able to perform it. Nor is there anything biological or hormonal to differentiate a male "substitute mother" from a female one. The biological argument for women's mothering is based on facts that derive, not from our biological knowledge, but from our *definition* of the natural situation as this grows out of our participation in certain social arrangements. (Emphasis added)[5]

If cultural definitions of "the natural situation" guide caregiving practices, how the Bay Area mothers define the absolute constraints imposed by the birth mother's "natural situation" should play a significant role in their parenting practice. In particular, practices around breastfeeding and infant care would seem an important area revealing how a birth parent and a nonbirth parent determine definitions of biological necessity and a critical point at which the conventional gendered assignment of tasks might be replicated and renaturalized or, alternatively, disrupted.[6]

Bay Area Mothers' Practice of Shared Primary Caregiving

Rather than one parent assuming primary care, as in Chodorow's analysis of heterosexual women's exclusive involvement and fathers' lack of involvement, we can justifiably speak here of shared primary mothering or caregiving.[7] Shared primary caregiving by the Bay Area mothers stemmed from their perceived need to *compensate* for, rather than *accede* to, the imperatives of the biogenetic tie of the birth mother as they defined them.

The Bay Area mothers seemed to be acutely aware of how infant care and feeding provided an opportunity for "bonding," a means of emotionally "tying in" the nonbirth mother that could be added to the means described in Chapter 2. Implicit in this was a belief that the birth mother *did* have a special status by virtue of having physically gestated, carried, and given birth to the child and having a genetic connection with her. As we saw in Chapter 2, even before conception, mothers viewed the biogenetic tie as highly significant, and now, postnatally, they reinforced that significance in their perception of the need to compensate for it in their care and feeding practices. That is, rather than viewing the birth mother's maternity as a reason for her to do exclusive primary caregiving, they believed that it set up an *undesirable* relational advantage or privilege for her and attempted to compensate for this perceived advantage. Their valuation of emotional and caregiving labor appeared to proceed from an entirely different principle than the heterosexual-couple response to women's maternity: one that viewed equality and balance among those involved in the life and care of the child as paramount.

Kathleen Peterson and Sharon Carlton explained how they would wake up together when their daughter Sophie, who had recently celebrated her first birthday when I met them, cried in the night wanting to breastfeed and be soothed. As nonbirth mother and birth mother respectively, Kathleen and Sharon both worked full time, but they were concerned to share equally the tasks and sleep deprivation associated with their infant daughter's nighttime needs.

KATHLEEN: For a long time she [daughter Sophie] was sleeping until 2:00 or 3:00 and I could just go get her and bring her to Sharon [to nurse].

SHARON: It's hard to do that at first, to get used to that when you're nursing, but to compare that to getting up and sitting up, in the long run it was better.

KATHLEEN: What we've done a little bit recently is that when she [Sophie] cries, I just go in and walk around with her, 'cause even though she sleeps for a couple of hours, she's still tired, especially if it's early, like if it's 4:00 instead of 5:30. And Sophie does go back to sleep. We both put her back to sleep.

Birth mother Jamie Ruiz and comother Marsha Holmes, both with full-time jobs as a public defender and commercial artist respectively, had similar ways of talking about their routine with their one-year-old son Colin:

JAMIE: Yeah we sort of had a routine: she'd go get him—particularly since he had moved out of our bedroom—and change him, and bring him to me.

MARSHA: Or if it was one of those nights where it was just too long, it'd be like, "Okay, I [Jamie] did my, you know, whatever, hour, you go." So we'd [Marsha and Colin] dance and crash out on the couch a lot and try to let Jamie get some sleep. But um, that's kind of always been our thing.

Cathy Lotti and Katrina Smith described a similar practice with their daughter Lauren, though they articulated what felt like difficult emotional dynamics associated with Cathy's breastfeeding, while at the same time speaking of how they were the envy of heterosexual women as a result of their shared primary parenting:

CATHY: She [Katrina] would go get the baby every time, change her, and then bring her in to me. I was so exhausted that she did as much as she could. I rented a pump and started pumping so that Katrina could feed her as much as possible. But the thing that was hard was Lauren did not want the bottle at all. So instead of it being a positive thing for Katrina it ended up being almost worse in a way because it made her feel rejected, and Lauren would just scream, she hated the bottle, and it just took a long, long time.

KATRINA: Yeah, that was hard. I didn't miss breastfeeding, but I had a real problem: in the beginning she would cry and there was nothing I could do, 'cause what she wanted was to breastfeed. And so all I could do was hand her to Cath, and so I, the end of my interaction was that she [Lauren] was crying, and then Cath would breastfeed her and then she'd be all happy and fall asleep. So it wasn't really the breastfeeding per se but it was that there were many many times when I couldn't console her [baby Lauren] and it was sort of a hard thing. And Cath would just breastfeed her and then she'd be all happy. So she was able to get her from crying to happy. And I missed that, I missed being able to do that for Lauren; to get her, to make her feel happy. So that was really hard.

CATHY: But, having two moms is the way to go. And everybody has said that, including my mom, I mean, I can't tell you how many people have said, "Two moms? Oh my God! Is that the way to do it?" You know women, straight women, who have a hard time with lesbians, acknowledge that it is the superior family structure! (laughing). Oh, and the other thing that a lot of straight women are really envious of, like, I'm thinking in general most recently, people at work, you know, they'll say, "Well, are you going to have another one [baby]?" And I'll, one of us will say, "Yes, but Katrina will probably have the second one." And they go, "Oh that's great!" Like it never crossed their mind that . . . cause the only way they can have another baby is to have it themselves. So there are a lot of women who are very envious of the fact that we can share that too. It doesn't all have to be on one person. Because it's not easy to be pregnant either, it's hard, it's tiring, it's very hard.

When I asked Cathy and Katrina hypothetically whether they thought they might have done things differently with Lauren had they not been planning for Katrina to bear their next child, they responded:

KATRINA: It's [the question] very valid in that I may not get pregnant, I mean, I may not be able to, let's say. And so, um, I don't think I would have done anything differently because as I said earlier, I wanted to be part of absolutely everything. I couldn't have been any more involved, or any closer to what Cath experienced, than I was. There wasn't anything else I could have done except . . .

CATHY: There wasn't anything else.

KATRINA: The nursing or something.

CATHY: Which is how we would have done it either way, I think, whether one of us was going to do it [give birth] or not.

The practices around primary caregiving and feeding were much the same for couples in which the nonbirth mother would not be giving birth to a second child in the future. Caitlin Simonds and Belinda Tarpin, nonbirth mother and birth mother respectively, explained a routine they had with daughter Cassie:

> CAITLIN: The main bonding for me was just, especially at night, if Cassie would nurse and then if she didn't go to sleep after having nursed for however long, Belinda would say, "Okay Caitlin, it's your turn." And what I would do is . . . we [Caitlin and baby Cassie] sat in the rocking chair, that glider-rocker, and I would hold Cassie and sing to her. And sometimes for hours at a time. That was our thing. And when Cassie got older and she had words for it, I think she called it "mama-song."
>
> BELINDA: She'd have "mommie-milk" and then "mama-song."

Belinda's and Caitlin's practices with Cassie, and the words that Cassie later used for the types of care and need gratification each mother provided, point to modes of differentiation that mothers and children established that militated against the birth mother becoming dominant in their intimate relations with one another.

This mode of differentiation became especially crystallized in a pattern many mothers described as "food mother, fun mother." They suggested that when their children were still infants, and especially when they breastfed almost exclusively, refusing the bottle as Cathy and Katrina's daughter Lauren had done, they distinguished between the food source mother and the mother who represented fun, stimulation, or other non-nursing forms of interaction and intimacy—like Caitlin's "mama-song" role. Food and fun, I heard repeatedly, became an early mode of differentiation when an infant would not accept a bottle and made the nursing mother the absolute food source.

Emily Trindall and Nina Tarangetti, comother and birth mother respectively, were acutely aware of this early distinction and even explained their practice of Nina's getting up to breastfeed baby David without help from Emily in biological determinist terms. But as Emily later pointed out, the food source role transferred from Nina to Emily once baby David started appreciating other types of food besides breast milk:

NINA: And for the first three months since I was off, and I didn't have to worry about being at work, I was always the person who got up. And obviously I was the person who had to breastfeed him and so, it wasn't going to do her [Emily] any good to get up. Well, and you know it's like, it's such a weird thing, because there's nothing you can do about something like that. Those aren't even roles, that's just, the biological mother's got to get up, you know, you've got to deal with the kid, 'cause most of the time he's crying because he's hungry and that's just it.[8]

Emily explained how she later became the preferred food provider:

EMILY: I'm a big cook. And Nina is a finicky eater. So I've always said that this kid is going to eat with me. Vegetables and swordfish and everything. I like to eat, so he and I can sit in the kitchen and eat while we're playing.

NINA: And that's one of my pleasures with him being with Emily is that, he can eat from her. They can share all the food, because it makes me . . . I am a very finicky eater. I just won't eat a lot of things and I have a really hard time making something I don't like to eat or the smell of it. So, you know, he just, his whole body, his whole face, lights up when Emily is going to eat.

EMILY: That's been fun, 'cause the food stuff is getting transferred to me. Still the breast stuff with Nina, but breast stuff is security. And he really likes the comfort of breastfeeding, more for the security than he gets from the food. But I now puree all his food and freeze it in ice cube trays and put it in ziplock bags so that when I come home I just plop it into the little containers and zap it in the microwave. Put David in the chair . . . he's so cute . . . you put him in his chair, he sits up on the tray . . .

NINA: On the tray, and he just yells . . .

EMILY: "Let me eat eat eat!"

It is important to reiterate, even though I have already noted it, that Nina and Emily were the only mothers I talked with who took the view that because the birth mother had to breastfeed it made sense that only she should get up in the night to attend to the baby. All other couples who mentioned their nighttime routine described some version of the scenario where the nonbirth mother would get up, change the baby, and bring her or him to the nursing mother while the latter remained in bed or a favorite nursing position. And nonbirth mothers would also get the child back to sleep, either alone or with the birth mother's help. Nina and Emily saw the breastfeeding as inevitably dictating a certain practice, which as we have seen, actually can be performed in a number of ways and which supports the notion that there is nothing naturally given about a parturient and lactating woman's exclusive early caregiving.

The food-mother/fun-mother distinction appealed to many couples as an explanation for a number of different emotional and relational dynamics that occurred among the two parents and child/ren: feelings of jealousy, exclusion from intimacy, concerns about not being able to provide appropriate stimulation and "play" activities, and other such issues. Because of their candid acknowledgments and assessments of such deeply personal feelings—and these were experienced by birth mothers and comothers alike and thus did not only revolve around a perceived advantage of the birth mother—mothers were able to extend their own analyses and reflections to encompass the fuller context for the relational and emotional patterns they described. Thus, while Lee Lanier, comother and part-time weekday caregiver to her toddler son, Nathan, wistfully described herself as being secondary to her partner Danielle Walton in Nathan's affections, Danielle spoke of Lee's parenting relationship with Nathan as fully present and equally important to Nathan as his other parent.

LEE: The sun rises and sets on this mom [pointing to Danielle], you know, not on this one [pointing to herself.] Like when she [Danielle] was gone to the conference that she went to for three days in a row, I got all the good loves and hugs and stuff that she usually gets [from Nathan]. So that was fun, that was nice. [When Danielle's home] I get some, but not like I get . . . because he just, he lays on you and just, pats your cheek, you know, he's really affectionate anyway. And you just get more of that when "mom" isn't here.

DANIELLE: Yeah but he relates to Lee like the other parent, "Where's Lee?" I mean he's attached to her. The other day we were both leaving at the same time, Nathan was with me, and he was crying,

"What happened, where're you going, Lee?" And all this . . . And this was just starting to happen with him with Lee. He's attached to her as another parent and he knows that she's the other person that's there for him.

Since Lee was twelve years older than Danielle and had herself borne and raised a daughter from a heterosexual relationship well before her relationship with Danielle started, her parenting and intimacy needs, she indicated at one point, were different from Danielle's and thus may explain why her feelings of not being included in the "good loves" more often from Nathan were not seen by the couple as more of a problem. Further, and perhaps attesting to the power of language, Danielle and Lee were one of only three couples who had not instigated forms of address as "mama and mommie" or some other scheme that would have had the effect of defining Lee more explicitly as "mother." Nathan referred to Lee as Lee, though, as Lee pointed out, "He calls me 'mom' sometimes when he gets mixed up, and he does once in a while, I've noticed, he's started doing that. He said, 'Lee-mom' or something the other day."[9]

Another couple specifically mentioned jealousy arising out of the perceived advantage of the birth mother in a way that gave me the impression that they worked especially hard at trying to understand and work through the disappointment and pain they associated with it. Nonbirth mother Kim Richardson, who had herself tried to get pregnant before the couple decided that her partner Natalie Dalton would (and did), described feelings she has had with respect to their daughter Melanie in carefully weighed words. The couple began describing these feelings openly by first talking about the more legal mechanism for "tying in" the nonbiological mother—the all-important surname:

KIM: We sort of decided from the beginning . . . we were going through the biological/nonbiological mother conversation. . . . I felt like, when I was trying [to get pregnant] I felt like, you know, [the baby] should have Natalie's name. It's sort of like, you're not getting to do the rest of it so you can have some kind of balance to it. So the nonbiological mother would get the name part.

NATALIE: Yeah, it was sort of like a tradeoff, the one who didn't get the biological tie could have the name.

KIM: Which was like, you know, a kind of tie, whereas when biologically you've got that, *you know*. It just felt like a good balance.

NATALIE: Fair. We're into fairness in this relationship. We both have big issues about "fair," I think.

KIM: Well I think, each, every position's got its own stuff, and I think being nonbiological before she [baby Melanie] was here I was more afraid that it would feel like she was all Natalie's. But I think the bonding's been such that it's never been . . .

NATALIE: Well I think it was harder when I was nursing. At the very beginning she [baby] was sort of more attached to me.

KIM: I was jealous, I mean I've been jealous of the time that Natalie had off from work and stayed home with her and stuff. I took a little time off, I've taken some time off. But, yeah, I mean, I'm not saying I wasn't jealous of the nursing and sometimes her responding much more to Natalie because Natalie was home more. But, um, it's easier when, you know, when you get to be home for a while and you realize it switches [child's attachment] a little bit, you know, and you kind of feel not bad about it when she's [baby] more into you. Because if I spend time with her [exclusively] she's more into me a little bit. But . . . but I'm also jealous that she's got Natalie's genes. So we can look at baby pictures and see how much they look alike. Even though that feels great to me sometimes, to look over at them sleeping together and feel like they look alike. But you know, it is an issue to always deal with when people start talking about who she looks like. And so I am jealous. Actually, Natalie was really jealous for a while of me and Melanie 'cause Melanie would always crack up [laughing] when I came home. I could make her laugh.

Kim's reference to making Melanie laugh prompted me to ask, with the food-mother/fun-mother distinction vaguely in mind, whether Melanie came to each mother for different needs. They responded:

NATALIE: You know, I don't think so much anymore, do you? (to Kim)

KIM: No, I mean when you were the food, that was tough. (laughs)

NATALIE: Right, or I probably, when I was the food was probably also more the nurturer and Kim was more of the clowny fun kind of mom. But I don't think anymore. She really, I think she goes to both of us.

I present this segment of conversation at some length because Kim's and Natalie's candid remarks get to the heart of what is perhaps the most extreme case of how the biological credential, the breastfeeding nexus, and the food-mother/fun-mother distinction all get taken up and processed in a complex of relational dynamics. Most Bay Area mothers clearly perceived the biological relationship between birth mother and child as enormously salient to everything from their parenting practices to their own relationship to issues concerning intimacy to how others would perceive them. When Kim said, above, that with a biological tie *"you know,"* that is a reference not just to oneself "knowing" one is connected to a child but to extrafamilial others "knowing" that as well. The statement reflects cultural and legal discourse that has constructed biological relatedness as legitimate and defining of family, which has in turn become "common sense" such that there is no ambiguity in relationships when two people can be known as biologically related. Like any credential, the biological credential operates through knowledge, the circulation of that knowledge, and what people do with it and about it in their practices. As we have seen, most mothers here construed the biological tie as conferring privilege, accepted this construction as reality, and then accommodated it, usually by compensating for it, as Kim and Natalie's implementation of their fairness principle shows.

But it is not only the birth mother–child tie in its biogenetic significance that precipitates compensatory practices. The intimacy, security, and comfort that often flow both ways in the breastfeeding relation between nursing mother and child, as Emily Trindall observed earlier, are not only about the satisfaction of an infant's nutritional needs. The breastfeeding nexus amounts to a relational dynamic in which the possibility exists—as a consequence of the physiological and family-structural fact that one woman has given birth and is lactating—that one partner may have her emotional and intimacy needs met for a relatively short period of time through the breastfeeding relation.[10] The attachment with the child, and the infant's own coming-into-being, continue long after nursing has ended. However, the potential for temporary exclusion and jealousy, as we saw with Kim and Natalie, is considerable. What couples do with this possibility and potential is the key question, and most, as we have seen and as typified here by select parents' accounts, compensated for the potentially exclusive emotional cathexis between breastfeeding parent and child by providing for the comother's active and engaged infant care in every other way possible.

When the nursing relation was construed more in terms of food than "bonding," the food-mother/fun-mother mode of differentiation became emphasized, but, as birth mother Marilyn Weiss confirmed about her and her partner Brenda Jacobson's practices, it did not have to be linked to a biological/nonbiological mother arrangement once other forms of nutrition and comfort were introduced:

> Brenda and I can complement each other. I, um, I'll rough Michael up, you know, we play Cirque du Soleil, and I put him up in the air on my legs and we do tumblesaults and I put him over my back or over my shoulders and do those kinds of physical things that babies like. It's a lot of physical stimulation. And Brenda will sit and read with him and she does more of the passive things with him, although she's taken him to gym class and swimming too. So he gets that, you know, that stimulation that's well-rounded.

Further, when the food-mother/fun-mother relation did develop, it appeared to be a temporary dynamic, not a sustained distinction between mothers. And even when a birth mother did become fairly exclusively associated with food/comfort versus fun/stimulation, as with Molly England and Jolene Tyson, it could not reasonably be said to have been the result of hormones or physiology or even "feminine" personality. As birth mother Molly and nonbirth mother Jolene explained their parenting, it became clear that their family backgrounds, specifically their *class* backgrounds, might have conditioned them for the particular activities and needs they fulfilled as parents to daughter Sid.

MOLLY: I feel like [Sid's] already created . . . This is the play person [pointing to Jolene] and I'm the one that feeds her. She knows that. Like [Jolene] pointed out to me yesterday, "See, [Sid] only nuzzles into you." Like she'll suck on my shirt or nuzzle into me, looking for my breast. But if I'm feeding her and she's not too hungry, and she hears her [Jolene's] voice and kind of knows that she's in the vicinity, she'll like, keep whooping her head around and laughing till she gets [Jolene's] attention, and then they start playing and laughing. I mean it's hilarious. And like, [Jolene's] the one that really, when it comes to children, she knew a lot more about playing with them than I did. I just knew how to take care of a child, I didn't know really the playing end of it.

When I asked Jolene how she knew about playing, she said:

JOLENE: I don't know, I guess it just kind of comes to you. I don't know, [Molly] had a lot more of, she took care of her younger brothers and sisters. She pretty much raised them since she was like seven or eight. So, I mean, I was able to play my whole life, you know, my parents kind of let me do, play around the house, or you know, whatever. I never had responsibilities like she had. I had just one brother. So we pretty much, you know, they [Jolene's parents] didn't really want us to work even when we were in high school. And when I went to college they didn't really want me to work. They said, "Yeah, live in the dorms, have a good time." Basically that's what the whole thing was. You know, "You're gonna have to work when you get out of college so you might as well enjoy life now." You know, and when I got my first job when I was a senior in high school, like my parents were like, "Don't do that. You're going to have to work later. Just, go play sports, go hang out with your friends, do your homework, have a good time." Yeah, [their financial support] was really nice. So, I mean, . . . so I know how to play! Yeah, where she was totally the opposite. Where, you know, come home and take care of the kids.

MOLLY: I had a brother and sister who were younger than me. And a brother and sister above me. And I took care of the brother and sister below me. Because my mom worked and she was a single parent. And so she wouldn't be around, so I'd do all the laundry, all the cooking, changing the diapers, everything. Just basically whatever needed to be done I took care of it. So I knew how to raise children in that sense, you know, the . . . I won't say raise because it wasn't interacting with my brother and sister. It was just taking care of . . . more of the survival needs. I knew how to meet their survival needs. I can definitely do that with Sid, but it's learning how to interact with the baby that's new to me. You know, and that's what I get to watch [Jolene] do, and I learn a lot of how to do that. Like how to roll around on the floor with her and those kinds of things that I didn't do with my brother and sister because I didn't have time.

JOLENE: Or even have thought that it would have been okay.

MOLLY: Right, right.

In mothers' descriptions, it's clear that a certain emphasis was placed on maternity, that mothers viewed a biological tie as somehow identical with ontological connection: that one could not be closer with another human being, and therefore this tie was irrevocable. These concepts of the natural enter mothers' assumptions and practices, which in turn have the effect of producing the biological credential, which then must be compensated for if standards of fairness and equality are to be met.

For the most part, parents viewed their arrangements as equally shared primary caregiving. All but one of the Bay Area couples in fact stated explicitly that they were fully "coparents," "equal," "unified," or engaged in "we" parenting, or they referred to their children as "ours."[11] Such terms, if nothing else, reflect intentionality on their part; they reflect parents' conscious decisions to be involved equally in parenting, however they define that. If the foregoing discussions of their practices around feeding and care are any indication, their efforts to implement these principles of "unified" parenting were effective to the extent that mothers were able adequately to deal with issues of evolving attachments and jealousy and to compensate for the biological credential.

We must now ask, what are the implications for the reproduction of mothering and, by extension, the reproduction of gender? What might we be justified in thinking about the fate of gender difference and the social structural division of labor when families headed by two women practice shared primary caregiving?

THE REPRODUCTION OF GENDER
OR THE EXPANSION OF INTIMACY?

Mothering, Chodorow argued, is reproduced in women as a result of the sexual division of labor, in which women provide exclusive primary care of children as compared to noncaregiving husband-fathers. The mechanism is gender personality differentiation—which is itself the product of this "asymmetrical organization of parenting which founds our family structure."[12] That is, women's exclusive or near-exclusive mothering and men's nonmothering, the sexual division of labor, and psychosocial gender difference itself occur in part because men do not assume or share the primary care of infants and children. The important elements in the cycle are the not sharing and the fact that the nonsharing parent is male—that is, "not mother/female." In addition, heterosexual mothers are thought to be emotionally deprived in their relationships with male partners.

Among the Bay Area lesbian-mother families, these elements are different in crucial ways. I propose that families headed by lesbian coparents who share primary parenting may disrupt the cycle of gender reproduction in ways that are unachievable by simple heterosexual "role reversals" or equally shared parenting by heterosexual men.[13] If the type of masculinity that ensures that men will not mother—and correspondingly the type of feminine personality that ensures that women will mother—is produced psychically within the context of familial object relations, then the intervention necessary for breaking the cycle must occur at the level of social-psychic sedimentation; it must occur when familial objects and object relations are "introjected," split, reintegrated, and so on, as part of children's developmental process. If fathers who share primary parenting still project the same type of masculinity (emotionally distant, punishing) as those who do not, or if (heterosexual) mothers are incapable of sharing with fathers the emotional connections with children, the shared primary care is unlikely to make a difference intrapsychically for children. So not only the perceived "maleness" and "femaleness"—sexual difference—of heterosexual parents but the entire complex of gender-coded, libidinal cathexis relations sets up the oedipal drama of classic and object relations psychoanalytic theory and must be reconstructed for the necessary transformations to occur. The advantage lesbian comothers have for effecting and sustaining these transformations is, first, the absence of *paternal masculinity* in the familial psychic field; second, the sharing of primary caregiving; and third, parental satisfaction in the couple relationship. To interpret their likely effects for children raised in lesbian-coparent families, these three elements may be traced analytically through the psychosexual developmental stages known as the preoedipal and oedipal periods in psychoanalytic theory.

The Preoedipal Situation

Chodorow argued that the "omnipotent" mother in children's intrapsychic and external object world arises in nuclear (heterosexual-parent) families in which the father is mostly absent in terms of day-to-day care of infants and children and the mother engages in exclusive or near-exclusive caregiving. This absence of the father is different from the absence of a father figure in lesbian-coparent families precisely because in the latter a second parent is emotionally and physically present. As Bay Area birth mother Jane Kyle explained to her own mother, who was concerned about the lack of a father: "The important thing is that the child will have two loving parents who are very capable of supporting them financially and emotionally, and they'll have grandparents, and if you want male, uh, what do you call them . . . role models, there's my father and my brother, and many, and Carla's [partner] brother, and many other male people in her life. So I don't think that's much of an issue." In heterosexual-parent families, because of the emotionally closed dyadic structure of mother and child, and because mothers are women who are unlikely to have their own intimacy needs met in the adult (heterosexual) relationship, mothers extend the preoedipal period of mother-infant fusion and primary love with daughters. "Because they are the same gender as their daughter and have been girls, mothers of daughters tend not to experience these infant daughters as separate from them in the same way as do mothers of infant sons." In contrast, the early mother-son relationship "is likely to emphasize phallic oedipal issues along with preoedipal individuation issues," such that boy infants are seen by the mother and respond to her as separate *because* they are male, or rather, because their perceived maleness is emphasized. "A mother, of a different gender from her son and deprived of adult emotional, social, and physical contact with men (and often without any supportive adult contact at all), may push her son out of this preoedipal relationship to her into an oedipally toned relationship defined by its sexuality and gender distinction. Her son's maleness and oppositeness as a sexual other become important, even while his being an infant remains important as well."[14] Thus begins psychosexual differentiation at the earliest moments of infant psychic development.

For the Bay Area mothers, one of the most striking and important elements demonstrated by their parenting practice is that no single omnipotent mother arises. The preoedipal period for daughters and sons of lesbian mothers who share primary parenting occurs, not in a dyadic relationship, but in a triadic one. The intensity of the early fusion (if that term still applies) is actually "diffused" among three individuals, diminishing the possibility that the absolutely dependent child will experience separation-individuation in relation to only one female parent. In her 1985 doctoral dissertation, the psychologist Ailsa Steckel hypothesized precisely this possibility, even though her description of the parenting practice of her lesbian mother informants did not reach the level of "unity" and "sharing" of the Bay Area mothers here because she had prelabeled her lesbian couples as "mother" and "co-parent," and thus the assumption of a primary parenting figure in the form of the birth mother informs her analysis.[15] Even so, Steckel wrote,

> [T]he child of a lesbian couple would theoretically be able to struggle less intensely with one parent, knowing the other parent was available to ally with. Such a child might experience the regressive pull to mother as less focused and more diffuse, because of the greater daily availability of the co-parent. The child may then not feel compelled to pull away from the mother with such force or to express her/himself in such a domineering way.[16]

Steckel's psychoanalytic work supports the assumption that no omnipotent mother arises or, at the very least, that preoedipal processes are distributed within a triadic structure in lesbian-coparent families. From this significant presumptive and empirical point of departure from the heterosexual-parent family theorized as foundational to psychosocial gender personality development, one can trace the implications—first for preoedipal daughters, then for preoedipal sons.

If heterosexual mothers in a dyadic preoedipal relationship with infant daughters extend that period because they see their daughters as "like me," and consequently establish relationality as a core element of feminine psychic life, it is very likely that lesbian comothers, having already experienced the "like me" dynamic in the couple relationship, will be less inclined to identify so intensely with daughters. Further, because they are more likely to have their own needs for emotional connection and intimacy met in the couple relationship, as has been confirmed by numerous studies, lesbian coparents like the Bay Area mothers do not suffer the emotional deprivation experienced by heterosexual mothers—which encourages the exclusive dyadic relationship with the child in the first place. The lesbian family psychologist Valory Mitchell observed this in her study of planned lesbian families: "Because the lesbian couple consists of two women, both partners will have more of their emotional needs met in the couple relationship, thus reducing the likelihood of emotional overinvolvement with the children."[17] Lesbian mothers have no reason to develop overly intensive cathexes with children due to the emotional mutuality and reciprocity derived in the couple relationship. Along with this, mothers who share primary caregiving have scant *opportunity* emotionally to overinvest in children in the way heterosexual mothers do because the effect of two, equally present, primary parents is diffusion and circulation of emotional energy—expansion of intimacy.

Preoedipal daughters of lesbian mothers who share primary parenting are unlikely to become for the parents "narcissistic extensions" of themselves, as has been described for heterosexual mothers of preoedipal daughters. This means that daughters separate from their lesbian comothers in a less tense, but still supportive and inclusive, object world. This, in fact, was precisely Steckel's psychoanalytic finding: "This study concluded that the presence of a female co-parent, rather than a father, does not adversely affect the child's progression through the separation-individuation process, but does establish a qualitatively different separation experience for the child, on the basis of having two female parents, rather than a male and a female parent, from whom to separate."[18] The qualitative difference is that children of lesbian mothers experience "a less aggressively tinged" separation, but they do separate successfully (establishing autonomy and a sense of self with secure ego boundaries but also capable of altruistic love and intimate connection with others). The advantage for daughters of not experiencing an extended period of fusion with single omnipotent mothers, as Chodorow saw it, was that "[f]eminine personality would be less preoccupied with individuation" and it "would help women to develop the autonomy which too much embeddedness in relationship has often taken from them."[19] In other words, girls' early identifications would be based on an internalized association of "woman-mother" with autonomy and independent selfhood.

For preoedipal sons, the difference in the experience of this phase for children of heterosexual versus lesbian parents turns on whether lesbian mothers sexually "other" their sons—whether they introduce sexually tinged oedipal issues into the relationship, curtailing the preoedipal phase, which results, according to feminist object relations theory, in a sharper, more emphatic (for Steckel, aggressive) separation process and simultaneous establishment of core elements of masculine psyche.

Do lesbian mothers sexually "other" their sons? The answer depends on what is meant by sexual "othering." In traditional psychoanalytic formulations the sexual otherness of boys/men derives not only from their having different sexual organs but from the desirability of the phallus as representing power, privilege, and pleasure. Sexual othering of sons by heterosexual mothers is thus libidinally motivated. Sexual othering can also simply mean perception of sexual difference without libidinal overtones.

Even though lesbian mothers and their children live in a heteronormative world where the phallus represents power, privilege, and often pleasure, these cultural meanings do not necessarily hold sway in the lesbian mother household. Bay Area mother Jill Collins had this to say about her three-year-old son's growing awareness of genitality:

> He takes showers with me on a regular basis because I find that's the most convenient way to bathe him. He's been talking about his penis. And James's [friend] penis. And my penis. And I keep telling him I don't have one, you know, and he likes to look, and now he's saying, "Jillie doesn't have a penis. Mommy doesn't have a penis. Auntie Kate doesn't have a penis. James has a penis. John has a penis. *Danny* has a penis." He's got it! Except for he really doesn't know what that means. He knows where his is, but he can't know where mine isn't. It's like he doesn't see that it's not there, you know.

If it is safe to assume that lesbian parents have no need to develop libidinal investments in boy children, then the argument that heterosexual mothers "push" preoedipal sons into libidinally tinged oedipal dynamics because sons are "like father/male partner" will not hold for them. Moreover, even if lesbian mothers, like Jill Collins, "other" boy children in the more libidinally neutral sense of perceiving boys' anatomical differentness—where boys' sexual organs are merely different, with no special valences attached to them—it still makes little sense for there to be any "pushing" of sons into oedipal dynamics. Sometimes a penis is just a penis. In fact, it is quite conceivable that there would be no oedipal phase at all—for boys or girls. (I take up this question in the next section.) Finally, as with preoedipal girls, the shared caregiving practice of the Bay Area mothers also inoculates against aggressively tinged separation for boys because, once again, there is no omnipotent mother from whom rigorous separation is required for the establishment of self.

The preoedipal separation-individuation process, then, is unlikely to have the same psychic effects for children of lesbian comothers as for those of heterosexual parents. Before an examination of the oedipal phase, in which incipient sex/gender components of psychic structure supposedly become consolidated for children, the question of "double dosing" of feminine mothering by lesbians needs to be addressed. Double dosing of mothering implies, not a diffusion of cathexis relations and deconcentration from an omnipotent mother-child dyadic relation, but a doubling of female mothering and therefore a doubling of the omnipotent mother effect.

Because mothers have themselves been socialized as women with capacities for nurturance and needs for emotional connection and intimacy, the argument goes, both mothers in lesbian-coparent families may overinvest in the child relationship. Some possible results, according to Steckel, are that "two female parents [who] do more things for the child . . . may overprotect the child and subtly reinforce a self-image of helplessness" and thus impede separation, individuation, and the achievement of independence. Or "two female partners would focus on maintaining the relationship at the expense of healthy aggression, if aggression were perceived as threatening the relationship."[20] For boys, Steckel notes in relation to the double-mothering effect, "Chodorow's work [may] suggest that lesbians' boy children differentiate more easily because both female parents perceive them as distinctly 'other.' " Finally, there is the possibility that "two female parents, both deriving their identity from relating rather than separating, would both focus too much on the relationship with each other and with the child, resulting in inadequate room for the child to separate."[21] The latter suggests enclosure rather than expansion and diffusion of emotional energy. After raising these possibilities, however, Steckel concludes that they are not supported by her findings, with the possible exception of the double "othering" of sons by two female parents, allowing for unambiguous separation by sons—a scenario Steckel does not attempt directly to address.

Because these possibilities relate to *mothers'* gender identity in relation to their children's preoedipal period, it is important to examine the role of gender and untangle theoretically whether double dosing occurs and any implications. Another strand in psychoanalytic theory actually offers an explanation for Steckel's findings of successful separation of children of lesbian comothers and why double dosing may be ruled out.

In the psychoanalytic understanding of the operation of the primary love, preoedipal relation between infant and (heterosexual) mother, the preoedipal situation is sometimes referred to as the pleasure principle because the id runs riot, unchecked by the rules and prohibitions of the external object world. In the heterosexual-parent family, a mother who does exclusive caregiving in the absence of caregiving by the father is for an infant child an extension of the infant's presymbolic, internal affective environment and eventually comes to represent its own developing self (external ego); thus the infant does not see the mother as separate or as having needs or interests of her own. "She is the person whom it loves with egoistic primary love and to whom it becomes attached. The infant comes to define itself as a person through its relationship to her, by internalizing the most important aspects of their relationship."[22]

Fathers, on the other hand, are said to represent the reality principle, since they come and go discontinuously in the child's field of external object relations; they represent for the child its earliest sense of an object or other that is not its self and thus impose the "reality" of external object relations in a way that mothers, in symbiotic relation with infants, do not.

An important element in the child's introduction to "reality" is its mother's involvement with other people—with its father and possibly with siblings. Father and siblings—or other important people in the caretaker's life who are perceived as coming between caretaker and infant, but *do not do primary caretaking themselves*—are in some ways more easily differentiated from the self, because the infant's first association with them involves envy and a perception of self in opposition. Father and other [noncaregiving] people are important as major constituting elements of the "reality principle" and as people enabling differentiation of self and differentiation among objects. (Emphasis added) [23]

Thus the asymmetrical organization of parenting in heterosexual-parent families codes the pleasure principle versus the reality principle in specifically gendered terms.

In lesbian-coparent families, because both mothers represent the pleasure and reality principles, lesbian parents' gender in their children's pre-oedipal period serves to delink or undo the gendered coding of these domains as feminine and masculine. The conventional gender typing of pleasure and reality principles is not possible when, representing both domains, women do primary caregiving and other familial and extrafamilial tasks. Rather than a doubling of feminine mothering, then, it would seem that the distribution of necessary object relations for infants successfully to separate and individuate occurs without gender differentiation of such processes. To put it schematically, mothers' gender does not pile on top of itself vertically but is distributed horizontally throughout cathexis relations. Pleasure and reality, nature and culture, are represented by women.

Danielle Walton, whom we met earlier in this chapter, spoke directly to this issue in reference to parenting with partner Lee Lanier:

DANIELLE: I think that he'll [son Nathan] have a different view of women, not even so much from me but from Lee. Because Lee can do anything. I mean, she cooks, she cleans, she builds, she does gardening, she's just a very powerful person in herself in a not-so-traditional way. I have my own power too; I step out there too and I'm not passive. But that's what I really value about Lee. I think Nathan's going to, I don't think that Nathan's not going to lose not having a man. I think that he's um, you know, he's going to have the loss on some level of not knowing who his father is and not having that person here in his life, but Lee puts my brother-in-law to shame!

LEE: We [Nathan and she] won't be able to pee over the railing together and this sort of thing.

DANIELLE: But I mean, he [brother-in-law] can't do anything, and Lee can do it all. And so, in terms of talent and what he's [Nathan] going to be exposed to, he's got a full set [of parents].

Steckel's findings of successful (if superior because less aggressive) processes of separation-individuation of lesbian coparents' children make sense when the child does not have an omnipotent mother from whom to separate—in single or doubled form—but still has "a full set of parents."

The Oedipal Situation: Crisis? What Crisis?

The oedipal crisis, as it is thought to normally occur in heterosexual-parent families, is different for boys and girls. Chodorow described the oedipal girl's dilemma in the following way:

> When an omnipotent mother perpetuates primary love and primary identification in relation to her daughter, and creates boundaries and a differentiated, anaclitic love relation to her son . . . [and greater independence], a girl's father is likely to become a symbol of freedom from this dependence and merging. A girl is likely to turn to him, regardless of his gender or sexual orientation, as the most available person who can help her to get away from her mother. The turn to the father, whatever its sexual meaning, also concerns emotional issues of self and other. *These issues tend to be resolved by persons in roles that are systematically gender-linked, not because of qualities inherent in persons of either gender but because of family organization.* (Emphasis added)[24]

The implication here is that an oedipal girl will turn to whoever represents "not omnipotent mother" in order to distinguish her self from her mother, thus propelling her into the oedipal phase. It happens that in heterosexual-parent families the "not omnipotent mother" is father, a man. This is one reason gender coding occurs: the object turned to happens to be male. Two elements are different for lesbian-coparent families as a result of mothers' shared primary practice: again, there is no omnipotent mother to turn away from; and, if a single, omnipotent mother even temporarily arises, the object the child will turn to will be another woman, not a man.

There is a second gender-linked reason, according to feminist object relations theory, that girls in heterosexual-parent families make a (partial) turn to fathers. Because a daughter has become for the heterosexual mother a narcissistic extension of herself, and the daughter sees that people unlike herself receive "special" treatment from mother (because they are sexual others in possession of penises), the daughter seeks ways to secure this "special" love. "A girl turns to her father in defense, feeling angry, like a rejected lover. She wants her father for the special love she cannot get from her mother and she wants his penis, which will *allow* her to get this love. She wants mother and father both."[25]

Girls consolidate (heterosexual) feminine personality by retaining a primary identification with mother but desiring what father has (and thus father/males). Curiously, though, a girl desires what father has, not for its own sake, but as a means of pleasing or having mother. The (partial) turn of the girl to father is thus motivated by *mother's* heterosexual libidinal stance. Both reasons for girls' oedipal turn to fathers—that he is "not omnipotent mother" and that he also appears to "please mother"—have to do with the heterosexuality of the parental couple. The "resolution" of the oedipal crisis for daughters, Chodorow wrote, is when "[a] girl identifies with her mother in their common feminine inferiority and in her heterosexual stance."[26]

In lesbian-coparent families, there is no phallic figure and therefore no model of feminine desire of the masculine, no "special" treatment of, or gratification from, things masculine. Oedipal girls in lesbian-mother families—if we may even speak of them as oedipal girls—thus will not value masculinity as a means of either pleasing mother or escaping mother because there is no mother and there is no father.

Is there an oedipal crisis for boys? In Chodorow's reading of the oedipal son of heterosexual parents:

A boy gives up his mother in order to avoid punishment, but identifies with his father because he can then gain the benefits of being the one who gives punishment, of being masculine and superior.

A boy must attempt to develop a masculine gender identification and learn the masculine role in the absence of a continuous and ongoing personal relationship to his father (and in the absence of a continuously available masculine role model). . . . Psychologically boys appropriate those specific components of the masculinity of their father that they fear will be otherwise used against them, but do not as much identify diffusely with him as a person.[27]

Boys must cobble together a masculinity for themselves that is made up of elements having little to do with their actual personal relations with fathers or men—because fathers and men have themselves denied the interpersonal, emotional relationality of which they might once have been capable had they not themselves rejected their love for mother and the maternal relation more generally. "In boys," wrote Freud, "the [Oedipus] complex is not simply repressed, it is literally smashed to pieces by the shock of threatened castration."[28] Fathers and men thus have few psychological resources with which to develop the personal relationships with sons capable of averting this precipitous "resolution." The smashing of sons' capacities for altruistic love is the price of conventional masculinity. For Chodorow, "Masculine identification processes stress differentiation from others, the denial of affective relation, and categorical universalistic components of the masculine role."[29] Categorical, universalistic components are those that are culturally distilled and defined as masculine.

The sons of lesbian comothers are unlikely to have their capacities for nonself-love and relationality "smashed." It *is* the case that they must cobble together a masculinity from the available elements. What is crucially absent from lesbians' sons lives, however, is the source of masculinity that is associated with punishment and with possession of mother: *paternal* masculinity. The smashing of the oedipal son's love for mother is accomplished by the fear of *paternal* punishment. Paternal masculinity as a source of identity for sons is a particular masculinity, with its own positional and categorical prerogatives, even while it is a subset of societal hegemonic masculinity/ies. Because for the oedipal son of heterosexual parents paternal masculinity is proximal but impersonal, unreal yet palpable, it wields its force psychologically at the same time that it is endorsed and affirmed sociologically. "A boy's identification processes are not likely to be so embedded in or mediated by a real affective relation to his father."[30] Paternal masculinity is present in heterosexual-parent families whether fathers are around or not. It is not present in lesbian-comother families and therefore cannot trigger oedipal processes for sons.

The Bay Area mothers spontaneously offered their opinions on the missing paternal element in their families: most volunteered that fathers were an unnecessary and undesirable component of their family life. Marlene Fierer declared:

> I just didn't think that that was really necessary from everything I've seen in my life. That's just my experience. I know our house [family of origin] would have been better off without a man, a father. So I never did see that as a necessary ingredient. If anything, I thought it might be useful—I know it's on tape but—not to have a man, a male figure. And then being in recovery for so many years as I have, I've just heard over and over and over from, you know, of course women in A.A., but even women who aren't in A.A., there's just so many violence and incest issues. I mean, this kid is not going to be harmed, in my book, not to have a male parent in the home.

Jill Collins offered this opinion:

> A lot of women that I would talk to would say that, you know, their attitude was, "All those straights who think that it would be horrible to raise a boy without a father or even a girl without a father, you know they just don't realize that you don't need a man. You don't need a man around to raise children." And it's true, you don't need them in the house.

And Kristen Frantz had this to say:

> We have male friends. We have grandpa. We figure grandpa can teach him how to pee in the woods, you know stuff like that. Yeah, we've got, not a bunch, but we have male friends.

These views about having male role models turn on the distinction between fathers and simply "male role models." There is a difference, psychoanalytically and sociologically, between men who are perceived as potentially punishing, possessive of woman/mother, and dominant fathers and men who are perceived as benignly masculine and who choose to involve themselves in the lives of (lesbians') children. The absence of paternal masculinity means that the initial psychoaffective inscriptions of gender for these children are likely to be much less emphatic. They will not have the same (unconscious) emotional charges that they have for sons of heterosexual parents.

If "successful" resolution of the Oedipus complex for a boy consists in perceiving paternal threat and repressing his love for his mother, gaining for himself the privileges of paternal masculinity, gender identification occurs for him in a shifting emotional complex embodying fear, envy, rivalry, hatred, and contempt, most of which become a factor when the father becomes a more continuous figure in the object relations world of the child. For lesbian-coparent families, what is strikingly different—and made manifest in the Bay Area mothers' observations—is that both "phallic power" and perhaps the more pernicious aspects of the emotional complex precipitated by it are absent. Children may see mothers and themselves as castrated or candidates for castration, but the precise agent of that castration, and the purpose for that agency (the maintenance of a credible threat and possession of the mother) have no reality in the relationships within their family organization.

Sons and daughters of lesbian coparents still achieve gender identity, whatever one thinks of that. Especially for sons, nonpaternal sources of gender identity will (and do) play a greater role in the development of their sense of gendered selfhood. Like the Bay Area mothers quoted above, most couples I spoke with expressed interest in having some men in their children's lives; male "role models" in place of fathers seemed to be the most urgent concern.[31] It follows that, for boys, the "boyness" they display may have no discernible connection to the kind of masculinity associated with the oedipal resolution. But they will still (and do) display boyness, as was abundantly evident to me in the numerous 49ers jerseys, baseball caps, trucks, and fire engines I saw in the homes of Bay Area mothers with sons. When sons of lesbian mothers are exposed to real adult men with whom they have personal relationships minus oedipal issues, they are more likely have richer, personally meaningful sources of masculinity with which to identify.[32]

For girls, because they are likely to have separated from two co-primary love objects rather than ambivalently turning away from an omnipotent mother in partial favor of father, their resulting sense of self is likely to be one secure in its autonomy and ego boundaries and capable of self-love and love of others. The sources of feminine identity are not attached to painful processes of partially rejecting the primary love object, and thus there is no "rejected internal mother object" for them to turn into self-hatred. But the cultural epiphenomena and props of femininity—dresses, dolls—are still there for them to appropriate.

For lesbian-coparent families, then, since this is an expansive parenting model, one of diffusion and abundance of emotional intimacy, there is no need for children to turn *away* from overinvolved exclusive mothers or turn *to* fathers out of fear or feelings of inadequacy. If there is any turning, it is to another woman. These observations suggest that all the gendered oedipal identifications occurring in heterosexual-parent families, as theorized in the traditional and some feminist object relations psychoanalytic accounts, will be at most peripheral to lesbian-coparent families. For children, masculine/feminine identifications are not attached to the emotional and libidinal energies circulating within lesbian-coparent families in which primary parenting is shared and the couple relationship is emotionally satisfying to both partners.[33] Whatever patterns of deep attachment and identification occur between children and parents, and whatever psychic inscriptions these produce for children, will not be linked to gender.

This delinking of gendered identifications from extremely intense emotional and psychic experiences could produce the result, finally, that

> [m]asculinity would not become tied to denial of dependence and devaluation of women. Feminine personality would be less preoccupied with individuation, and children would not develop fears of *maternal* omnipotence and expectations of *women's* unique self-sacrificing qualities. This would reduce men's needs to guard their masculinity and their control of social and cultural sphere which treat and define women as secondary and powerless, and would help women to develop the autonomy which too much embeddedness in relationships has often taken from them.[34]

In lesbian-coparent families, the expansion of intimacy, brought about by a sharing of primary caregiving, together with the absence of paternal masculinity, might well signal the beginnings of a generation free of the psychic costs of gendered power within the family.

Chapter 4 | UNDOING THE GENDER DIVISION OF LABOR

Coparents Bobbie and Mindy Covington legally changed their own surnames to Covington so as to fashion a family name for themselves and their two children, Trevor and Abbott. They were the only Bay Area family who created an entirely new family name for themselves, believing that, symbolically, the family name would unify them. Bobbie, who was originally from Australia and expressed strong opinions about the "sexist" culture there, gave birth to both children, while Mindy, originally from Texas and giving hints of her fondness for the country music and sensibilities she grew up with, had legally adopted them. Though Mindy was considerably taller than Bobbie, they had been mistaken for sisters on more than one occasion, since, as they surmised, they both sported blonde ("to cover the gray"), feminine hairstyles and shared a taste for 14k gold jewelry.

But despite their common, conventionally feminine appearance, they worried that, among those who knew they were coparents, they would give the impression that they followed "gender roles" in their work and family practices. They feared that, even though both mothers were self-employed in the environmental consulting firm they operated together, because Bobbie had given birth to both children and did the firm's accounting and office work, often at home, while Mindy did the on-site field work, they would be understood as "doing gender," as doing "mother" and "father" respectively. Nothing could be further from the truth as far as they were concerned, and they made conscious efforts to dispel any such impression.

> BOBBIE: I think the thing that I had the most difficulty with is people's perception of our relationship. Particularly on this year-long contract where Mindy is out of the house and off to work and then coming home at night. And we're starting to get known in the neighborhood. That they perceive this as a male-female type relationship. And that does worry me. And added to it, Mindy's a lot taller than I am, she's a bigger person, she's [possibly perceived as] the "man of the house" type thing. And I've started going to a local mother's group where all the kids get together on Tuesday morning and I'm concerned at this point that that reinforces what people might see as I'm the mother who stays at home with the children. And that is not how our relationship is and that's not how I want gay relationships to be perceived. So what we're going to do is when it's our turn to have all the kids and mothers over, Mindy will stay home that day and I'll go to the office just to break, people will think, "Oh, we really have two mothers here." And not one playing as the man.

Bobbie and Mindy's worries about the impression they gave attested to their own awareness of how gender functions as a mechanism distributing power and rewards inequitably between (heterosexual) parents. Bobbie intimated that her awareness developed while growing up in Australian "sexist" culture, where, as she put it, "They were still running commercials with women selling power saws in bikinis, and the men congregate and drink beer and the women congregate and whine about the men congregating drinking beer."

But closer to home, in a suburb of San Jose, the couple's awareness of gender and the division of labor between parents was reinforced every time they picked up or dropped off their kids at day care, where they drew the envy of heterosexual mothers:

> BOBBIE: The question most asked is, "What's it like with two mothers?"
> MINDY: We get that a lot at day care. The mothers . . .
> BOBBIE: The mothers asking, "Is it different, do you think, from us?" And we say, "Pretty sure it is."

MINDY:	Yes it is!
BOBBIE:	Most of them are struggling with . . . mothers doing . . .
MINDY:	All the work.
BOBBIE:	Most of the mothers work [for pay], obviously, if they're at day care. But they're falling for all the children things. You know, they have to get them up, make the sandwiches, get them to school, pick them up, and, you know, so they, you know, working outside the house and then falling for all the motherly things. And they're asking us, you know, "Is it like that for you?" And we go, "No."
MINDY:	"Sorry!"
BOBBIE:	"Sorry. It's very equal." And one of the mothers said, "Who does Trevor go to, you or Mindy?" And I'll say, "Well it does fluctuate from week to week; he has favorites for the week." And I say, "But equal." She said, "Oh, that would be great (making sighing noise). My kids always come to me. 'Mommy will you do this? Mommy will you play with me? Mommy will you come to my room?' They just don't go to their father as much." And I said, "No, it's not like that."

"NOT LIKE THAT": THE SEXUAL DIVISION OF LABOR

The "that" is the sexual or gender division of labor that has historically plagued heterosexual women who are mothers, and all women within the larger economy, and it represents one component of the larger social organization of gender, or sex/gender system. Labor here involves both productive and reproductive labor, the paid work people do to materially support themselves and their families and the unremunerated work involved in maintaining a home and cleaning, feeding, socializing, and caring for family members, particularly dependent children. For analytic purposes I am distinguishing this complex of paid and unpaid work that parents do from the primary infant care and relations among parents and child/ren from the last chapter, since the latter constitute a familial structure of cathexis that involves a particular distribution of affect, intimacy, and needs gratification. While these interpersonal and psychological dynamics clearly involve (mostly emotional) labor and are not necessarily experienced as distinct from other forms of work people do for and within their families, the focus in this chapter is more on the material labor parents perform, as that labor necessarily inserts them in a field of economic relations and affects the distribution of power and rewards.[1]

Historically the division of labor within modern, Western nuclear families headed by heterosexual couples has been based on gender conventions in which men assume primary responsibility for breadwinning in the paid labor force and women assume primary responsibility for unpaid or low-paid household maintenance and child care in the home. Feminists have argued convincingly that this division of labor by gender—influenced to a large degree by the historic movement of productive activity to the public sphere of market relations, leaving reproductive activity to the private sphere of domestic caregiving—has profoundly diminished women's status and power both within the family and in society as a whole. Marxist feminists have suggested that because domestic and reproductive labor in capitalist economies remains largely devalued and socially unrewarded, women, who have traditionally performed this labor and continue to do so disproportionately to men, remain economically dependent and disadvantaged, as Engels himself outlined meticulously in *The Origin of the Family, Private Property and the State*.[2]

The disadvantage of this arrangement for heterosexual women is meted out in its most severe form when married couples with children divorce, and wives, having deferred opportunities for earnings and occupational development while child rearing, now face the breadwinning responsibility with considerably limited options for earning even subsistence income.[3] This division of labor by gender for women in heterosexual nuclear families has also limited women's power to make or influence important decisions that affect themselves and their children. According to some social scientists, within a nuclear family, the partner who contributes the most material and financial resources, who often controls the distribution of valued goods both within and beyond the family, or who confers the highest social status on the family by virtue of his or her occupation and education typically exercises more power in family decision making.[4] Men, therefore, historically have had more power than women to influence major family decisions concerning, for instance, buying a home, moving, changing jobs, educating children, and even whether they will do housework.[5]

Heterosexual women in dual-income families who work in the paid labor force now have greater autonomy and power to make important family decisions, and studies conducted in the late 1980s and 1990s located a few families in which men and women appeared to share labor equally.[6] But because women in general earn roughly 30 percent less than men, on average, the vast majority of women in heterosexual marriages still most often sacrifice personal and career interests to meet family needs, and they still do a significant majority of child care and household work.[7] Women's "second shift," as Arlie Hochschild famously dubbed it in her 1989 book of the same name, while always prevalent for working-class mothers, appears to be a relatively stable structural feature of modern, middle-class heterosexual family life, even among couples who consciously attempt more egalitarian work and family arrangements.[8]

Without Gender, a Measure of Equity

If the division of household, child care, and paid labor in heterosexual nuclear families continues to be based on gender, presenting women with impossibly "hard choices"—as sociologist Kathleen Gerson memorably put it in her 1985 book of the same title—and maintaining their socioeconomic disadvantage and dependence on men or the state or both, might lesbian-coparent families like the South Bay's Covingtons alter this structural dynamic?[9] The vast majority of Bay Area couples I spoke with, twenty-nine of the thirty-four, had allocated their work and family labor such that neither partner disproportionately assumed responsibility for a particular form of labor; or when she did, it was understood as temporary, and any disadvantage associated with it they compensated for by shifting certain valued responsibilities—whether materially valuable or subjectively defined as valuable—in the direction of the "disadvantaged" partner. The Bay Area mothers viewed housework, child care, and paid work, in one sense, as a total complex of familial tasks that needed to get done day to day, week to week, month to month, and so on, and assumed that their distribution would be taken up by two fully capable, socially unrestricted adults. By *socially unrestricted* I mean that there was no social category to which one partner had been assigned that invited a priori a certain arrangement. Couples did not see gender, or for that matter any other arbitrary social category, as a basis for allocating paid work and family work. Comother Naomi Raley put it this way: "Not having the roles there, we have to struggle with them, we have to argue about them. We have to figure it out, and it adds a whole other level of stuff that we have to do. That if we were straight we wouldn't have to do; we would just assume that, you know, the male would paint the house and blah blah blah, the woman would, whatever it is, take care of the kids." While Bobbie and Mindy Covington worried that they would be perceived as "doing gender" when in practice they felt they were not, Naomi, like most of the parents in this study, viewed doing gender as an impossibility—that as a mechanism for sorting labor, gender was not only unavailable to lesbian coparents but impossible for them to produce if they wanted to.

This observation stands in direct contrast with one 1985 "New Home Economic" analysis of heterosexual-parent families as "tiny firms" with "household production functions," in which, as the author Sarah Berk contended, not only is parents' labor allocated by means of gender, but gender both "affects and is perhaps effected *through* the division of household labor."[10] Gender is itself produced in and through the work that husbands and wives do, as "the 'shoulds' of gender ideals are fused with the 'musts' of efficient household production."[11] In other words, in Berk's analysis of heterosexual-parent families, gender and work are mutually constitutive; gender and gendered power are integrally linked to productive and reproductive household labor.

Among the Bay Area mothers, however, couples' practices reflected the proposition that, whatever their perception of it, gender was autonomous from and not constitutive of their labor. Whether they conceptualized gender as a generally efficient (because established) but unavailable mechanism of labor allocation, as did Naomi, or as a pernicious set of "roles" lurking in the culture and capable of subsuming hapless couples within its template, as did Bobbie and Mindy, mothers' labor practices reflected a refusal to exaggerate or otherwise attach sustained social significance to the relationship between birth mother and nonbirth mother. Beyond the initial differential pattern of taking leave from (paid) work and the physiological exigencies of parturition and breastfeeding, mothers generally exhibited no clear patterns of labor distribution according to a birth mother/nonbirth mother dichotomy, and, for that matter, there was no correlation between self-display of masculinity or femininity with maternity. The Bay Area couples viewed birth mothers as no more responsible for or equipped by virtue of their maternity to do "typical" female/mother tasks than nonbirth mothers.[12] Moreover, when a partner in a given family did take on a disproportionate share of the child care and housework responsibilities, she was no more likely to be the birth mother than the comother.

This suggests that these parents' individual gender identities were not bound up with the gendered meanings conventionally attached to the tasks of breadwinning, maintaining a household, and caring for children. This is not to say that individual mothers did not have a personal gender identity or that they did not "perform" gender in their self-displays of particular traits and styles typically associated with masculinity and femininity. Rather, it means that, in relation to each other, partners' self-image and felt experience of gender did not depend upon heterosexual significations of labor. Thus Pat Keating and Sarah Alton, comother and birth mother respectively, both described themselves as "on the butch side." They played softball in a city women's league, wore "typically" masculine clothes, and had an intimate, practical knowledge of what goes on inside a gymnasium. When I strode up to their doorstep on the day of our interview, Sarah greeted me wearing army fatigue pants and a gray, army-issue T-shirt and ushered me into the living room where a Soloflex machine stood in one of the corners, gleaming impressively like the chrome on a vintage automobile in show condition. Sarah's body looked as if it knew the machine well and was itself in exhibit condition, making it difficult to believe that she had given birth to Steven less than a year before. Pregnancy and childbirth were probably the most "feminine" events in her biography following years of serving in the army and later working for United Parcel Service, driving trucks and delivering packages. But Sarah said she had always wanted to have a child, to give birth, and had felt that desire since she was very young.

According to heterosexual conventions, where a feminine gender identity equates with a desire to give birth, which in turn makes a woman somehow more qualified for and interested in domestic work ("women's work"), Sarah was clearly anomalous, or rather more complex than this gender track would suggest. The kind of (paid) work Sarah was most qualified for and preferred is traditionally thought of as "men's" work. But as it happened, in Sarah and Pat's current practice, Sarah cared for baby Steven full time while Pat worked as a data processing manager, an arrangement the couple had decided made economic sense because Sarah had difficulty getting work again as a driver after she had changed jobs earlier. So when Steven came along, Sarah took on full-time homemaking and caregiving, but not because she was more qualified or experienced by virtue of her maternity or because she had more desire to do domestic labor. Rather, according to them, it was the couple's economic situation— more specifically, the disparity between Sarah's and Pat's class statuses— that made Sarah's full-time domestic labor appealing.

This example illustrates how personal gender identity is constructed by a complex process that may or may not articulate with stereotypical expectations and how it need not correlate with work defined by an opposition of male and female. In fact, for lesbian-coparent couples, the framework of "women's work" and "men's work" is infinitely more complicated if it applies at all, since there are so many ways in which the particular fusions of identity, desire, self-esteem, and productive activity with gender that the sex/gender system enforces unremittingly upon heterosexual women can fail to take hold.

Not only did Bay Area mothers not employ gender as a mechanism for allocating labor, but the vast majority did divide labor equitably, a finding I think is reasonable to conclude results from their nonadherence to gender as their guide. Among the thirty-four Bay Area families, twenty-nine of them, or 85 percent, detailed distributions of housework, child care, breadwinning, and financial management such that neither partner was disadvantaged economically or rendered vulnerable, and this in turn appears to have resulted in a balance of power such that partners exercised similar degrees of influence in family decision making. Moreover, this pattern of equity among the twenty-nine couples was consistent across income levels, from those at the low end who relied on friends and family to help with child care to those with six-digit family incomes.

Five couples, including Sarah and Pat, did describe their division of labor as adhering to a full-time breadwinner/full-time caregiver-homemaker arrangement, in which stay-at-home caregivers depended heavily if not completely on their partners' income with little if anything in the way of material compensation. This latter "Rozzie and Harriet" pattern may not necessarily constitute inequality in terms of the distribution of rewards to partners who happen to value full-time parenting and domesticity, as many clearly do. But to the degree and length of time that "Harriets" are engaged in full-time domestic work that is socially devalued and economically unvalued, the balance of power within these couples is likely to shift in favor of the "Rozzies," as I observed (and discuss later in this chapter) for two couples whose work and family arrangements had been organized this way for a longer period of time than the others.

In contrast, however, both partners in nineteen of the twenty-nine equal-sharing couples said that they worked full time and paid for some form of day care. Eight of the equal-sharing couples claimed that the partner with the more flexible (paid) work schedule did more child care during the week while the other partner contributed more in the way of housework and weekend parenting. In the remaining two equal-sharing families, the mothers said that they had consciously reduced their work hours proportionately so that neither parent was assuming an unequal share of responsibilities relative to her partner. The mothers in one of these couples alternated taking Fridays off from work each week, and their twelve-month-old daughter stayed at home with a caregiver for the remainder of the week. Among these equal-sharing couples, few partners expressed overt dissatisfaction with the arrangements or with each other,[13] a result, perhaps, of their having already "argued" and "struggled" to "figure" them out, as Naomi observed.

PORTRAITS OF EQUITY— ACROSS THE CLASS SPECTRUM

Parents who had equitable divisions of labor and were among the more affluent Bay Area families had greater financial latitude to negotiate their work-family-leisure tradeoffs and did so fully aware of the benefits and options available to them. Those couples in which both partners earned professional salaries were generally also those who, to use Berk's phrase, "marketized" their domestic labor: they paid for quality day care, hired housecleaners, and ate out or consumed more prepared foods. Even so, these Bay Area dual-career couples could not marketize all of their family labor, and some expressed concerns over the costs to the quality of their family life of living in a socially progressive, gay-friendly, but expensive urban center that demanded high incomes.

Kathleen Peterson, thirty-three, was a labor union public relations consultant and comother of daughter Sophie, who had just celebrated her first birthday when we met. At forty-five, her partner and birth mother to Sophie, Sharon Carlton, was a self-employed personnel consultant who worked at home when she was not on site with clients. In 1994 Kathleen earned roughly $55,000 per year, while Sharon's annual income, which fluctuated month to month depending on client billings and collected accounts, approximated that amount. Educated at top-notch universities and having developed the occupational skills and experience to establish stable career trajectories, Kathleen and Sharon would seem so firmly middle to upper middle class that they could pay others to perform the labor and tasks that have historically been "women's" unremunerated work. In practice, they did have a day care provider for four of five days during the workweek, and they hired a housecleaner on occasion. But they also mutually planned for both to take two Fridays off per month so that daughter Sophie would be in the care of one of her parents for a full day during each workweek. In addition, they routinely made chore lists and schedules in their attempt to organize and make explicit equitable arrangements for the tasks and responsibilities that they did not "farm out," such as cooking, shopping, and daily tidying.

But even while their arrangements equally distributed responsibility for paid and unpaid labor, and the parity of their income levels certainly facilitated this, the need to earn such high incomes in the first place disturbed their socially progressive sensibilities. They were concerned not only that raising a family in San Francisco required two incomes but that for same-sex-parent families the two-income requirement constituted a "queer tax":

SHARON: This last year it's been really hard for me to not have Kathleen come home [from work] when she says she's going to or when I'm expecting her to. Most of the time she can't help it, the job demands it, but this is part of the problem. Which makes us all wonder why we shouldn't just, you know, move to South Dakota where they're not income machines. But we'd probably be shot and run out of town.

KATHLEEN: It's a queer tax. One salary, we'd be able to afford to live on one salary. I *never* thought I'd make this much money in my life. I mean, there's Gay Pride that we're volunteers for and our kids can be exposed to that, but it's expensive to live here. If we weren't gay and didn't need to live in an environment where we'd be safe we wouldn't need to afford [all of this].

Other dual-career parents, particularly those living in suburbs, described their negotiation of egalitarian work and family arrangements as less fraught with concerns about quality of family life. Indeed, for one family, in which both parents worked full time in different divisions of the same county parks and recreation system and earned salaries similar to those of Kathleen and Sharon, the comfort of their suburban community and tri-level home exemplified the upper-middle-class American Dream. Each day on her way to work in the morning, birth mother Alana Resnick drove the couple's son Brian to day care, and each day on her way home from work in the afternoon, comother Eleanor Paltz picked him up. Brian's morning and evening meals were usually prepared by the mother who took him to or picked him up from day care.

Though Alana and Eleanor paid for some housecleaning, they both did household work according to their personal proclivities: Alana liked to do "major" jobs and projects, often during the weekend, compared to the more diffuse tidying that Eleanor did as a matter of habit, since, as she explained, she was "the neat and tidy person." But Alana's "major" jobs were not the kind of tasks and projects that men typically do—vis-à-vis overworked wives—those that may be done on a discretionary basis and are inessential to the maintenance of the family's well-being, such as yardwork or repairs. Alana's "major" jobs consisted in such activities as doing an accumulation of laundry, spending an entire weekend day cooking the next week's meals, scouring the oven, cleaning the refrigerator, or vacuuming the carpeting throughout the couple's substantial home. The entire operation, the mothers felt, ran relatively smoothly, as they put it:

ALANA: [It's] [p]retty equal at this point. It's been good for both of us.
ELEANOR: It's better for both of us, 'cause at this point, [Brian's] all over the
          place. So one person chases and one person cleans up.

They had developed the routines and patterns that made the operation run smoothly partly in response to baby Brian's severe allergies: there could be no disagreements about providing an impeccably clean home environment or about both mothers doing the allegist appointments, since both needed to accumulate the practical knowledge and develop the relationships with medical professionals necessary for maintaining Brian's health. Moreover, as Alana and Eleanor explained, they each brought different cognitive "skills" to the management of Brian's health with professionals:

ELEANOR: I'm a better question person.

ALANA: She's a very good question person and I'm more of a process . . . I want to kind of know what the process is going to be. Eleanor's much more of the "Take it when?" and "At what time?" and "What does this mean?" [person], where I don't want to know what it means, I just want to know what the outcome is. So that's helped us in the long run too.

Both mothers therefore did the doctor appointments, and both were committed to maintaining a high standard of cleanliness in the home. In the main, despite the challenge of Brian's illness, Alana and Eleanor's visible satisfaction with their lifestyle suggests that their socioeconomic status went some way toward mitigating such challenges, while simultaneously facilitating equitable labor practices between partners.

If the parallels in partners' salary levels and paid work schedules made it easier to distribute the unremunerated work evenly, it is worth noting how equal-sharing couples with disparities in earnings and occupational demands between partners still managed to achieve a measure of equity. For, in the case of heterosexual couples, higher-earning men generally reap the rewards of leisure and influence in family decision making vis-à-vis women, who are paid less and often work fewer (paid) hours so as to attend to the needs of children and home. For the Bay Area mothers, however, even with substantial disparities in earnings between partners—which might have tilted the distribution of rewards and power in favor of the higher-earning partner, as I believe was true for two of the "Rozzie and Harriet" families discussed later in this chapter—equal-sharing parents managed to transform "women's second shift" into two equally distributed "quarter-shifts" of a decidedly different feel and quality. And in the process, they compensated for the economic disadvantage of the partner doing more family unremunerated work by giving her nearly complete control over the family purse.

In one Berkeley family with a substantial income disparity between partners but with an overall family income still reaching six digits, birth mother Karen Shaw, a highly specialized emergency room nurse, earned $90,000 per year to her partner Arlene Roesner's $15,000 part-time computer technician salary. Arlene provided part-time, stay-at-home care for their five-year-old son, Bobby, throughout the period following Bobby's birth and Karen's return to her intense, full-time work. This child care arrangement was later supplemented with the services of family day care providers, a favorite of whom was a Chinese family provider that Arlene and Karen, who were Jewish, actively sought, as they felt it important that Bobby be exposed to the Chinese aspects of his ethnicity (Bobby's donor was Chinese American). The couple hoped to use this child care provider on a more permanent yet flexible basis, since, as Arlene stepped up her search for full-time employment, Bobby's after-school hours would eventually require supervision.

During the workweek, while not at her part-time job, Arlene performed the daily maintenance and provisioning tasks necessary to keep the family functioning. When Karen returned from her emotionally and physically exhausting days at the hospital, Arlene had prepared dinner, allowing Karen to enjoy "quality" time with Bobby. Karen's time with Bobby involved reading to him, playing with him, bathing him, and tucking him into bed. The "second shift" that full-time working heterosexual mothers face after putting in their hours at their paid work *feels* like more work, so much so that Arlie Hochschild, in her more recent book *The Time Bind,* reported that women are staying longer on the job, working overtime, because the burdens of family, borne in the past with little to no help from male partners, now feel unbearable.[14] For Karen Shaw, however, coming home to feed and bathe and lull her son to sleep was a pleasurable proposition because Arlene had attended to so many of the other tasks—like preparing dinner for them—that can combine to create what feels like an overwhelming, if not impossible, burden when shouldered by one person. Arlene described the tenor and quality of their "quarter-shift system" in this way:

> I take care of Bobby in the morning, get him off to school, fix his lunchbox and all that stuff and at nighttime I let Kate spend time with him, 'cause she likes to come home and play with him and you know, I've got things to do. I

mean, we share, or whatever. But she's usually the bath giver. And she plays guitar while Bobby's in the bathtub.

To compensate for Arlene's economic disadvantage from her lower earnings and her doing more unremunerated work during the workweek—not something the couple consciously sought to ameliorate but achieved in practice—Arlene did all the financial management for the family, investing the portion of Karen's considerable salary and her own such that Karen "doesn't have to worry about it." Karen and Arlene preferred this arrangement, as Karen explained: "She likes to do that, she enjoys it, and I'm happy to just turn it all over to her." The equity achieved here worked as follows: Karen's full-time job was intense and demanding, and the salary she earned rewarded her for this; but by "turning it all over" to Arlene to manage, she was in effect relinquishing or trading power deriving from her superior earnings for the reward of spending time with Bobby that felt pleasurable to her rather than labor intensive. Arlene's job consisted in (part-time) paid work that generated a modest income and (part-time) unremunerated family labor; but because her job also afforded her greater autonomy and flexibility, she was able to pursue personal interests and projects that were pleasurable to her, one of which involved the management of the family's finances.

For most equal-sharing Bay Area mothers, their process for deciding how their paid work, domestic, and family responsibilities would be divided appears to have followed an egalitarian principle of shared rewards and responsibilities.[15] This applied across income levels and class categories, such that, though struggling with fewer material resources and the stress accompanying economic insecurity, lower-income families still managed to distribute domestic and child care labor equitably between partners.

What was at issue for lower-income families in particular was the allocation of unremunerated work that they were financially constrained from "marketizing." These families had fewer resources with which to "farm out" housecleaning and yardwork or pay for quality child care, as did their higher-income counterparts: unable to afford household help, and paying small amounts to friends or relying on family for daily child care, they faced greater strain in making ends meet and felt the demands of domestic and family responsibilities acutely. Some, like Nora Duncan and Jill

Collins, simply "let some things go." Nora worked for a city parking division as a meter collection supervisor and was the birth mother of three-year-old Danny, whose growing fascination with genitals Jill narrated in Chapter 3. Nora had long, flaming red hair and pale skin, attributes she had passed along to Danny with the apparent help of the couple's (anonymous) redheaded donor. But beneath the glow of Nora's wondrous hair her face betrayed a weariness, her demeanor a certain resignation, that I came to understand as the product of years of work she didn't care about but that enabled her to claim self-sufficiency. She had received from her mother a message inculcated in many children of working-class families: not to depend on anyone for material or other support but to survive and make a life for oneself, by oneself, because no one would be there to help. Nora had taken this message to heart, she told me, and had worked for over ten years in the same city agency in the same position in which she had started until her recent promotion to supervisor. Nora's options had been limited by her lack of a college education. Thus, while her city job itself offered her a small measure of security, the promotion opportunities presented very little in the way of real occupational mobility, and although the pay over the years was enough to get by on, she was never going to get rich.

At thirty-five, Jill had recently become employed full time as a computer technician for a geological research center—only in a temporary position. Having finished a baccalaureate degree in geology literally one week after Nora gave birth to Danny, Jill now had a credential that theoretically could steer her into better jobs and away from those she had moved in and out of all of her adult life, jobs such as stockroom clerk and ditch digger. But even the job she landed with her new credential was poorly compensated, as Jill explained: "It's less pay than digging ditches. It's really lousy pay, you can't live on it." At roughly $18,000, Jill's income combined with Nora's for a total family income of $46,000, an amount that could go far in some regions of the United States for a family of three, soon to be family of four. But in the Bay Area, where the cost of living is among the highest in the country, as Kathleen and Sharon lamented, the two incomes earned by Jill and Nora inadequately covered basic necessities.

When Jill recounted her history of tenuous workforce attachment, her attitude toward it seemed cavalier compared to Nora's deep sense of economic fatality. But both Jill's and Nora's remarks about their financial predicament, in light of their plans for expanding their family, betrayed an acute apprehensiveness. For, in fact, Nora would have loved nothing more than to quit working for a while or move into part-time hours so as to gain an extended respite in preparation for the arrival of their second child, to whom Nora would also give birth. Her hope was that Jill's job would become permanent so that the couple could take advantage of the employer's on-site day care. But Jill and Nora had no illusions about how important Nora's income was:

NORA: I would like to quit working, but I can't, especially since we want to sell this house [in Oakland] and buy another house over there [in Daly City]. There's no way that I could quit.

JILL: Even with this mortgage we couldn't get by on my salary.

NORA: It depends on what happens with [Jill's job]. I mean, Jill's working with [the research center] now and we're on the waiting list to get on the child care [there], and as long as she's working there and it's convenient for us to take him [Danny] there, then . . . I mean, once the new baby's born, and once I go back to work, then after that the new baby will also go to the day care. Hopefully. This is what our plans are, we don't really know how this is going to happen.

JILL: Money is going to fall out of the sky on us.

Both Jill and Nora saw clearly the constraints they faced in making ends meet and appeared to regard the family and paid work that had to be done as their joint responsibility, even while each partner contributed different personal abilities and emotional resources toward the accomplishment of that work. While I visited with them in their Oakland home, the one they hoped to sell because it was located in a neighborhood they considered unsafe, these differences were enacted in the course of our visit.

Exhibiting apparently boundless, almost childlike energy, Jill continually jumped up from the family's worn sofa to help Danny with his clothes, to check on him while he played in the backyard, to deposit him in the bathtub when he came in from outside, and to retrieve file folders that contained his legal and medical documents when we were discussing his birth. It was Jill whose lap Danny sat on to be toweled off and cuddled following his bath. Nora, on the other hand, evoked calm and maturity amidst the kinetic energy generated by Jill, Danny, and the family pets, who seemed to be in perpetual motion. For Danny, it was Nora whose lap was soothing when playtime was over, whose words were spoken softly and with care, whose ministrations were ever mindful of conveying her love for him. It was Nora who had doled out crackers and cheese and money for sodas at the picnic where I first met them.

Nora and Jill approached household labor, from which more affluent families buy themselves relief, as a matter of personal taste and preference, apparently in accordance with their different reserves of energy and patience, health requirements, and aptitudes for particular tasks. Neither partner expressed complaints about the division of household tasks and responsibilities, but they did imply that whatever sacrifice was required for them to keep the family functioning, that sacrifice was made in their housekeeping standards. In response to my initial question of "who did what" in the way of housework, the couple responded with their characteristic mix of playful sarcasm and resignation:

JILL: Well, look around . . . Danny!

NORA: Danny does the housework!

JILL: Danny does the majority of the housework!

NORA: Actually we shop together, but we don't cook that much.

JILL: The breakdown of the cooking is supposed to be, she cooks and I do the dishes, except for breakfast on the weekends, I do the breakfast, cook breakfast. I always have. We don't really cook other than that, so I do everything! I don't know, I would say it's a pretty even split as far as the housework goes because she does all the inside stuff because I'm allergic to dust.

NORA: Jill does the dishes and she does the garbage and she does, probably like half of the cooking that's done, and the other half of the cooking that's done I do and I do the vacuuming.

JILL: She gets positively vicious if I touch her laundry.

NORA: But the work outside of the house, Jill does a lot of that.

JILL: I'm in charge of the cars. I do most of the oil changes and stuff like that. Last weekend I was out here with the pushmower, I'll do the pushmower, but I don't like the gas mower. Which is why our lawn never got mowed before because you couldn't push the pushmower through it. One of our neighbors came down and cut it all down, chopped it as far down as he could, the weekend before, so that I could push a pushmower through it.

Though there was something of an inside/outside split in their division of domestic tasks, Jill's inside work still consisted in essential tasks that had to be performed daily and weekly, as opposed to the outside work, which, as Jill's story about neglecting the lawn suggests, was more discretionary. It is worth remarking again that men in heterosexual-parent families, especially working-class men, derive a sense of what it means to be a man in part by doing this "outside" household labor over which they exercise discretion.[16] If gender identity involves the identification of one's felt sense of self as predominantly masculine or feminine with cultural gender ideals, and the achievement of that identity occurs in part through the performance of historically gendered ("sex-typed") work, the example presented by Jill and Nora's division of labor is instructive for understanding the conditions under which that process founders.

Jill's outside household work, though "sex-typed" as masculine, did not do for her what it does for men, namely, reinforce gender identity. Not only was it not signified as masculine (defined oppositionally to tasks signified as feminine) within the specific context of Jill and Nora's domestic labor, but Jill did not benefit from or exercise her prerogative more frequently than Nora as a result of doing more of the discretionary domestic tasks. In other words, the inside/outside split in domestic labor did not have the same meaning for Jill and Nora that it does for conventional heterosexual parent-couples where men are able to "capitalize" the value of the difference in the forms of labor performed, enjoying greater leisure and personal autonomy than women. So even though the "surplus value" arising from the difference in household labor—as it is valued in terms of time—is a material one, that difference itself derives from a gendered semiotic one: the prior labeling of household work as men's or women's. In heterosexual-parent families, men and women perform sex-typed tasks because those *meanings* resonate with ongoing gender identification and performance. Heterosexual couples accept the gendered meanings of the tasks, consciously and unconsciously, and then act on these internalized meanings in their labor practices, thereby producing the material difference in the value of their labor: by doing work that requires less continuous attention and affords personal autonomy, men, their work and their time, are valued more highly than women, their work and their time.

The example of Jill and Nora's division of domestic labor shows how this process fails. Jill did not accept for herself the culturally gendered meaning of her outside household work; her self-concept did not "need" its masculinized meaning, since it had no relevance in her relations with Nora. In turn, she did not "capitalize" on her outside work being discretionary in the same way as do men who see it as their domain *and* who realize and act on its benefits. Acting on the gender restrictions placed on their household work, men in heterosexual-parent families take advantage of the discretionary nature of it; for them it is an opportunity that may be exploited. The gender restriction did not exist for Jill, so she proceeded—past the "exploitable moment" as it were—to do inside and child care work as well, spending considerable energy and time with Danny, as these activities were not defined as someone else's; they were not defined as not hers. The result of Jill's sharing of both inside and outside work was that neither Jill nor Nora enjoyed greater leisure or appeared to exercise greater influence in family decision making.

In light of this picture of egalitarianism, the contrast between these equal-sharing parent-couples and those who chose a vintage 1950s arrangement is stark indeed. The latter arrangement, which I refer to as the "Rozzie and Harriet" pattern, generally consisted in one partner assuming full-time responsibility for the household and child care while the other partner bore full responsibility for breadwinning. This organization of labor, when heterosexual couples adopt it, bears a specific, gendered significance for wives and husbands that may be traced to the immediate postwar culture in the United States. The family and gender norms of this period are familiar,[17] but why lesbian coparents in the 1990s should find these arrangements appealing, and whether the latter hold the same meanings for them, is important for understanding whether gendered power is still operative in an archaic (gender) structure when the actors ostensibly have no particular interest in the maintenance of gender.

THE ROZZIE AND HARRIET PATTERN

The work and family arrangements of the five "Rozzie and Harriet" Bay Area families fit the 1950s white, middle-class model of full-time breadwinner/homemaker and appeared to produce the same types of problems for lesbian coparents who did this as for the white, middle-class heterosexual wives whose "problem without a name" was articulated by Betty Friedan in *The Feminine Mystique*.[18] The lesbian version of Ozzie and Harriet assumes many of its predicates—a family wage earned by one adult, usually the higher-status adult; a stay-at-home caregiver and domestic worker who supports the breadwinner emotionally; and children who are primarily the charge and responsibility of the homemaker. What the Rozzie and Harriet version does not carry forward from this 1950s throwback is the assignment of the functional roles according to gender. Functionalist theorists writing in the 1950s held that women, because they give birth and are thereby naturally suited to caregiving, perform "expressive" tasks within the family, while men, who are by nature more rational and goal oriented and thus more suited to navigating markets and generating income, perform "instrumental" tasks.[19] Both the expressive and instrumental tasks and the gendered roles through which these are carried out are necessary for the maintenance of the family and for social order more generally, since a highly functional family system contributes to the ordered functioning of society as a whole.

In the Rozzie and Harriet couples here, however, birth mothers were no more likely to be the full-time homemaker/caregivers; indeed, only two of the five stay-at-home mothers were birth mothers. The potentially gendered basis for the allocation of tasks even within this historically sex-segregated, sex-typed functional arrangement was thus precluded from the outset. Birth mothers were seen as no more qualified for expressive caretaking than for instrumental breadwinning, and nonbirth mothers were not disqualified from becoming homemaker/caregivers.

Nevertheless, couples who chose to divide their labor in this way, depending on the length of time they practiced it, demonstrated how structurally disadvantageous it is for the full-time homemaker/parent. Stay-at-home partners themselves expressed dissatisfaction, concern, and anxiety with their arrangements, though some did so obliquely. Of the five Bay Area couples who had adopted a primary caregiver/primary breadwinner arrangement, two had been following this pattern for a greater length of time (approximately six months and four years respectively) than the other three, who had only recently initiated this arrangement. But the primary caregivers in the former two couples offered profoundly dispirited accounts of their daily lives.

"I Felt So Devalued by Her"

Clara Mueller and Madeline Lovadas's fifteen-year relationship began when they were undergraduates at a midwestern university during the late

1970s and early 1980s. For Madeline, who admitted she was "infatuated," Clara would be her first and only love interest, and Madeline remained committed to the relationship throughout their college courtship and afterward. For her part, Clara was also deeply committed to Madeline, and the two of them generally decided by mutual agreement the path their joined lives would take.

The decision to start a family was not exactly mutual, however, nor was the path to parenthood obvious to them. Madeline had always wanted children and began in the mid-1980s researching whether and how lesbians could have children and the legal avenues available for protecting their custody. At the same time, both Madeline and Clara were considering applying to master's programs out of state as a way to leave home for good and start the next phase of their lives. Having both been accepted to programs in the same northern California university, the couple moved and each partner began her graduate work. But Madeline, unable to set aside her desire for children and becoming increasingly dissatisfied with her master's program, dropped out after a year and stepped up her family planning research. Clara went on to earn her master's degree in agricultural management and took a nonacademic job with the university. But throughout the course of these geographic and occupational changes, the interest in starting a family remained lopsided, as Clara told me: "Madeline wanted kids. I didn't really want them, but she did." Clara eventually acquiesced to Madeline's desire for children by way of noninterference, as Madeline described the day the couple traveled seventy miles to obtain the semen for Madeline's first insemination attempt: "Well, she didn't really like it but when we were on our way to the sperm bank in Oakland, I told her that if she really didn't want to do it she could pull off of [the interstate] at the next exit and turn around and go home. But she kept right on going. She had the option to not go through with it."

When I met Clara and Madeline, they were the parents of Andrea, five, and Ethan, three, to whom Madeline had given birth and of whom Clara spoke proudly (and publicly). But it was Madeline who knew and described every detail of the children's lives, for she was also a full-time homemaker and mother, having given up any occupational aspirations, at least for the period of Andrea's and Ethan's lives that she felt they would need her. Madeline organized children's activities at the church the family attended, but this work was completely voluntary and, like her household and child care labors, monetarily uncompensated.

Madeline described her decision to stay home with the children simply as reflecting her desire to mother them in the fullest way possible but stated that over time she had begun to feel a "lack of support" from Clara. For Clara, being the sole provider of the family's income as an agricultural public relations specialist meant that home and children were strictly Madeline's domains. But Madeline's domains comprised twenty-four-hour days with no time off. During one of my interviews with Madeline,[20] she recalled painfully how the "lack of support" from Clara felt:

> This was a very difficult time for us because I thought that even though I was the one who wanted the kids, when you care about someone, when you are in a relationship with someone, you support them. You are supposed to help the other person, encourage them and support them in what they are doing. I felt so devalued by her. Nothing I did was of any value. The most value I had to Clara was as an object that could keep the kids quiet. I was an object. I couldn't do anything to please her. Whenever I wanted to do anything else other than work, anything that took me out of the house, this was too much for Clara. I couldn't go anywhere without feeling like I was neglecting Andrea [their only child at the time]. I couldn't leave her with Clara. Clara would complain to me when I came home that all Andrea did was cry and need constant attention. I couldn't do anything right. The most important thing I could do was to keep Andrea quiet while Clara was home. If Andrea cried, no matter what I was doing, it was my responsibility to quiet her down so that she wouldn't disturb Clara.

Clearly Madeline's "domains" represented work for her; when she was at home with the children she was "at work." But because this work occurred in the home, was not structured by shifts, and had no monetary or even social value, it became coded for Clara as that from which she was exempted as part of her status and privilege as breadwinner. It was her "right" to be literally relieved of it.

The couple had since worked through some of the emotional distress from these difficulties with the help of their church pastor, a woman who was also a family counselor. But while much of it might have arisen from the original, nonmutual decision to become parents, as Madeline alluded, the difficulties might also be artifacts of the Rozzie and Harriet arrangement that instituted the home as "Madeline's domain" in the first place. Madeline's position of total economic dependence on Clara—whose income fell in the mid-$30K range—seems to have translated into a diminished capacity to negotiate for her needs, especially as they related to the children, who had become, by definition, her responsibility. Indeed, in this arrangement, Madeline's needs were singularly synonymous with children and home, which in turn dispossessed her of personal autonomy and nonfamilial sources of human capital such that any capacity to exert influence in the matter, any leverage she might mobilize, was completely foreclosed to her. Madeline well understood her lack of power as related to the children: "When the kids were younger, [Clara] really resented it when I asked her to do anything or help out with anything. So it was like I would have to do everything. I really couldn't talk to her about what I wanted. I was good for nothing since I had the kids. I didn't know what to do." Clara's original lack of interest in having children most likely explained her reluctance to assume responsibility for caring for Andrea and Ethan, and these (negative) preferences merged with her (positive) career interests in defining her role as not involving caregiving: "I prefer to work full time than take care of the kids. I would say that that is a fair statement. I like to work more than watching the kids." Implicitly leveraging her earlier "sacrifice" in consenting to start a family with Madeline in the first place, Clara located her role outside the domain of domestic caregiving, giving Madeline strong motivation to assume full responsibility for it. This had the effect of polarizing and tracking their responsibilities into ever narrower specializations such that over time—going on four years—their homemaker-caregiver/breadwinner roles were cemented and Madeline's economic dependence was normalized. Madeline's devalued status and resulting lack of power thus stemmed most dramatically from this structured economic dependence, for only in the context of this rigidly specialized division of labor did the children make Madeline "good for nothing."

Besides ambivalence or lack of interest on the part of one partner to become a parent, another factor that may both influence and result from a 1950s-style division of labor among lesbian coparents is one partner's greater earning power. The full-time caregivers in all five families with a primary caregiver/primary breadwinner arrangement reported a lower income, sketchier job history, or lower level of educational attainment than their breadwinning partners. Income disparities between partners did not necessarily lead to inequity between partners, as we saw with Arlene Roessler and Karen Shaw, one of the equal-sharing couples whose sizable income gap they dealt with by having Arlene maintain control of the distribution of Karen's nearly six-digit salary. But when lower-earning partners completely forewent or deferred indefinitely their own earnings and labor force participation to assume primary responsibility for the household and child care, it was more likely that they would not have an equal say in how the breadwinner's salary would be distributed, whether they could count on receiving "help" with domestic labor, or whether their preferences in any number of personal and family decisions would be honored.

"I Just Needed an Hour"

Marilyn Weiss was a mid- to upper-level corporate manager and birth mother of six-month-old Michael, while her partner, Brenda Jacobson, was his full-time caregiver. Before Michael was born, Brenda had owned and operated a small clothing boutique for a number of years in a resort town about an hour and a half's drive north of San Francisco. But Brenda and Marilyn had decided even before Michael was born that one of them would, in Brenda's words, "stay at home and become the housewife or whatever." But which one of them would become "the housewife" seemed to be a foregone conclusion: since Marilyn's career goals as a quality assurance professional had dictated a corporate track, in realizing those goals she had committed herself, in a sense, "to the life." Thus, whether or not flexibility existed in Brenda's work before the discussion of Michael's care had come up, it materialized over the course of the talks, and Brenda was slated to become the Harriet in this family.

By the time of our interviews Brenda had cared for Michael full time since his birth, over six months, having turned the day-to-day management of her shop over to a young manager. While Brenda's income had always been lower than Marilyn's corporate salary and total compensation package, her transformation from *petite* merchant to housewife precipitated a decline in her economic status such that, in her domestic relations with Marilyn, her capacity to negotiate for the things she wanted became increasingly limited. In our interviews she talked about wanting to take time off from mothering, have time to herself, and give Michael her last name.[21] Brenda's account of some of these instances reflected a desire to support her partner, but her "cover-up" failed inasmuch as her own distress resounded forcefully through her words. Here is how she spoke of the discussion of the baby's surname:

> Yeah, [his name is] Michael Seth Jacobson Weiss. One of the motives for that was because of the significance in a last, in names. Some people really put a lot of credibility to a name, and when I take him to school or when I sign him up for swimming or you know, he has my name and Marilyn's name. And then along the line he'll be dropping Jacobson off and he'll just be Michael Weiss.

When I asked how it came about that Michael would be dropping off Brenda's last name, evoking Marilyn's bio-ontological privilege, Brenda responded:

> Well, Marilyn picked out Michael, and Seth was her best friend. And Jacobson came kind of later. I guess I never really . . . you know, I didn't really bring it up but I really wanted Jacobson to be in the name. I would have liked it to have been Michael Jacobson. But she was really attached to having Seth. She's the biological mother and um . . . so I didn't really say anything only I thought it, you know, that I would really like Jacobson there. And then we were sitting around a table at her shower and all of her friends said, "Well I would want the name Jacobson to be there." You know, and so I said, "Well really?" And then they started talking to Marilyn about it and we talked when we got back, and I said I'd really like his last name to be Jacobson-Weiss hyphenated. And so that's what was on the birth certificate. But then my sister was here one day at the table and she says, "Well you know all of that won't fit into a computer and it'll wind up dropping one of the names." And Marilyn says, "Well I don't want them dropping Weiss." And so I said, "Well, okay, that's true, let's just make it Michael Seth Jacobson Weiss." So we dropped the hyphenated form. And that's fine. A lot of people have two names. Whether he uses [Jacobson] or not, all of his life he will be a Jacobson-Weiss.

Though Brenda attributed Marilyn's greater influence in this struggle over Michael's name to Marilyn's maternity, that she found it necessary to explain it in terms of the biological credential was symptomatic of her powerlessness, which, I believe, must be understood as related to her diminished economic position. For in effect, once Brenda's work was defined as less important, less valuable, and once she had assumed all domestic and caregiving responsibilities, this reduced her capacity both to produce and control material and financial resources within the family *and* to advocate for her own physical, emotional, and psychological needs ("I really wanted Jacobson to be in the name"). When I asked Brenda how her full-time caregiving and homemaking vis-à-vis Marilyn's full-time breadwinning was working out for her financially, she responded:

> I'm definitely sacrificing income. But Marilyn is subsidizing me. She pays more of the mortgage on the house, and then the tradeoff is that I'm staying home with Michael. She makes more than I do, so we divide the bills up like that, which is really . . . Like, I just stay home and Marilyn is always at work, full time. We don't really have any problems monetarily, although I do because I'm not making as much as I would, you know, so it's harder for me to accept the fact that . . . yeah, I can't do what. . . . I'm watching my money more. I'm not spending like I used to. Who knows what's going to happen to my business, the business is very volatile. I have a manager who does all the general ledger and does the buying, but she's going to school so she'll only be around for another two years, and then I'll either decide to sell the business or do something down here. But, I mean, Marilyn really wants to have a second child, almost more than she wanted the first. And everybody says to wait a year before you even think of having another child you know. So there's a part of me that says, "Sure, I'll stay home for the next five years, run my business, and raise the kids until they're in school." And then there's the other part of me that's scared because I'm, I'm going to be forty-six years old and don't have any energy as a thirty-year-old would have or a twenty-five- or twenty-six-year-old would have, so I have some fears around being able to, you know, do it.

Brenda described her once thriving and personally gratifying retail business as volatile now that almost all of her time and attention were devoted to caring for Michael—and possibly a second child. Since her de facto occupation had shifted from independent retail owner to unpaid domestic, her economic position now required subsidization—a subsidization that here, in fact, accrued as an equity asset in Marilyn's name.

Brenda's fears about whether she could "do it" seem warranted, given the way the labor she accomplished as the traditional housewife in an untraditional family left her physically and emotionally exhausted by the end of the day. But her day usually did not end when Marilyn came home from her ten-hour day on the job. While Brenda spoke of "her shift being over" and "turning Michael over" to Marilyn, she still felt *responsible* for Michael and described being unable to steal away for a precious single hour that she needed alone without feeling the need to keep a watchful eye on him—even while Michael was in the care of his biological mother.

> When she [Marilyn] gets home at night, I'm at the door with Michael after like ten or eleven hours, and I'm ready to turn him over. I say, "My shift's over." And I need like an hour, you know, to take a bath, read the paper, whatever, and that's why I say you really need two people to do this. Marilyn's very good, she's really good. She has a lot on her agenda when she gets home, she wants to do her bookwork, she wants to talk on the phone to the East Coast. The other day she came in . . . it was one of those days when I really knew that I needed an hour, you know, and that's not always . . . but I knew I needed some space since he was at that time cranky all day. And she comes in here and she's on the phone and I'm reading my paper and she leaves Michael on the floor and walks out there and I said, "Would you get that kid in here!" [Marilyn says] "I'm on the phone to the East Coast." I says, "Take the child with you to the other room to talk on the phone." But . . . I've got a long day, I've got ten-, eleven-hour days with him and he doesn't nap a whole lot and, you know, I take care of the house, I do the food shopping, I do errands, and I still manage my business, I drive him up there with me about once a week.

Brenda talked about "needing an hour" or "needing space" in the same hungry way that Hochschild's working heterosexual mothers from the 1980s study talked about sleep. The similarity between Brenda's account of her days and the daily lives of working heterosexual mothers points to the ways in which this division of labor not only compounds income gaps between partners but produces leisure gaps as well.[22] Moreover, the specialization of material labor into productive and reproductive ("unproductive") tasks in Brenda and Marilyn's arrangement seemed to have taken its hold over their allocation of mental labor as well, as Brenda still felt responsible for Michael and found herself worried about him while he was in Marilyn's care. This strongly supports the idea that biological maternity does not ipso facto qualify one for caregiving and that the exclusive assignment and distribution of unpaid tasks to one person shapes that person's practice in such a way that her cognitive map tends to cover only the terrain of practice. Thus, because Marilyn's normal practice when she got home from the office still involved job-related work and communication, these activities, rather than her son, occupied her mental landscape.[23]

I asked Marilyn and Brenda whether they had ever discussed making adjustments to their arrangement by having Marilyn scale back on her work hours. Brenda responded with a nervous giggle:

BRENDA: I asked that. We needed some couples' counseling around the second baby and some other issues. We did like five sessions, and it was great just to go in. And I, in negotiating on this second baby thing, I [had] thought, "Well hey, I may as well just ask for the moon, you know." So I said [to Marilyn], "Well, how about getting a job that you're not away ten hours a day." And she looked at me like "I didn't think that was part of the negotiation." But I thought, Well, . . . I can ask for things. You know? It would definitely be wonderful. But it's probably not a probability. She has a good career. She would not, she doesn't like working ten hours a day. I mean, that's just the demands of the job.

MARILYN: They'd like me to work eighteen-hour days.

BRENDA: But we are talking about things like getting someone to help clean the house, maybe, someone coming in during the day to help. So [Marilyn's] very amenable to doing whatever it takes.

In addition to differences in partners' original interest in parenting, and disparities in their income levels and occupational ties, a final factor concerning couples' decisions to adopt 1950s-style divisions of labor had to do with providing, as one couple put it, "a strong sense of family." Shannon Cavner and Marian Gould-Whitmer, who had plans for Marian to quit her full-time work as a driving instructor to care for eighteen-month-old Andy, suggested that they chose this arrangement so that their son would feel secure in who his family was and would internalize their values. When

I asked them what precipitated their decision to discontinue the employment of the day care provider who had been coming to their home for over
a year, they responded:

MARIAN: She's [caregiver] been very good and Andy adores her and she
basically does a good job. But it's still not the same as one of
us. And we're working it out so that we have the opportunity
to do that, that I can be home. We moved here [less expensive
house and neighborhood] so that we'd have less expenses. So
that I don't have to be working as much. We'd rather have one
of us taking care of him rather than a nanny or a sitter.

SHANNON: Well, especially the older that he [Andy] gets. When it comes
to the point of disciplining them and, you know, encouraging
them or learning your values as opposed to somebody else's
values . . . because we don't have the same values as Marie
[caregiver] does. She's quite young, she's only twenty-three
years old. Now she has this child out of wedlock by a black
father, not that that is neither here nor there but it's . . .

MARIAN: A different set of values . . .

SHANNON: It's a different set of values. He's not even her boyfriend
anymore. If he took some responsibility for the child and did
something like that, you know, but he doesn't, and she doesn't
really, it's sort of like, "Well, that's the way it is, that's the way
men are and that's what you do." And it's like, "Well, maybe
you should have thought that through a little more before you
had the baby."

When I asked what sorts of values they had in mind to teach Andy, Marian reflected for a moment and said: "Well I guess a much more secure
family, family kind of picture, rather than her [caregiver's] extended kind
of family. I guess she's got a sort of extended family. But much more secure family." Tinged with a disconcerting racial observation—one that I
suspect signaled a deeper process at work than Shannon's dismissal would
have it—the couple's values seemed to be in line with those dominant in
U.S. culture before the sexual revolution of the 1960s and 1970s. In their
criticism of the "irresponsibility" of Marie and her ex-boyfriend, Shannon
and Marian betrayed an affinity for the image and values of heterosexual
family life and sexual mores prominent in the 1950s, when out-of-wedlock

pregnancy and childbearing were managed through shotgun weddings and (often involuntary) adoption. Invoking the 1950s intact nuclear family as personally preferable to the 1990s extended, nonmarital, multiracial postmodern family, Shannon and Marian's values and division of labor epitomized heteronormative assimilation and replication, the negative effects of which family legal scholar Nancy Polikoff has warned about and the neoconservative writer Andrew Sullivan celebrates.[24]

There is more than a little irony in this situation, both in the mothers' disapproval of "deviant" sexual and family values when their family type was itself nonconformist, and in the heterosexual family model they had chosen to appropriate. I do believe these mothers felt a deep need for family security; against the backdrop of homophobia and brutalization of gay people in the larger culture, securing one's family from such a heartless world would seem only rational. But the adoption of a familial division of labor promoted by a patriarchal state and effectively institutionalizing economic dependence and subordination for caregivers seems a high price to pay for security—and judging from the practices of equal-sharing couples, perhaps an unnecessary one. But some of these mothers had taken seriously certain 1990s family values arguments against working mothers who let "strangers" care for their children. The argument that a lack of parental control and responsibility contributed to social problems associated with, among other things, juvenile criminality appears to have resonated with some mothers here, as Marilyn and Brenda suggested:

MARILYN: Yeah, I had said that I think there's a lot of merit to women staying home and raising children or men staying home and raising children but to have one parent at home with a child. Because if you look at the kids today, you know, half the reason why all these kids are so into crime is because they're in dysfunctional families where their parents aren't teaching them family values, you know. Where they're not taught the difference between right and wrong, and they're not taught the value of life. They have absolutely no respect for life.

BRENDA: There's a day care that we were considering putting Michael in at [Marilyn's company]. There's a hundred and fifty kids in there, and they're [mothers] all professional women and the kids are there all day long and my feeling is, you know, they're professional women, they can afford it, and these children will suffer being raised in a day care environment totally. You know, I don't think there's anything that replaces parents.

Advocating the 1950s-style family and its values as not only practically but morally superior, the family values rhetoric of the 1990s seems to have reached audiences across class and sexual orientation divides. For Shannon and Marian, whose socioeconomic status was considerably lower than that of Brenda and Marilyn, the impulse to "secure" their family from increasingly complex sexual and kinship practices of the larger culture reflected a certain fear, when it came to their child, about who was doing the "imprinting" and what that imprinting consisted of. Similarly, Brenda and Marilyn's interest in having one parent at home with their son, even though they could afford "state-of-the-art" day care, involved the inculcation of a basic moral or ethical perspective that they believed could be achieved through a now-outdated division of labor between partners.

In effect, these couples were appropriating certain atavistic elements of heterosexual family life and values as a way of protecting their families from more current elements of heterosexual culture. The paradox is that lesbian coparents who implemented this labor arrangement achieved a conservative "ideal" according to which most heterosexual parents do not live.[25] In this attainment of the "ideal" they might, in one sense, compensate for their own "deviance" as gay-parent families. This ideal state, however, as we have seen, came at a cost to caregivers of enormous emotional, economic, and physical consequence: all the effects that had been visited upon women as the subordinate class in an unequal distribution of labor and leisure, responsibilities and rights, power and pleasure, both within the heterosexual family and in heterosexual society as a whole.

Chapter 5 | TRUTH AND RECONCILIATION

Families of Origin Come Around and Come Out

So far, chapters have examined lesbian coparents' practices in terms of primary interpersonal relations—giving birth to children and working through how best to balance breadwinning, child care, and emotional support for all family members. The focus now shifts to their relations with members of their own families of origin.

People who occupy important positions by virtue of their status as friends or members of mothers' families of origin inhabit a border territory between inside and outside the families mothers have created. They traverse the regions of inside and outside because they have been present as a force in mothers' lives before and often during the creation of their new families. Unlike casual acquaintances and strangers, mothers' families of origin represent a category of relationship that is implicated in almost everything they do, if for no other reason than that these ties are culturally defined as primary. In her study on the meaning of family for lesbians and gay men in the United States, anthropologist Kath Weston became convinced that "gay families [can]not be understood apart from the families in which lesbians and gay men [have] grown up."[1]

Weston's study examines the relationship between the "gay families" and "straight families" of gay people. According to Weston, a gay person's "gay family" comprises those relations chosen and affirmed as constituting kin, while that person's "straight family" comprises those individuals to whom he or she is related biogenetically—by "blood." Weston conceptualizes gay families as chosen in order to distinguish them analytically from blood kin and to draw out the tensions between them, both theoretically and empirically. With these categories she also disrupts the equation of gayness as being antithetical to family, the historically specific formula whereby claiming a gay sexuality meant not only that one was nonprocreative but also that one risked losing the family one had. Mostly, however, the categories of "chosen" and "blood" families, which Weston uses interchangeably with "gay families" and "straight families" respectively, are not so exclusive in the sense that, as she shows, an element of choice structures relations with blood kin more than is usually credited. The act of coming out to one's "blood" family, and the ensuing decisions and actions taken by all parties involved, reflect this element of choice, for, in Weston's words, "bonds symbolized by blood prove terminable precisely because they are selectively perpetuated rather than 'naturally' given."[2]

By the same logic, lesbian-coparent families may be understood as combining symbols of both chosen and blood relations. In this chapter, I refer to mothers' "straight" or "blood" families as their families of origin, but the focus is on questions similar to those driving Weston's analysis. How has the creation of lesbian coparents' own families with children affected relations with their families of origin? Are lesbian coparents with their own children now seen as procreative, thereby further dispelling the notion that gay equals antifamily? What is the significance for members of families of origin that their lesbian daughters and sisters are continuing "the blood line" by having biological children? Does this biological element smooth relations between a lesbian mother and her family of origin, relations that may have been upset by her coming out as a lesbian? How do mothers themselves manage relations with families of origin given the new development in their lives?

Although most of these questions are similar to those Weston sought to understand, her conceptualization of the gay person's created families is, in fact, broader, including a wide range of relationships that generally are not formed on the basis of biology. For Weston, "chosen" families are not "blood" families, the distinction being both ideological and a product of choice itself.

The entrance of biological children into chosen families makes problematic any easy notion of blood relations as exclusively associated with the family one grew up in—including the entire extended family traced by way of the genealogical grid.[3] The new addition of a blood relation in the form of a child to parents who were historically thought to be non-procreative—or who were procreative in heterosexual relationships before or in lieu of their coming out as gay—adds nuance to the matrix of considerations for analyzing gay kinship.

ACCEPTANCE, SUPPORT, AND DISAVOWAL

One of the most enduring questions associated with gay identity and relations with one's family of origin continues to be whether, and to what extent, disclosure of gay identity will result in the gay person's rejection by family members, especially parents. Weston details the experiences of her Bay Area informants in their narratives of coming out to blood relatives.[4] From talking with "hundreds" of lesbians and gay men, Weston understood that they expected coming out to their families of origin would yield insights into those relationships—answers about the "truth" of those kin ties. Would familial love endure? Was it truly unconditional love that characterized their relations with blood family, as was popularly represented and perceived? Disclosure of sexual identity in one sense would be the acid test of the integrity of blood kin ties. It would provide an "accurate assessment"[5] of where people stood with their families.

In her analysis, Weston was more interested in the experiences and stories of her informants than in "actual" rates of acceptance and rejection by members of the families of origin. Indeed, rates of actual rejection and acceptance are extremely difficult to ascertain (if that is even desirable or useful) for the reason that rejection and acceptance comprise complex, changing affective states. Moreover, no action or inaction on the part of families of origin is irrevocable: rejection and acceptance are not static conditions. Weston's participants overwhelmingly anticipated rejection as the outcome of disclosure so much that acceptance, for them, expanded to include "everything from grudging toleration to confirmations of lovers and a positive pride in gay identity."[6] Only a third of her informants reported incidents that they classified as signaling rejection when they came out to parents. Thus there is a disjuncture between anticipated outcomes and post facto incidents that are then classified as rejection or acceptance. In a separate, earlier survey of lesbians and gay men in couples, 40 percent reported that their parents invited them to family gatherings, 36 percent had not come out to their parents, 21 percent said their parents "treat their relationships as simply two friends living together with no commitment," while only 3 percent said their parents refused to see their son or daughter and his or her partner.[7]

It seems that the only "sure truth" about the nature of a gay person's ties to blood family, for which disclosure of sexual identity provides the litmus test, is the hard fact of rejection, which itself can take many forms but is unambiguous for those involved. But here again, rejection is also "reversible." Weston presents the story of a Catholic mother who had at one time disavowed her gay son but who, in light of the raging AIDS epidemic, reestablished ties by promising to care for him should he become HIV positive. The categories "rejection" and "acceptance" are, in the last instance, protean, and this changing character of relations with families of origin was highlighted among the Bay Area mothers I spoke with concerning the response to their motherhood by their families of origin.

Enter Baby

The most common response from the parents of Bay Area mothers was delight and enthusiasm about the arrival of a grandchild. Cathy Lotti's account of her mother's response was typical:

> I guess we'd [Cathy and Katrina] been together a couple of years when I told her [mother] that we were thinking of having children, and she had always really cared about Katrina and had expressed that to me. I would say our relationship was nice. We just sort of, we didn't spend a lot of time, it wasn't very deep, it was cordial and that was it. And I met her for lunch and it was her birthday and I gave her a picture frame. During the lunch I expressed to her that I had something I wanted to tell her and told her that we were thinking about having children. And she had this stunned look on her face for about sixty seconds and then all of a sudden she started to smile and she said, "Grandma! Grandma! I'm going to put the baby's picture in this frame." All of a sudden. . . . I think one of her biggest issues with me being gay was that she was never going to have grandchildren. So all of a sudden it was like, the old her started leaking out this little tiny hole behind the big wall that had gone up and it was like, "My God, this might be great!"

Cathy's mother's response was representative of most parents' ultimate response, as 85 percent of Bay Area mothers recounted them, but for many parents of the mothers this response occurred only after mothers had prepared them for the event, had communicated their intentions beforehand, and had actively worked to ensure that the ties would form, as Cathy did here. With the same meticulousness and reflection that the Bay Area mothers planned the incorporation of children into their lives, most if not all considered relations with their own parents both before and after their children were born, with a view toward establishing a clear understanding of what the relationship would involve. In similar fashion to the way that Weston's participants perceived coming out to parents as establishing the "truth" of those ties, the arrival of children put them to the test once again.

Mothers' expectations of their parents' and siblings' reactions ranged from pride of knowing that their children would be cherished and valued by their families of origin (based upon the existing strength of the ties), to ambivalence (blood kin could lean "either way"), to a certainty of rejection (based upon cool if nonexistent relations before the arrival of the child). But because the categories of acceptance and rejection are so fluid, not only were mothers' expectations and reactions from blood kin often discrepant, but relatives themselves, mostly parents, moved from positions of shock and concern to becoming the most doting of grandparents. Their perspective changed as they processed the information.

These changes in affect and regard must be understood as a product of time and of the times. In a heterosexual world, few straight families anticipate their children will be gay. Members of families of origin have needed time first to process the disclosure of gay identity. Moreover, as Weston notes, many straight family members assume that their gay daughters, sons, sisters, and brothers, being nonprocreative beings, will not be the source of consanguineal continuity, as Cathy's mother had believed. Now comes the revelation that gay family members are not only adopting and fostering children but producing children from the same blood and DNA that pulses through their own bodies. More time is needed to assimilate this information and its meaning.

The "times" are implicated here as well as the historical context within which individual family members understand the meaning of the possibility of kinship via their lesbian-identified daughters and sisters. Weston wrote,

The emergence of gay families represents a major historical shift, particularly when viewed against the prevalent assumption that claiming a lesbian or gay identity must mean leaving blood relatives behind and foregoing any possibility of establishing a family of one's own, unless a person is willing to make the compromise of hiding out in a marriage of convenience. Given that homosexuality became firmly allied with identity only at the end of the nineteenth century, and that the major period of urban gay population growth and institutional consolidation in the United States did not occur until after World War II, this entire shift has happened within a relatively brief period of time.[8]

Like Cathy's mother, for whom "sixty seconds" was sufficient for her to realize that a dream of hers had come true, relatives and parents commonly demonstrated temporal changes in their perspective—changes of heart, postbaby conversions—with the announcement of the imminent arrival of grandchildren, nieces, and nephews.

Coming Around: Postbaby Conversions

In addition to the typical response as exemplified by Cathy's mother, there were what I think of as "conversion narratives" recounted by mothers I spoke with in connection with their parents' (and other relatives') responses to the arrival of their children. Birth mother Megan Johnson and comother Penny Cipolini relayed the story of Megan's parents' adjustment to their news, with each parent "coming around" independently in response to the arrival of baby Kathleen.

MEGAN: I approached it from, I thought it was better to tell them from the very beginning what was going on so that they could get used to it, because that's been my experience with my mom at least. The sooner I tell her, she'll come around. Like my relationship is more important to her than her bigotry or whatever it is. Whereas my dad is . . .

PENNY: A bigot and a pig.

MEGAN: My dad's a pig. For instance, you know that [antigay] vote in Oregon? He asked me about it, and he wouldn't tell me how he was going to vote on it. My guess is he voted for it. So, anyway . . . though I'm not sure he would do it again. I think he is also in a process. Anyway, so my mom, I told my mom that we were thinking of inseminating. I told my mom every month that we did inseminate, I could be pregnant, we did inseminate this month. I talked to her about who the donor was, all that kind of stuff before I was ever pregnant.

PENNY: But her reactions were, "I don't want to hear about this, I don't want to know about it."

MEGAN: Right, but by the time I was pregnant, she was excited. She was thrilled. My dad, as always, was really quiet, not that my dad's quiet but he's quiet about like . . . he doesn't want to hear about it, he doesn't want to talk about it and so he never had any reaction. When Kathleen was born, they were in Mexico. They're both retired. They were in Mexico and were coming back a little bit early. So they decided to see her. They saw her a couple days after she was born. It was actually rather sweet. I mean, Penny only knows my dad through the way that I talk about him, which is not very positively.

PENNY: I only know of him as being a jerk.

MEGAN: Right.

PENNY: I mean an abusive jerk.

MEGAN: And he was very sweet with Kathleen. He really wanted to spend time with her. And then when Kathleen was about seven weeks old, Penny went on a four-day business trip and so my mom came and stayed here. *Wanted to. Asked if she could.* And that was, well, my family is fraught with all kinds of complex relationships, and I wasn't thrilled with the idea of having her around, but I felt like it was good. It was good for Kathleen. So we did it. My mom adores Kathleen. Kathleen is the only grandchild; none of my brothers or sisters are married. Jill, my youngest sister, was married and is divorced. So they, my dad's sixty-five, my mom's sixty, and my mom has said that she really thought that she was not going to have any grandkids. So she, she loves being a grandmother, she loves Kathleen.

A number of things are striking about this narrative. Both of Megan's parents are described as bigoted to varying degrees, father more than mother. And while Megan was more sure of her mother's "process" than her father's, she wasn't sure of their ultimate response to the arrival of baby

Kathleen, nor did she know exactly what she wanted from them. What *is* clear is that Megan wanted them to know Penny's and her intentions to have a child and wanted to communicate with them before and during the planning of the pregnancy and the pregnancy itself. She wanted to give them time to reflect and prepare, without knowing for certain that they would "come around."

Megan's parents were not pleased with her relationship with Penny. Megan's tone betrays the fatigue of one who has seen many battles in this family "fraught with complex relationships." Undoubtedly the gay issue brought to the surface "the truth" of her parents' bigotry. But with the arrival of Kathleen, the only grandchild and, ironically, born to the family member least likely to have produced a grandchild in pre–lesbian baby boom days, the grounds for estrangement were challenged. Faced with a living, breathing granddaughter, the indifference cultivated by Megan's parents before Kathleen's arrival melted away under the charm of a baby and the symbolic weight of biological kinship.

Other stories of postbaby changes of heart among members of mothers' families of origin reveal similar instances of relatives' coming to terms with what they reconciled as the priorities in their family relationships. Danielle Walton, Lee Lanier, and their son Nathan, whom we've met in previous chapters, lived on the country property Lee had bought when she sold her dog-grooming business to settle down in semiretirement while continuing to do "odd jobs" here and there to keep her afloat financially. Lee was in her early fifties, had married in her teens, and had had a child even while she was coming out as a lesbian during the heady days of lesbian feminist separatism. At that time Lee was ostracized by her lesbian friends and acquaintances who disapproved of her motherhood. Now, as coparent to Nathan, to whom Danielle gave birth, she had easily settled into the role of comother but was generally wary, and not a little weary, of dealing with people who did not accept or understand gay kinship.

Like Lee, Danielle was from a working-class family. Her mother had died young, after raising five children virtually alone, since Danielle's father, a "merchant seaman," was nearly always away at sea. Danielle's mother had worked as a waitress, the "epitome of the 1945 waitress," Lee told me with affection in her voice, "warm and loving and just, I loved her mother." And Danielle's mother loved Lee. By all accounts Danielle's relationships in her family were strong.

After her mother died Danielle realized that an important source of familial support and cohesion was lost to her and Lee and their prospective child. Danielle's mother had provided a tempering force against the harsh judgments of one of Danielle's sisters who, as a born-again Christian, had denounced Danielle's relationship with Lee. But when baby Nathan came along, Danielle's sister experienced another kind of conversion.

> DANIELLE: My oldest sister is a born-again Christian and she's not very accepting . . . When I got together with Lee she basically said I couldn't come to the [sister's] house with Lee. If I came I had to come by myself and spend time alone with my niece. That was really hard because I'm her [niece's] godmother and she was like the other kid I've been the closest to besides my own. And so that was really a major loss. But you know it's been interesting because *after Nate was born,* my sister and niece called and they wanted to come up here and see Nate and everything and that was kind of out of the blue. And they came and it wasn't, it was nice, you know, it wasn't deep, but it was nice. They don't shun us like they used to. I mean [before] they didn't even, wouldn't come to Christmas at my parents' house because Lee and I were going to be there the first year we got together. So it was pretty bad. Very painful for me.

Danielle's mother's advocacy for them as a couple had provided important support when their own relationship was in its early, delicate stages. But relations with Danielle's sister, not insignificantly the eldest sibling, had remained cool and painful for Danielle. For reasons that were not entirely clear from their account but that surely involved the arrival of Nate into their lives, Danielle's born-again sister softened the hard-line stance in which her faith had most likely played a role.

Far less dramatic but equally compelling was the postbaby conversion of Serena Walby's father. He had never believed that Serena's attraction to and love for women was a serious life commitment. His own commitment to his daughter was never doubted by either of them, but he questioned her lesbian identity and her relationship with Carrie. His postbaby conversion experience had less to do with accepting her lesbianism on principle and more with taking it seriously. Ironically, for him, it was necessary that his daughter bear a child for him to understand and support her as a lesbian.

SERENA: Until she [daughter Polly] really came, until he'd seen her, I think he was still convinced that this [lesbian relationship] was a little bit of a phase. Or a big phase. And more than that, he was convinced, he told me one day, sort of that I had been seduced. He thought I was seduced by a lesbian cult! He told me that he thought this group of lesbians—which actually [at the time] we lived in a neighborhood with a large gay and lesbian community—that they had seduced me and were using me as a breeder!

CARRIE: Good breeder stock here!

SERENA: He thought for the culture or something.

CARRIE: He must have seen it on Donahue or something. Probably something about lesbian cults.

SERENA: But since, after three months of pregnancy, he's been very . . . nothing but supportive. He ended up surprising me and just showing up for my due date. He actually came across the country from Memphis to be here and nobody else did. But in general my family's been supportive. Most of the years.

CARRIE: Both families.

SERENA: Yeah, both of our families.

Consanguinity is an important factor in these conversion experiences. Blood relatives are much more likely to "come around" with the birth of a child with whom they have a perceived biogenetic connection. The deeply felt and powerful cultural significance of biological offspring is demonstrated tellingly in the story of another couple, Kelly Kronenberg and Diane Chaucer, whom we met in earlier chapters and who represent the only Bay Area family in which both partners are birth mothers. Both mothers gave birth to sons by the same donor. Kelly gave birth first to Noam, and the mothers coparented him together until he was five years old before Diane decided she wanted to give birth to their second child, Oliver. Diane's mother's cool relationship with them following Noam's arrival, and her process of "coming around" with the arrival of her *biological* grandson, is instructive for what it conveys about the depths of meaning historically attached to consanguinity.

DIANE: My mother has always had a very difficult time with me being a lesbian. She's never been supportive of my relationship with Kelly, you know, never. Anyway, it was really horrible when Kelly got pregnant. She basically thought that I was getting screwed 'cause I was going to have this kid that I was going to babysit for but I would have no claim to. Or the kid would have no bond with me. It wasn't my child. And we actually didn't speak to each other for a year after Noam was born. A year and a half. She told me that she wasn't this child's grandmother, and I wasn't his mother. And I finally said, "Goodbye till you can get your act together." And she finally did. I mean it took a long time of not speaking to each other and she, she called up and said, "I'd like to come visit you and your son." So she finally came to her senses. And since then, she's had this gradual thawing. And then when I got pregnant [with Oliver] I think it was like, the moment of reckoning for her. What she ended up doing before I got pregnant was, she never referred to herself as Noam's grandmother but she came up with this name, a diminutive name, that she told Noam to call her. "Mamie." So that's what he calls her. And she would never introduce herself as his grandmother or refer to him as her grandson. But she obviously had to relate to him. And she acknowledged that I was his mother. At least to my face, I don't know what she did otherwise. The adoption I thought would make some difference to her, but it didn't really. Then I got pregnant, and she was acting really strange. I think it really hit her that she was going to have this biological grandchild and there was obviously no way that she could treat the one [Oliver] as her grandchild and not Noam. We had this big confrontation and ever since then, she's totally changed. Now she's like Grandmother of the Year. She tells everybody, she's totally into the grandchildren. [She has] no other grandchildren. So she's sort of changed.

KELLY: She wins the award for most improved.

DIANE: I mean, she was like at the bottom of the barrel.

KELLY: She was. And now she's good.

DIANE: Yeah. She's very sweet.

Again, time was a factor—"a year and a half"—in Diane's mother's process of "getting her act together" in learning how to relate to a grandson with whom she was not related biogenetically and whose parentage she did not accept as legitimate. By inventing a term of address for herself, she worked out a practical relationship with Noam and his mothers that allowed her to retain her ambivalence toward their familial unconventionality. Her position before Diane gave birth to Oliver, which Diane described as a "gradual thawing," might not have thawed completely had a biological grandson not arrived. The addition of Oliver to the family moved Diane's mother from "Mamie" to "Grandmother of the Year." And even this transition required a "big confrontation" whose outcome could have been very different. That Diane's mother did "come around" is powerful testimony to consanguinity, which takes on the character of a first principle in many of these reckonings of kinship with families of origin.

Diane and Kelly's story was unique among the Bay Area mothers, since they were the only family thus far in which both mothers had given birth. Their experience offers a comparative perspective on the operation of the biogenetic element in relations with families of origin. Another comparative perspective on the effect of consanguinity is the view of relations with family members on the side of the nonbiological mother. Consider again the experience of Megan Johnson, Penny Cipolini, and their daughter Kathleen. We saw how relations with Megan's parents followed a tortuous, often desultory path toward an uneasy and as yet unfinished understanding with them, even with Megan serving as the biogenetic link connecting grandparents to granddaughter. On Penny's "side" of the bilateral family structure, the path was even more tortuous. Megan began a narrative of a situation involving Penny's parents that the couple took to be representative of their relations.

MEGAN: At their [Penny's parents'] house, they have up all kinds of pictures of Brad [Penny's brother], like a high school picture, Brad with his wife, a wedding picture, Brad with the kids in a Sears photo session, you know all the stuff. And they had recently put up a picture of Penny, I think her high school picture.

PENNY: Ten-year reunion, they've had it up since my ten-year high school reunion.

MEGAN: Okay, so even in comparison, there's not as many pictures of Penny. Anyway, there's not one picture—even though we have sent them many, many pictures—there's not one picture of Kathleen up. And see I get overincensed about this. So I go over there, furious even before we get there, and then you're met immediately with this wall of photos. And so I just get so pissed at the idea that Kathleen is not up there. So Penny . . . See, I get mad at her. I get more mad at her than I do at them because I feel like *it's her job to advocate for us as a family* and I don't feel like it's my job. Or not only my job but not my place. Her parents don't see me as, I don't know. I don't know what it is. So anyway, so I tell her, "Damn it, make them put some pictures up of Kathleen." And I've heard her say it several times to them. "Mom, how about a picture of Kathleen up?" "Oh well we just haven't gotten . . . " What was the one [excuse] last time?

PENNY: We don't have pictures from K-Mart or wherever. Nice posed pictures.

MEGAN: Posed pictures. Whereas we have these gorgeous pictures of Kathleen, you know, at home kind of thing. Beautiful pictures.

PENNY: Adorable.

MEGAN: Adorable pictures. A lot better than you can get at Sears.

PENNY: We've taken twenty rolls of pictures anyhow.

MEGAN: Hundreds. So it's really, it's really irritating.

Penny described the family she had grown up in as ethnic Italian American, although they were members of a Unitarian church, whereas Megan, who described her ethnicity as northern European, had been raised Catholic. Penny had experienced class mobility as a highly paid chemist for a biotech company in the heart of Silicon Valley. For a variety of reasons she was not interested in giving birth to a child, so her parental status would be based upon the social and legal legitimacy the couple could establish through such means as coparent adoption (which was in process at the time of our interview), giving the child her surname, and relations with significant others in their lives, all of which are typical in lesbian coparents' repertoires of legitimating techniques in the absence of formal social recognition. Relations with her family of origin at one level were crucial for establishing the kind of continuity and social support that extended family could provide and that she and Megan desired for their daughter. At another level, the ties were important for the legitimating function they served.

Their story of the wall of family photos at Penny's parents' home says a great deal about the ways in which class and ethnicity are implicated in the obstacles the couple faced for acquiring legitimacy in and through their relations with blood kin, in this case, without the "benefit" of the bloodline of Penny's family being continued in the body of daughter Kathleen. The exclusion of Kathleen's photo from the wall of photos in the Cipolini family home was a statement that baby Kathleen was not blood kin.[9] It was not sufficient that Kathleen "had some Italian blood" via her donor, for it was not Cipolini blood. Penny's mother's excuses for not including her granddaughter's photo also expressed class: posed photos purchased at Sears or K-Mart represented the preferred family portraiture of lower- and lower-middle-class Americans. Here, in a twist on the usual direction of class prerogative, Penny and Megan's "beautiful" home photos failed the taste preferences of Penny's more traditional mother. The taste preference expressed by Penny's mother as a rationale for excluding Kathleen's photograph effectively constituted a class coding of consanguinity—or rather the absence of consanguinity.[10]

If blood was thicker than water in relations with Penny's family of origin, so too was lesbian identity. Penny's identity as a lesbian and her relationship with Megan were almost certainly equal in significance to the absence of consanguinity among the factors that made it difficult for Penny's mother proudly to display her nonbiological granddaughter's photo in the family home. Penny's mother had displayed comparatively few photos of Penny herself, and Megan could not say exactly how Penny's mother regarded her. For Penny's parents, lesbian relationships simply did not add up to kinship, which threw open and left unresolved the question of how "Megan's daughter" was related to them, if she was at all.

Megan's narration of the wall of photos story, a story she told with great animation like many mothers I spoke with when telling of their relations with families of origin, also revealed something about the intensity and never-ending nature of the kinwork lesbian coparents do.[11] Although Megan didn't believe it was her job per se to "advocate" for her family in relations with Penny's family of origin, there was no doubt that advocacy needed to be done. Implicit in her account was an assumption that advocacy work had to be done on both sides of the family, while explicitly she understood advocacy on Penny's side to be Penny's responsibility. Penny's repeated attempts to persuade her mother to display photographs of Kathleen repeatedly failed, a situation to which Megan responded with exasperation. The implication seemed to be that Penny could be working harder as an advocate, yet because Penny was not the biological mother of Kathleen, she did her kinwork from a position of "genealogical disadvantage" in relation to her own parents.[12]

Disavowal—and Renewal

Thus far these stories have depicted incidents and changes of heart that most mothers represented as generally positive, as moving in the direction of acceptance of their families by their families of origin. Much less often, as Weston and others have found, but no less important for the families affected, Bay Area mothers did speak of extremely dispiriting and hurtful incidents involving their parents, siblings, aunts, uncles, cousins, and other extended-family members. For some members of lesbian mothers' extended blood kin, raising children in a familial environment that they either did not recognize as *really* familial or abhorred effectively worsened a situation they saw as already reprehensible. The argument that it was unfair to children to subject them to a life of discrimination and social condemnation resulting from their parents' status and mistreatment in society, while unpersuasive from a social justice perspective, was not exactly the view of these blood kin who denounced their lesbian relatives' decisions to become mothers. The denunciation seemed to be based more on visceral response than rational appraisal.

Significantly, and not surprisingly, given the meaning and importance attached to biogenetic relations, family members of nonbirth mothers expressed this extreme disapproval more often than did those of birth mothers. In turn, both mothers in these families worked harder to resolve the tension with these relatives. Moreover, they consistently sought explanations for the hurtful behavior.

There's the reaction Marjorie and Sophie received from Marjorie's parents when Sophie prematurely gave birth to their son Zeke. Marjorie had counted on the last trimester of Sophie's pregnancy as the time to "prepare" her parents. Whether Marjorie's parents would have used that time to reflect calmly on the news will remain a question, since Zeke's premature arrival placed strains not only on his parents' plans for managing relations with extended family but on their emotional reserves for coping with the situation more generally.

MARJORIE: I came out to them a couple of years before, but it was the baby . . . I knew that that was going to be really hard for them, so I wanted to give them some time. I thought that they'd have three months to get used to it. And lo and behold it ended up, a couple of weeks.

SOPHIE: They would have been shocked anyway.

MARJORIE: [But they were] Nasty.

SOPHIE: They were awful.

MARJORIE: Zeke was born early. I mean, and you can, you just can't imagine the stress we were under. I mean, Sophie was in the hospital, I was still working off and on depending on circumstances, I mean, it was just awful. And then finally Zeke was born and he was . . . and we still had a long road. And my folks called, "I don't know how you can do this." It just sent me over the edge.

SOPHIE: Very unsupportive.

MARJORIE: Well, they're like that, I mean they flip out without thinking maybe I don't need any more of that. I mean I was over the edge.

SOPHIE: I think the thought of lesbians having babies is a wee bit far for them. I think that was truly a shock and that was why they reacted the way they did. Your coming out to them was not a big revelation.

MARJORIE: It was to my dad.

SOPHIE: Well he wasn't happy to have it confirmed. He was not happy about that. But the baby just sent him over the edge. *They just had no frame of reference for that.*

MARJORIE: So that's their story. And they're okay now, I mean, they're fine, they're fine. They call themselves Grandma and Grandpa. Sometimes it's Mrs. and Mr. Rubin (laughing).

Marjorie's relations with her parents were already strained, as Marjorie indicated ("they flip out without thinking maybe I don't need any more of that"). And once again, time might have been an ally, a resource for helping Marjorie acclimate her parents to the idea of her impending motherhood as a lesbian. In many ways Marjorie's parents' reaction represents the other side of the process of comprehension that Serena's father, from earlier in this chapter, experienced. For Serena's father, the arrival of a child clarified his understanding that his daughter's sexuality was not a passing phase or a coerced choice. The baby made her lesbianism real in some sense. Here too, for Marjorie's parents, the baby made it real; Zeke's arrival confirmed his mother's status as a lesbian in her parents' eyes, a status with which they had been uncomfortable.

The shock for these parents of lesbian daughters contemplating and having children came from their having little if any conceptual preparation for this next step. They moved from an uneasy adjustment to the idea of having a lesbian daughter, which was associated with nonprocreative sexuality (an idea that itself has been cast as the basis for a "species difference" attributed to gay men and lesbians), to the very real, nonabstract, flesh-and-blood reality of a grandchild.[13] The sense here was that things were moving too fast. Parents' and other blood relatives' comprehension of the *idea* of gay kinship lagged behind the actual families that were being created. The implication was that they did not recognize the partners and lovers of their sons and daughters as family to begin with. They seemed literally not to see their adult children's relationships as intimate unions like their own marriages, or their breakups like their own divorces. Their daughters' children, then, were not only born "out of wedlock" but born outside any context that meaningfully connoted family or kinship in this culture. Marjorie's parents, by her account, seemed to have experienced a kind of heterocentric culture shock: "I don't know how you can do this."

The incomprehension accompanying unsupportive words and deeds on the part of families of origin appeared to usually evolve into (often grudging) acknowledgment. Marjorie's parents finally did "come around," following a period of painful derision and denunciation, as Marjorie told it. Another couple told the story of relations with comother Eleanor's parents in slightly different terms, invoking ethnicity as a causal factor in her parents' initial (and to a certain extent continuing) denunciation of their family.

ALANA: When Eleanor and I were just a couple, that was kind of an intellectual thing. But suddenly, well, when we announced that. . . .

ELEANOR: Well, when we bought the house, they didn't really question that at all.

ALANA: No, that was a good financial investment! But then came the kid. And that really challenged them that it's *real,* that it was *real.* Your parents disowned you . . .

ELEANOR: Yeah, it didn't last long, but [it felt] devastating. They said it was the worst thing I'd ever done to them in their whole life. I think because they didn't think we should have kids. We told them that we were going to try getting pregnant in August, and then I didn't hear from them for a month, which was a little bit strange because I talked with them every week. And we're not close close but . . . But then there was no letter, no phone calls. And then my dad called me one night and said, "You know, this is really hurting your mother." And I didn't call her or anything. And then my dad called again. I think my dad came around first. He called again and came down to see me. No, they came down to have lunch, and my mom was still adamant that this was not okay. I think we saw them once, or twice, before Brian was born. And then, we went up there one time after Brian was born and my mom says, "Oh, why have you been away so long?" But [now] I [still] don't think that they consider themselves grandparents, and I haven't broached the subject, although Alana wants to broach the subject.

ALANA: There's another side of this that I think is going on is that deep down inside, your folks, as much as they say that they're liberal—they've been to gay bars before, they have lots of gay male friends, couples . . .

ELEANOR: They'd never told people! They'd never, I told them I was gay maybe fifteen years ago, and they never talk about it.

ALANA: And their reaction [to Eleanor's disclosure of sexual identity and Brian's arrival] was a typical Jewish reaction. Is that, if it's something that Jewish parents don't approve of . . . Eleanor's brother did something . . .

ELEANOR: Yeah and my mom ceased to talk to him and told my dad not to go over there.

ALANA: And your dad still maintains some minimal contact but certainly does it discreetly. I think it's a Jewish thing. I talk about this with other people who discuss this in therapy that this is typical of Jewish families.

Alana's explanation for Eleanor's parents' reaction to both her gay identity and her motherhood invoked an ethnic characterization of their means of coping as typical of Jewish families. That ethnicity played some part in how blood kin responded to their lesbian relatives' motherhood is not in question. What is important here, however, is Alana's and Eleanor's view of ethnicity as mediating their relations with their families of origin. Weston wrote that "[d]ivergent perceptions of the relation between family ties and race or ethnicity are indicative of a situation of ideological flux, in which procreative and nonprocreative interpretations vie with one another for the privilege of defining kinship."[14] This is another way of saying that the need for understanding parents' and other blood relatives' responses to gay kinship on the part of lesbian mothers themselves is great, and the invocation of more familiar categories of explanation—ethnicity, for example—helps makes sense of relations that have undergone a kind of cultural shock. Ethnic identity is a safe category of explanation for feelings and attitudes about gay kinship that are difficult to process and classify because they are new and "in flux." It is easier to say that one's parents are just acting how they usually act, how they normally act, in situations that are in fact new territory. Here Alana characterized the behavior as "typical of Jewish families."

These stories of initial denunciation by parents and other members of families of origin, and (often) subsequent warming of relations, could be understood as "postbaby conversions" according to the way I have characterized those changes of heart in earlier narratives. What is different here in these accounts of initial disavowal is the intensity of the feelings expressed by relatives and of the mothers' experiences of them. Words like *disown* and *devastating* expressed the pain of these reactions. In addition, relatives did not always "come around" in a way that could be meaningfully described as a conversion or transformation of affect and regard, as we saw with Eleanor's relations with her family, and with Marjorie's parents, who still referred to themselves as "Mrs. and Mr. Rubin" sometimes and not "Grandma and Grandpa."

For some mothers, relatives never do "come around." Lee Lanier, whom we met earlier in the story about her partner Danielle's sister, who apparently reconciled her fundamentalist Christian beliefs with her sister's gay kinship, experienced no such reconciliation with her own aunt, one of the only remaining members of her family of origin. Lee's relations with this aunt were already somewhat strained but not irreparably so. When Danielle and Lee became the proud and excited parents of Nathan, Lee's aunt drew the proverbial line.

LEE: Yeah, my aunt told my daughter that it was just disgusting that we were having a baby. And she cut off having anything to do with me, and pretty much I cut off having anything to do with her because it's very one-sided. She wanted me to always help her out and yet she wasn't really willing to talk about realities or anything. So it [the relationship] was kind of downhill before that. But then when she found out that . . .

DANIELLE: We had sent a letter to her. Remember it was around Christmas time and she was kind of sad 'cause she was over there by herself and [we thought] maybe we can straighten things out with her. And so Lee sent her a nice note and then we never heard back from her. And then she sent the nasty note back, and then Laurie, Lee's [adult] daughter, told us that she [Lee's aunt] thought it was disgusting that we were having a child and raising it together. You know, that kind of stuff. I mean it's, on some level you let go of it because you know the relationship was strained before that and everything. But really, it's painful.

LEE: Yeah, it's hard to let go. She *was* judgmental about Danielle's and my relationship [before Nathan arrived] and she knew about that.

DANIELLE: But she made an effort.

LEE: Yeah, she did.

DANIELLE: At that time, I mean, she had her reservations and things and she wasn't 100 percent approving for sure. But we'd have dinner together and she tried to include me as family and was nice to me. Do you know what I mean?

LEE: But she's like one of these people where she can be nice to your face and stab you in the back ten seconds later. And within earshot. I got tired of that. She was always disapproving of everybody that she knew. It's still, it's like I'm really angry. And there isn't really anything I can do about it. 'Cause I'm angry for a lot of things that she did to me when I was growing up even. So really, if I ever get the chance to say anything, a lot of stuff is going to come out of my mouth that probably shouldn't (laughs). Then we'll never be friends.

Here again mothers searched for explanations of their blood kin's denunciation of their family. Once again, they explained the reaction in terms of how normal and typical it was for this particular relative to behave in such a way: "she's one of these people." Invoking explanations that made sense and had made sense in other contexts was a way of normalizing a situation for which there might be no "rational" or obvious explanations available or forthcoming.

The impulse to normalize in this context may be associated with the intensity of the emotions involved with family members with whom one has lived or been raised to adulthood.[15] The anger Lee felt in connection with her aunt's treatment of her when she was a child suggests the importance of relatives who are or have been close. When those relatives express particularly severe views of mothers' gay families, it is all the more painful. When words like *disgusting, devastating,* and *nasty* are used to describe these relations, it is indicative not only of the level of emotional intensity but of the significance of a particular relationship. Lee's aunt was the "only family" she had other than her daughter from when she was a teenager, and the family she had created with Danielle and Nathan. Her aunt's disavowal upon the arrival of Nathan was difficult to accept given these circumstances, yet it is exactly this kind of clarification of a major (blood) familial relationship that gay kinship prompts.

If relations with members of families of origin are clarified in the sense that lesbian mothers learn "where they stand" with these blood kin, the arrival of children prompts yet another moment of extended-family clarification. The emergence of a generation born to lesbian daughters and sisters raises the question of how families of origin define *themselves.*

In a chapter on gay families in her 1996 book, *In the Name of the Family,* the feminist family sociologist Judith Stacey asked, What defines a family as gay, what "colors" a family gay? Is it the presence of one gay member? Gay parents? A gay cousin? It is nearly impossible to arrive at some ultimate defining criterion that makes a family gay, given the variety and multitude of family forms in which gay persons have lived or that they have themselves created.[16] Stacey suggests, however, that if anything, "What unifies such families is their need to contend with the particular array of psychic, social, legal, practical and even physical challenges to their very existence that institutionalized hostility to homosexuality produces."[17] In other words, the sociocultural structure of heterosexism forms the basis of a common experience not only for families but for gay identity itself.

As I presented at the beginning of this chapter, Kath Weston offered the alternative theory that the criterion of "choice" is determinate, that the families gay people choose to define as kin may be understood as gay families, and further that the families a gay person has grown up in may be understood as "straight family" as compared to the "chosen" gay families she or he creates. The element of choice in this conceptualization of gay families revolves around the gay person's subjectivity and preferences, from the friends and ex-lovers who are incorporated as kin to the children whose arrival is meticulously planned and celebrated. "Straight" family is organized by the symbols of blood, biology, and heterosexual procreation, all immutable, intractable, and thus not amenable to change by active selection (even though the deployment of such symbols is itself an act of election).[18] Moreover, straight family members are presumed to be nonaccepting—by Weston's informants themselves—of the gay person before she or he has even come out to them. For all of these reasons, straight families represent the absence of choice, the absence of options, in this conceptualization. The rupture of "chosen" families from "straight" families is total. What then colors a family gay, in Weston's formulation, is not only choice but a radical rupture from or refusal of the elements that color a family straight.

Both Stacey's and Weston's conceptualizations go far in explaining the experience and practices of lesbian-coparent families and their relations with their families of origin. However, the arrival of children in the lives of lesbian parents, especially those who are themselves blood kin, challenges the straight/gay family opposition in Weston's formulation. Children constitute a generational link. Whatever their subjective response to the birth of this new generation, families of origin (or "straight families" in Weston's formulation) do not ignore, perhaps cannot ignore, these new grandchildren, nieces, and nephews. As we have seen, members of families of origin may still express disapproval of the lesbian relationship of the children's mothers, but they must reckon with the idea that these children are connected to them, whether they define that connection as social, biogenetic, or both. In sum, children conceived through donor insemination, born to and raised by lesbian mothers, bridge the straight family/gay family divide because their very presence prompts relatives to reassess the meaning of the gay/straight opposition.

I suggest further that the arrival of this generation of children born to lesbian couples in fact redefines "straight families" as gay—that this generation prompts the coloring of a family as gay insofar as members of families of origin *come to face the same heterosexist oppression* as the lesbian daughter or sister, in a way that they were not forced to confront when she had no child. The notion of public versus private acknowledgment is important to this claim. Some parents of lesbian daughters with children, in their *public* acknowledgments of this generation of kin, "come out" as gay. Others may acknowledge and accept children and mothers as members of the extended family and thus *privately* recognize those kin relations—as we have seen in the first section of this chapter. But though recognized and often honored, those relations may still remain privatized, contained in the domain of the two-generational family.[19] What is decisive in either case is that the families of origin face the same disclosure dilemmas with their own friends, extended family, and colleagues as do the mothers themselves.[20] And this, I suggest, creates phenomenologically the experience of heterosexist oppression for the "nongay" members of families of origin in a way that indirectly but no less powerfully "makes them" gay.

For the first time, with the arrival of grandchildren, many parents of the Bay Area mothers realized they could no longer remain closeted about their own children's gay identity. When it was just one adult child who had "never married"—one of many vague explanations that could be offered for their child's nonconformity to the heterosexual order—the secret could be successfully maintained. With grandchildren in their lives, it was nearly impossible. Why this was so was presented tellingly by mothers in their accounts of their parents' public reckoning and acknowledgments.

Birth mother Marcy Callahan described with affection her parents' decision to "come out" to their friends and neighbors in San Francisco:

> When I told my parents about having a baby, [at first] they were very concerned for the baby, all the stuff that we'd already talked about and thought about. They didn't really bring up anything new. But they were sort of just, oh, "What about us? What about the neighbors?" And "Don't come down here pregnant." See, they had never really come out to anybody. My mother's known about me for twenty years but she's never talked to anybody about it. Then I got pregnant. Now you would think it was their idea! They absolutely adore her [daughter Gina]. My mom ended up coming out to like everybody she knew. She just decided, "I'm just getting it all out now, I'm tired of secrets, I'm not going to lie to anybody anymore." 'Cause I told her, "Just tell people I'm a single mom if you don't want to tell them everything." She says, "Nope, I'm getting it all out." She's now telling her whole world my life! But it was great, we got baby gifts from all of their neighbors, a lot of their friends, and it's really changed a lot of things for them. A couple of her friends called her up right away saying, "Oh, congratulations, you're going to be a grandma."

For the parents of lesbian daughters with children fully to claim their own status and identity as grandparents, which most appear to desire, public acknowledgment plays no small role. As we will see in the next chapter, social interaction with external others not only educates those individuals and groups to the existence and ways of lesbian-coparent families but serves to legitimate families themselves. And as the story of Marcy Callahan's parents' coming to terms and coming out suggests, the arrival of grandchildren inspires grandparents to reveal what they once kept hidden within the privacy of the family. It seems grandchildren exert pressure to reassess choices about the level of secrecy to maintain and thus expose the lie and the injustice of the repression of gay identity.

Comother Kathleen Peterson told the story of her mother's first serious encounter with the coming-out dilemma prompted by the planned appearance of Kathleen with her infant daughter Sophie at the funeral of

Kathleen's grandmother. In this account, Kathleen's mother had been waiting for Kathleen's legal adoption of Sophie to be completed before she would come out to her extended family and friends:

> Another thing that's really weird about her [Kathleen's mother] is when my grandmother died, you know, it was one of these drop everything and fly home kind of scenarios. And I said, "I think I'm going to bring the baby with me." 'Cause Sharon [Kathleen's partner] was working. And my mother, her first reaction was, "My God, I haven't told anybody about the baby, I wasn't going to tell anybody until you adopted her." I said, "Well you can just tell people that I did adopt her or that she's a foster child if you want!" I mean she lives, she works in this conservative religious community, you know, and my grandmother, both my grandfathers are preachers and so my grandmother was married to this devout preacher and it's not like she had any idea that I was a lesbian. So all of her friends were going to come to this funeral, like all of these ninety-year-old Seventh Day Adventists. It's not like you can say, "Oh, here's my lesbian lover and our child." You know, forget it, just don't even bother. So anyway my mother was like, "You can't bring the baby, I haven't told people." And then she, after about a couple of minutes she sort of pulled herself together and she said, "Honey, just bring the baby and it'll be fine. We'll figure it out." You know, so she really is trying very hard.

It is no small matter that second-parent adoptions are available for non-birth lesbian mothers in a growing number of states and counties in the United States.[21] Second-parent adoption renders the comother a fully legal parent and guardian to the child without abrogating the rights and status of the birth mother. It confers the same legal status automatically granted to heterosexual men who are legal spouses or otherwise whose genetic paternity is known, even when those men have no intention of parenting or supporting the child. Without the right to civil marriage, second-parent adoptions provide lesbians and gay men the legal mechanism for ensuring and protecting their parental status.

The same may be said for what it does for their social status. Even in the eyes of "tolerant" members of one's family of origin, the official adoption of a nonblood child secures the familial connection in ways that could not be achieved otherwise. Here Kathleen suggested to her mother that she could say that Kathleen had adopted, which would confer automatic social legitimacy on her relationship with her child in the eyes of her grandmother's conservative friends. Saying that Kathleen had adopted (or was fostering) Sophie did not identify Kathleen as a lesbian. Kathleen's mother would not be forced to come out at all, as Kathleen could be depicted as a single adoptive parent. As we will see in Chapter 6, comothers are in a unique position compared with their birth mother partners in that they are faced with explaining their relationship to their children more frequently than are their partners and thus more frequently strategize whether and how to disclose sexual identity. Like Kathleen herself, her mother might have chosen to continue to conceal Kathleen's lesbian identity, a decision that might not have arisen at all but for the imminent physical appearance of baby Sophie.

Whether or not Kathleen's mother came out fully to her own mother's friends and family, as did Marcy Callahan's parents, it was not the coming out per se that colored these families gay but *the encounter with the disclosure dilemma*—that is, that particular complex of shame and secrecy created by the social fact of systemic, institutionalized oppression of gay people. Kathleen's mother had to "figure it out," had to figure out how to represent her lesbian daughter's relationship with her own child to people deemed important to the family. This is a quintessential moment of negotiating the obdurate reality of heterosexist oppression. This is individuals bumping into a particular, oppressive, social structure. It is similar to the way in which the structure of racism prompts some relatives to conceal an interracial marriage in a family or to outright reject the "offending" son or daughter. It shares some qualities with other such structures of oppression as they affect the internal dynamics and public representations of a given family.

The experience of heterosexist oppression is felt deeply by members of families of origin; the arrival of grandchildren appears to prompt an even more emotionally complex confrontation with it than the nongay family members had in connection with the daughter's lesbianism. The addition of a human link in the family who would experience homophobic hostility at some point in her or his life seems to expose the injustice in a way that the same hostility experienced by the lesbian daughter could not. Before the arrival of children, nongay members of a lesbian mother's family of origin could disidentify with the daughter or sister when she was presumed to be nonprocreative and her lifestyle did not touch their lives or implicate them in some way. The lesbian daughter herself could be seen as an "isolated case" within the family, and unlikely to have children, so that "the problem of homosexuality," in a sense, could be contained.[22] But with children born to and adopted by lesbian daughters and sisters, it is easier for nongay family members to see that the only "problem of homosexuality" is the problem of societal hetero-sexist organization—that simply by virtue of their connection with their lesbian parents, children would be exposed to vicarious discrimination and hostility. With the arrival of the child comes the reidentification of family members with the daughter or sister, a family member who was now no longer an "exile from kinship," as Weston put it. The child provides the basis for shared experience, including now the experience of heterosexist oppression.

Birth mother Kristen Frantz and comother Clarice Hart, who lived in a small mountain town in the South Bay, explained how Kristen's father sought to avoid the potential physical danger their son Troy might face at the "redneck" schools he would most likely have to attend.

CLARICE: We were talking about schools for Troy and where we were going to send him to school. We're not going to let him go to a school that's . . . It's very redneck and inbred [around here]. It's very lily white up here, it's kind of scary socially. There's some good people, but, there's a lot of backwoods, like . . . there's a cat that hangs out around here and we discovered he had a bullet in him that can't be taken out, probably been there for years. So we don't do a lot of socializing.

KRISTEN: They're the kind of people that, the rednecks go to family reunions to pick up a chick. Scary.

CLARICE: So we were talking to grandpa [Kristen's father] about that. And that that's where he's [Troy] going to go to school. And he said, "Well, you need to come here, you know, we just bought this property and you can come live with us." And he had no [hesitation]. It was "Of course he can go to school here. Anybody that messes with him we'll just have to deal with it." He's just, he's a total champion.

A lesbian daughter's parenthood tests anew her extended family's loyalties and reservoirs of courage. To fully embrace and support a lesbian daughter's personhood, for which the arrival of a child provides the opportunity for reassessment, means that parents themselves are willing to "take on" the experience of her oppression, as we saw with Kristen's father.

Conversely, however, the reassessment may lead to the conscious or unconscious decision *not* to confront the effects of bigotry within the self. Birth mothers and comothers alike recounted interactions and conversations with parents who either could not come out to friends and extended family or crafted elaborate explanations and end-runs around the gay issue. The mother of comother Carrie Johnson simply did not come out to her own extended family, even while she supported Carrie, partner Serena, and their daughter Polly in every other way.

CARRIE: My mother I notice doesn't tell her extended family, back in Maryland. They just know that I have an adopted child. She keeps it closed. But she's always been very positive to us. My father's dead, so it's mostly my mother, brother and sister. We're very close.

SERENA: And they're all here [in the Bay Area].

CARRIE: Wonderful and supportive. Very, very supportive. My mother actually does child care for us.

Birth mother Marilyn Weiss spoke candidly about her mother's inability to accept her relationship with partner Brenda, even while her mother adored grandson Michael, to whom Brenda was a legal parent. In her public presentation of the addition to the family, Marilyn's mother chose to remain closeted.

MARILYN: My mom, she has a lot of shame around my being a lesbian, probably has to do with my shame about my being a lesbian too. But she's come a long way.

BRENDA: She didn't want Marilyn walking in the neighborhood when she was pregnant.

MARILYN: Now she shows everybody the pictures. She shows pictures of Michael all over the place. But she identifies me as a single parent.

The relationship between private, intrafamilial acceptance and public secrecy is complex, and it tells us something about how shame operates as a mechanism of social control. As we have seen, many parents and other members of families of origin may accept and support the lesbian motherhood of a member of the family within the protective domain of the family itself, while sealing the information off from the rest of society—or from significant extended-family members, as Carrie Johnson's mother did, according to Carrie. This position allows one authentically to support and embrace the lesbian daughter or sister and the family she has created and choose not to take that public. But in remaining socially closeted, this position surrenders to society's heterosexist familial norms. Apparently a compromise occurs at the level of the self: one's strongest loyalties are to society, but because one is keeping a secret from the public, the self is crucially burdened with the maintenance of that secret; one remains isolated from society and "a stranger even to self," in Weston's words.[23] Marilyn's mother's position was like this, in which her inability to move beyond her own shame over Marilyn's lesbianism honored the heterosexist system that produced that shame. At the same time, the shame crippled her capacity to fully and freely embrace her daughter's total person, including her relationship with partner Brenda.

Alternatively, when parents and nongay members of families of origin personally accept the motherhood and lesbian identity of a daughter or sister, they reject the societal heterosexism that produces sexual deviance in the first place. Their position of personal and intrafamilial acceptance, coupled with public acknowledgment, expresses an empathic regard for and openness to the experience of the lesbian mother or daughter or sister. Because of this empathic regard, the nongay family member feels the cold injustice as though it were trained upon the self, as indeed it is. And because of this empathic regard, the nongay family member who has developed it is likely to remain loyal to self and family. So instead of saddling the self with the burden of a secret born of social shame, these family members are able to shun that element of society that produces it. They reject as *antisocial* the construction of gayness as pathological or deviant. The statement made by one parent in Parents and Friends of Lesbians and Gays (PFLAG) in a collection of interviews with other such family members entitled *Beyond Acceptance* sums this position up eloquently:

We parents speak because we too feel the personal pain of being in a stigmatized minority, and we hate having to bear a penalty alone. We speak because we question the fairness of the stigma. We properly want justice for our children and ourselves. Finally, we speak because we want to work to change the prejudice of society. We have learned that our negative inner messages are merely antiquated judgments based on a lack of truth. We have a deep desire to correct a misinformed society. This is how human society has been changed throughout history.[24]

This position thus runs the reverse risk of rejection by (heterosexist) society. In turn, however, because this framework promotes greater consistency of interior psychic life, interpersonal affect and practice, and social (public) presentation, it also constitutes a more radical rejection of the mechanisms of social control asserted by heteronormativity—including shame. In Weston's words: "In coming out, a person acts to create a sense of wholeness by establishing congruence between interior experience and external presentation, moving the inner into the outer, bringing the hidden to light, and transforming a private into a social reality."[25]

It is no accident that the feeling evoked by one's rejection of shame is pride. Shame and pride form one axis that is linked to the dialectical relationship of self to society. The social psychologist Charles Horton Cooley stated this relationship most directly in his 1902 work *Human Nature and the Social Order,* in which he characterized the dialectic as "the looking-glass self." The looking-glass self is a process comprising three elements:

the imagination of our appearance to the other person; the imagination of his judgment of that appearance; and some sort of self-feeling, such as pride or mortification. The comparison with a looking glass hardly suggests the second element, the imagined judgment, which is quite essential. The thing that moves us to pride or shame is not the mere mechanical reflection of ourselves, but an imputed sentiment, the imagined effect of this reflection upon another's mind.[26]

The "imagined judgment" constitutes identification with the imagined normative social order. Being the opposite side of shame, pride is still a self-feeling generated as a response to a perception of social adjudication. In a letter written in 1929 to his parents in Madrid while staying in New York, the Spanish poet Federico Garcia Lorca characterized a strong identification with normative social appearances as peculiarly American: "For here nothing is frowned upon, and everything is tolerated . . . except social scandal. You can have a hundred mistresses and people know it and nothing happens, but just wait until one of them denounces you and whips up something in public. There is no hope for you socially. This is something really appalling. Appearances are what they live for, reality matters nothing."[27]

Combining traditional Japanese cultural norms with Lorca's appearance-oriented American perspective, members of Amy Takata's natal family perhaps throw into sharpest relief the relationship between self and society and the role of shame on the part of families of origin. Amy described her parents as "very traditional" Japanese, especially her father, who passed away before Amy and partner Jocelyn, who was also Japanese American, officially came out to their families. Amy and Jocelyn speculated that their lives might have been very different had Amy's father not died. Moreover, Amy invoked "the concept of shame" attributed to traditional Japanese culture to explain why her mother still could not see herself as Grandma to the couple's twin babies or bring herself to tell her own extended family.

AMY: My mother is very loving to me, but I think . . . well I know that she doesn't see these children as being my children. And has not been able to tell my aunt and my grandmother. She's having a real hard time. There's this concept of shame. My family is very much still traditional Japanese, much more so than Jocelyn's family. So, for her it's really hard. But we talk every week. She just can't quite . . . She likes Jocelyn and she'll always ask, "How are the children, how's Jocelyn? Make sure you both are getting enough sleep." And blah blah blah blah blah, but, she doesn't see herself as their grandmother. It was funny, she sent a card and the card was addressed to Jocelyn and to me, but on the inside, it was only written to Jocelyn, and the check was written to Jocelyn. My mom sends checks. Where on the other hand, my sisters will send something that will be addressed to all of us or addressed to the babies but inside it's always addressed to Jocelyn AND me.

JOCELYN: Her sisters have always recognized our relationship.

AMY: And the checks are always written to me, but with my mother, it's a different kind of situation. In her heart she's not grandmother to the babies.

JOCELYN: She doesn't see them as her grandkids. She already has two grandkids.

AMY: Now my dad, my dad passed away a long time ago, about ten or twelve years ago. My dad was very traditional. My sister met a guy up in Japan when she was teaching and they came back to Hawaii and they were living together, and my father just thought that that was the worst thing in the whole wide world. To him she was just a whore for doing that and it was such a shameful thing. So you can imagine what he would have said . . .

JOCELYN: I think had her father not died, I think our relationship would have been really different. And I don't even know if we'd be together still, had her father not died. Because she was so much into doing what would make her parents happy, her father happy.

AMY: I think it would have made him very upset. It would have been really hard for him. I would have to have thought long and hard about it.

This account of Amy's relations with her natal family demonstrates perhaps most comprehensively the range of feelings and regard, and definitions of kinship constructed around those feelings, within families of origin. Amy's siblings acknowledged and appreciated her "chosen" family, while her mother, unable to move beyond the feelings of shame that Amy's socially transgressive behavior ostensibly visited upon her and the entire family, disavowed any familial connection with Amy's children. Amy's father, had he not died, most likely would have imposed even more severe sanctions, perhaps complete estrangement, given his adherence to traditional Japanese norms, including his prescribed duties as patriarch. Weston points out that her informants expected their mothers to be more accepting and easier to come out to than fathers, a notion reflecting gendered stereotypes of feminine emotionality and masculine reason, while they saw their siblings as more likely to be accepting and easier to come out to than their parents.[28]

Amy's mother had crafted a compromise between loyalty to family and to society that promoted interior anguish: "She's having a real hard time." Shame prevented her from claiming her status as grandmother, even though she obviously cared for "Jocelyn's babies" as though they were her own grandchildren—that is, Amy's babies. Clearly the lack of a biogenetic connection to the children played a role in Amy's mother's inability to see herself as the children's grandmother. For, as we saw with Marilyn Weiss's mother, whose relationship with Marilyn and Brenda's child was defined as biogenetic since Marilyn was the birth mother, that connection allowed her to see herself as a grandparent, even though she refused to accept Marilyn's relationship with Brenda.

This is to suggest that the ability of members of families of origin to overcome the shame of internalized heterosexism is assisted by a biogenetic tie to the children that prompts the reassessment of relations in the first place. However, if the shame is strong enough, if the orientation to Lorca's social appearances is powerful enough, even with a biological connection to children, family members may still be incapable of rejecting the harsh "imagined and real judgment" of society, as Cooley put it. Family members of nonbirth mothers may be less equipped to accept the families created by their lesbian daughters and sisters by virtue of the social value and emphasis placed on blood relations, but the primary factor involved in their capacity (or not) to come to full acceptance of and public disclosure of gay kinship is the same complex that "colors" a family gay: the operation and effects of endemic, institutionalized heterosexism.

Chapter 6 | BECOMING FAMILIAR IN THE COMMUNITY OF STRANGERS

In their 1990 book *What Is Family?* the sociologists Jaber Gubrium and James Holstein analyzed the processes by which family as a socially recognized entity gets produced in the contemporary United States. Arguing that practice unifies ideas and things, they asserted that family emerges as an object of what they called "descriptive practice." The family, as a thing separate and distinctive from its component members, is a practical accomplishment. But if the practical accomplishment of family depends on unifying ideas and things through descriptive practice, it first requires an idea through which family may be signified to the rest of the world. Families that are relatively new to the public imaginary lack the benefit of having the idea of their particular family form circulating and thus, like the "six characters in search of an author" in the play of that name by Pirandello, find that their existence needs representation, it needs an author.[1]

Because the concept of two-mother families has yet to be easily grasped outside lesbian, gay, antiheterosexist, and progressive communities, members of lesbian-coparent families must work harder in their practical accomplishment of family than their more traditional counterparts. This is particularly true for nonbirth mothers in lesbian-coparent families. Birth mothers may rely on their identity as the biological mother in their descriptive practice. Nonbirth mothers, in contrast, have no such category and thus no identity by which they may represent to the world who they are in relation to their children. Their story is one of creating a sociofamilial identity that is distinct from that of their partners and has not previously existed. This chapter examines how, through everyday lived experience and interaction with strangers, these comothers construct their sociofamilial identities and how the lesbian-coparent family itself materializes as a socially recognizable form.[2] Through the accretion of countless social encounters and face-to-face interactions, in public places and sites of extrafamilial interaction, nonbirth mothers learn how to represent themselves to nonintimate others. In the same way, family members as a collective unit emerge from the veil of invisibility as a distinct social form.

THE COMOTHER'S PREDICAMENT

Comothers in lesbian-coparent families have no cultural category by which they can signify their identity as parents. They are not daddies, though sometimes, as we have seen, they are primary breadwinners; they are not nannies, aunties, or grannies, though often they are presumed to be by strangers. They must write their existence as parents into the public imaginary and thereby invent a sociofamilial category with no guidance from the idioms and norms that have governed the hitherto dominant heterosexual family forms—except for the unsatisfying option of defining themselves in the negative, as "not that." On the more positive side of identity formation, the truly constructive sense of social construction, comothers foster their children, with whom they share no blood tie, and their partners, with whom they share no legal tie, by means of resilient socioaffective cathexes.

Comothers in two-mother families also perform a public educational role because they occupy a unique position compared to their partners in that they may choose, but often feel compelled, to reveal their relationship with their children to curious others in public places. Unlike a birth mother, who may confidently lay biological claim to a child, or an adoptive heterosexual mother, whose relationship with a child is culturally sanctioned, the lesbian comother who utters the truth about her relationship to her child "outs" herself and her family. The decision to disclose and the form the disclosure will take, like all phenomena of the closet, weigh mightily on the shoulders of the comother. The spontaneous risk assessment and emotional calculus these mothers face in managing what literary scholar D. A. Miller called "the open secret" feel more onerous when there are children who factor into these disclosure calculations and whose relationship with comothers is not culturally recognized, much less legitimated.[3] This point was summed up nicely by Bay Area comother Kim Reynolds:

> When you're just dealing with yourself and this is your identity, and how you perceive yourself and people perceive you, it has only to do with you. But in this case, it has to do with a relationship with children, and so it's much more complex. And everything you're taught about a mother's role to the child and involvement is a lot different than just who you are in terms of your personal identity.

Comothers, then, who cannot "pass" because there are few if any intelligible family categories whose labels they can assume bear a substantial proportion of the collective burden of educating uninformed members of society. When they offer an account of their identity, they simultaneously create a new sociofamilial category and disproportionately bear the political and social burden of education.

No Rest for the Wary

A lesbian birth mother often will experience social respectability or legitimacy for the first time on the basis of her biological maternal status, which is more culturally acceptable than her lesbian status, in part because others often presume that she is a heterosexual mother and in part because she herself feels and projects a greater sense of being a woman more fully and completely than before she had a child. As sociologist Arlene Stein noted in her 1997 book *Sex and Sensibility: Stories of a Lesbian Generation,* the equation of motherhood with heterosexuality is so firmly rooted in mainstream culture that some of the lesbians she interviewed, who were also biological mothers, experienced their sexual identities as being effaced by the more acceptable status of motherhood. One of Stein's interviewees reported that she felt acceptable for the first time because she was a (biological) mother, an unambiguous—indeed sacralized—status given her social interlocutors' presumption of heterosexuality, which this particular mother often did not attempt to dispel.[4] While not disabusing one's interlocutors can evoke feelings of shame in the politicized gay person, this passing and feeling socially legitimate represents a choice that will always be available to a lesbian birth mother.

In her daily rounds, the birth mother can confidently share details of her motherhood with individuals and strangers, persons most likely predisposed to the heterosexual assumption, knowing that disclosure or nondisclosure of her lesbian identity is fully in her control. In her "descriptive practice" she can share stories with interested others about her labor, delivery, breastfeeding, and countless other practices, events, and emotions that will have the socially legitimating effect of persuading her audience that she is *the* mother, as Bay Area birth mother Resa Frank explained: "When I'm carrying the baby and there's other women with babies and we smile at each other, ask what the baby weighs or whatever, I love that stuff. And I do it all the time. And it doesn't occur to me that I need to tell them I'm a lesbian when I'm doing that."

In contrast, the comother, regardless of whether she would want to, cannot pass as *the* mother on the basis of the accurate information concerning her biological relationship with the child, even though she, like the birth mother, also shares stories with others in face-to-face interactions. But because she has no recourse to existing social categories, the comother is acutely burdened with the work of explaining, defending, or concealing—in effect fabricating—her relationship with her child and thus her social identity. As Stein indicates about the nonbirth mothers in her study, "[H]eterosexuals who saw a lesbian accompanied by a child generally assumed she [interviewee] was straight and married. She had to keep telling them otherwise. This was particularly true of women who were the nonbiological parents of children: not only did they have to challenge the equation of motherhood and heterosexuality, but they also had to introduce to people the notion of nonbiological, or social, motherhood."[5]

But nonbiological or social motherhood doesn't quite capture the social-psychological complex of experience that dynamically and relationally constitutes the particular situation of the nonbirth lesbian parent. The sexual identity of comothers cannot easily be effaced by their maternal identity, as with many birth mothers. In both random and routine encounters with extrafamilial others, a comother is confronted with inquiries about her particular relationship with a particular child with whom she appears to be close and for whom she appears to be responsible. The truth is that she is the mother of a child who has two mothers. A birth mother may use this line or some variation, but she is not compelled to do so, as a comother is if the comother wishes to be accurate. And the comother must be fully disclosing if she is not to be discovered later as having lied, if it is likely she will encounter the individual again, or if it is impossible for her to pass as the birth mother (for example, if it is apparent that she is too old to have given birth, in which case she may be taken for the child's grandmother and must decide to pass as that or disabuse her interlocutor).

Her information management, then, may take the form of outright, self-conscious deception, so as to shield herself and her child from unwanted further questioning or attention. Or she may be vague in her responses to interested others, lying, in turns, through omission and obfuscation. Or she may opt for "full" disclosure. The particular words or script she uses will depend upon the language used and questions raised by the interested other. The interaction may begin innocuously, at least from the perspective of the curious stranger, who might say something like "Your baby doesn't look like you, must look like the father." But no interaction begins innocuously for many comothers, who often dread but then come to steel themselves for these quotidian encounters, even while others find them easy, even humorous.

The comother must decide when and whom she will educate about her family in the myriad and initially unpatterned encounters she has with individuals whose attitudes about homosexuality and about gay parents she cannot know in advance. Her face-to-face interactions with grocery store customers, department store clerks, parents at playgrounds, and countless other strangers with whom she may have the occasion to exchange words or briefly become acquainted become for her a type of recurring game of identity poker. She must be vigilant to the people and situation at hand, assessing every possible sign concerning the risk of exposure she might take in entering what Erving Goffman called one of the primal scenes of sociology: the encounter between a "nonnormal" and a "normal."[6] In this case, the encounter is between the lesbian comother, who possesses a potentially discrediting attribute, and those heterosexual "normals" whose privilege as heterosexuals exempts them from having to manage information and tension about their sexual identity. Goffman pointed out that those who must strategize whether and how to disclose potentially discrediting information in mixed contacts will have to be alive to aspects of the social situation which others treat as un-calculated and unattended. What are unthinking routines for normals can become management problems for the discreditable. These problems cannot always be handled by past experiences, since new contingencies always arise, making former concealing devices inadequate. The person with a secret fail-ing, then, must be *alive* to the social situation as a scanner of possibilities, and is therefore likely to be *alienated* from the simpler world in which those around him apparently dwell. (Emphasis added)[7]

Being alive to social situations in ways that others may comfortably ap-proach without calculation and attention is not only (and somewhat par-adoxically) alienating, as Goffman suggests, but work. We might think of this mental, emotional, educational, and social labor that lesbian co-mothers do as identity work or construction work. It is constructive in the sense that comothers are creating new impressions of and expectations for a wider variety of hitherto unrecognized and preemptively delegitimated modes of human affinity. In effect, they are doing the discursive work of producing family, which, after all, according to Gubrium and Holstein, is simply "a way of assigning meaning to social relationships." As they de-scribe it: "Those concerned are social constructionists whose labors are definitely circumscribed by the conditions of descriptions, such as those arising around dinner tables, street corners, in hospitals, treatment centers, counseling agencies and family courts."[8]

A final question remains, however, as to why comothers feel compelled to offer accounts of their sociofamilial identity in the first place. If the so-cial circumstances they find themselves in are randomly traversed public spaces, as I illustrate in the next section, why are comothers required to offer identity accounts? What triggers such inquiries from strangers, es-pecially in gay-friendly urban and suburban areas such as the San Fran-cisco Bay Area, in which gay parenthood is already the most visible?

Part of the answer is that babies and young children are social magnets; they draw adult strangers together and provide a common focus and pre-text for conversation. A child elicits the amiable interest of strangers, prompting questions from them that the parent is then responsible for an-swering. Gubrium and Holstein refer to these promptings as "challenges" and the responses to them, and indeed the occasions themselves, as "family projects."[9] These challenges come in many forms, often with the simple purpose of establishing who is related to whom. When it is a lesbian non-birth parent with her children, the way she is related to the child is not clear if it has already been established that she is not the biological mother—as often occurs with the first question, as we will see. So one innocuous question is followed by more pointed ones, which then culminate in an interaction in which the gay parent is responsible for the entire (re)presentation of self-and-family. A lesbian without children negotiates her identity in public places with only her well-being, and perhaps that of her group or group politics, in mind. When one is with a child to whom one is a parent, however, the entire range of considerations changes. No longer is one negotiating one's own social-sexual identity.

It is here where, beyond the immediate attraction of children who draw strangers together, we find another impetus for comothers to provide an identity account: having children means that lesbian mothers are more public in general. They mix socially in straight society, in Goffmanian "mixed contact" fashion, more frequently as the needs of their children draw them into spheres where either they rarely entered before or, when they did, they could choose to be as "out" with their own identity as they wished. Now, many are mixing more in nongay groups and communities with their children, who elicit interest from strangers. Together these factors provide the conditions that lead to family "challenges," which, for the comother, become complicated information management problems, as Bay Area comother Penny Cipolini reflected:

Normally, if you're just a lesbian at work or something, normally when you go through life, you go to the grocery store, you do anything, and you can just go on and be who you are. You can choose to be out, like maybe wearing a shirt that says something. Or you can go about your life and just assume who you are and it's fine with you and anybody else. But I didn't realize that in order for me to explain how I was becoming a parent, other than that the child showed up from some adoption agency (and I didn't want to lie, I had already decided that), I didn't realize that in order to go through the whole process, I had to be totally out. And everything, from going through the hospital, the doctors . . . each time we went through a different thing it was another, I had to out myself. And I'm used to it now, but sometimes I wouldn't think about it beforehand and then we'd walk in a room and I'd think, "Oh my God, I've got to out myself again." That was a total surprise to me, it was absolutely, I just didn't expect that I would have to out myself in order to claim myself as a parent.

When I asked Penny's partner Megan why it was not the same for her, she responded:

'Cause I was a "single mom." I didn't have to explain it to anybody. I was big, I was pregnant. Nobody even asked. I saw a couple of people would look at my hand to see if I had a wedding ring on, that kind of thing. But if Penny says, for example at work, "I'm going to have a baby in two months. I want to go on . . . some kind of leave," there has to be some explanation.

FAMILY "OUTINGS," THREE STRATEGIES

Since a comother must offer some account, some explanation for who she is in relation to her child, she may decide from a range of (non)disclosure options in her information management given the circumstance she finds herself in with her children. So, in the absence of a more categorical resolution "not to lie," as Penny had decided, the kinds of discursive strategies available to comothers, strategies that go into their descriptive practice in particular situations, become all-important in the negotiation of their social identity. The scenes I describe in what follows highlight in detail three strategies a comother might employ—"full" disclosure, "partial" disclosure through obfuscation or omission, and outright deception or passing—not an exhaustive list but a rendering of the patterns we might begin to think of as movement along a learning curve as comothers become more experienced inhabiting and performing their identity as lesbian comothers. I begin with the "full disclosure" strategy, since new comothers, relatively inexperienced with interacting with strangers in this role, struggle to find words and phrases that allow them to control their own utterances about who they are. They enter social situations unprepared with experience and scripts and thus find themselves struggling to convey the truth of the matter, which constitutes "full disclosure," or as I think of this strategy, Telling It Like It Is.

The scene, as recounted by Jocelyn and Amy, the Japanese American mothers from the previous chapter, was a gleaming suburban mall in the South Bay, where one could easily disappear in the large crowd of anonymous consumers. Jocelyn and Amy strolled their infant twins in a lateral two-seater in search of a suitable place for lunch for the twins. Birth mother Jocelyn would breastfeed both infants. (The mothers thought it impractical to induce breast milk in nonbirth mother Amy in order to share the nursing, as some lesbian coparents have been rumored to undertake, although it could be a particularly handy arrangement for a couple with twins.)

They went to a department store dressing room, where Jocelyn began to nurse baby Todd, and Amy held and played with his twin sister, Hannah, just outside the dressing room area. As Amy narrated it, an encounter with a store salesperson progressed in this way:

> The salesperson comes over, "Oh, she's really cute, is this your baby?" I sort of stop in my tracks 'cause I know any moment Jocelyn is going to come out and she has a nursing top on and the double, twin stroller, and, I said, "Well, yes, sort of." And she's [salesperson] like, "You're sort of her mother?" And I said, "Yeah, sort of." And here comes Jocelyn, you know, she has a nursing top on, and so I said, "Jocelyn is the birth mother and I'm the co-mom, we're coparenting the children." Jocelyn said later that I didn't have to tell the salesperson that she's the birth mom. But, you know, Jocelyn was wearing a nursing top! We haven't quite gotten things down. It's easier for Jocelyn because people recognize her as being the mom and they address her as being the mom. I haven't quite learned when I should and shouldn't say it, and how to say it. I think it's a matter of practicing, rehearsing it, I'm not real comfortable with that part yet.

What would make that part of Amy's identity work more comfortable for her?

> If I could just tell them simply that I'm their mom, without having to explain it. And that she's the mom and I'm the mom and that that's another kind of family unit. Where right now you can't really say, "Well, I'm the

mom and Jocelyn is the mom" and everyone says, "Oh, that's really nice." They sort of stop in their tracks. In settings where it's not a personal situation I never receive an affirmative reaction.

The scene at the department store described by Amy is important for what it tells us about the disclosure strategies available to her. The clearly visible signifiers of Jocelyn's biological maternity (the nursing top) limit Amy's discursive range; they limit her repertoire of symbolic evidence for passing as something recognizable, something familiar. They compel her rhetorically toward "full" disclosure—that is, to a discursive point beyond the reach of deniability. In a sense, she is a marked woman precisely because she is not marked as something comprehensible and cannot provide comprehensible material evidence for who she is. This is why comothers bear a particularly difficult burden in lesbian-coparent families: they are in the process of creating a category of kinship and social identity that has not existed in modern Western (nonenslaved) society and for which there is no language that would make it intelligible.[10] Amy's words articulated her experience of this labor-intensive process best: "It's really hard, it takes a lot of energy to have to think about how you're going to deal with these situations and what you're going to say and what you're not going to say. You have to work so hard at it." Like Penny and Megan, both Jocelyn and Amy agreed that social interaction in public places was a little easier for Jocelyn insofar as her biological relationship to the children often automatically gave her normative status. Jocelyn put the point succinctly: "Well, since people think there is only one mom, they automatically assume I'm the mom. So that puts Amy in the position, 'Well, what am I?' "

The full disclosure strategy involved not only new comothers, like Amy, earnestly wanting to learn and help others to understand who they are in relation to their children. It also was a choice available to and made by more seasoned navigators, like Melissa Goldstein, who seemed to have mentally catalogued all the possible situations in which she would have to interact with people vis-à-vis her children and who deployed her disclosure strategies with laser precision. Here she "tells it like it is":

We were at preschool one day, just before the end, and we'd taken a day off or something I don't remember why we [parents] were both there. Anyway,

Amanda [daughter] was being clingy and she asked me to sit down with her. And so I did. This little girl sitting next to her said, "Who are you?" And I said, "I'm Amanda's mom." And she said, "Oh well, who's his mom?" and pointed at Jeremy. And I said, "I'm Jeremy's mom too." And she kind of looked at me and she looked over at Linda and she said, "Well, who's she?" And I said, "Well, she's their mom too." So it was, "Oh, you mean grandma." I said, "No, Jeremy and Amanda have two moms."

After this exchange, apparently the five-year-old asking the questions simply looked at Melissa "like I was crazy."

The concept of two moms may be difficult for the young and old alike to wrap their minds around, but it is the most direct and nondefensive way for a comother to describe "fully" her relationship with her children. And because the two-mother concept is so difficult, there will always be the occasions where one mother, usually the comother, will be taken for a nanny or granny or auntie before, during, and sometimes even after the explanation is given (as with the little girl in the encounter just described), regardless of the disclosure strategy used. But Telling It Like It Is still is the strategy most conducive to the promotion of understanding, however incomprehensible it may be initially, as comother Brenda Jacobson explained in her rationale for choosing it:

I find myself having to come out all the time as a lesbian with Michael because they immediately think he's mine and they'll ask, "Oh, did he kick you when he was in utero," you know. And I have a choice to kind of like avoid the question, but what I do is I say, "No, my partner had the baby and I'm adopting him." You know, I don't feel totally comfortable with my answers yet but I'm kind of getting it down.

It is important to note that comothers still have no language, no name, for describing precisely who they are. The two-mother concept describes the family form, and the comother is simultaneously and tacitly inscribed in that configuration. But the comother's specific sociofamilial identity still has no name of its own. And as we have seen, the identity work, the construction work of comothers, what we might even think of as the meaning-making and being-making work of the comother, takes patience, emotional and mental energy, and a willingness to pursue certain opportunities for fostering understanding.

Sometimes a comother's desire to Tell It Like It Is may conflict with the abruptness of the turn in conversation or directness of inquiry. She may then find herself uttering partial truths, equal parts fact and fiction, a disclosure strategy I call Speaking Half-Truths to Power.

Speaking Half-Truths to Power

Alana and Eleanor, the proud parents of Brian, the sweet-tempered toddler with asthma from Chapter 4, recounted a story in which comother Eleanor actually had to exit a social situation because she wasn't prepared with a script and the truth proved too unwieldy to convey.

> Ninety percent of the time we tell people the whole story. But one time I got caught off guard. I had been staying at home with Brian when he was three months old, and I decided to go out and give blood. Because he was so little they said to me that my iron level was really good after giving birth. And I said, "But I didn't have him." And the only thing I could think of was that I adopted him, but then the woman said, "Well, did you get him from an agency?" And that threw me off totally to the point where I just got up and left! I didn't know what to say!

For those comothers finding themselves "caught off guard" and not knowing what to say, this scene suggests something about power that is worth noting. We can see how a comother's "innocent" interlocutor may seem something of an accuser to her (and she the accused) if we understand that ignorance is the flip side of knowledge in assorted power/knowledge nexuses, especially in the organization and management of knowledge around sexuality. Literary and queer theorist Eve Sedgwick suggests that ignorance may be just as productive and efficacious as knowledge in its modes of manipulation and coercion, its "opacities," and most importantly, its effects.[11]

In her attempt to pluralize and specify this discursive terrain of ignorance-as-power, Sedgwick first exposed the duplicitous imputation that ignorance is passive or innocent. Instead, she argued, ignorance is quite generative.

> If ignorance is not—as it evidently is not—a single Manichaean, aboriginal maw of darkness from which the heroics of human cognition can occasionally wrestle facts, insights, freedoms, progress, perhaps there exists instead a plethora of ignorances, and we may begin to ask questions about the labor, erotics, and economics of their human production and distribution. Insofar as ignorance is ignorance of a knowledge—a knowledge that may itself, it goes without saying, be seen as either true or false under some other regime of truth—these ignorances, far from being pieces of the originary dark, are produced by and correspond to particular knowledges and circulate as part of particular regimes of truth.[12]

The capacity of ignorance to appear innocent and passive may well be an operation of its power, while the appearance itself of innocence and passivity may be one of its effects. The apparently innocent question posed to Eleanor by the blood worker in the scene described above constituted in effect not an innocuous conversational gesture but rather a seizure of Eleanor's freedom and authority to describe her own socioaffective relations and to name her own sexual desire. To put it another way, the blood worker held most if not all of the rhetorical leverage; she controlled the terms of exchange by virtue of her ignorance and the presumed right to interrogate residing within that ignorance. For her part, Eleanor, "caught off guard" and not knowing what to say, saw her epistemic authority usurped in a single thirty-second exchange of words. In this moment of panic, the flight impulse was apparently stronger than the calmer one of fostering understanding, suggesting that the occasions for employing the strategy of Speaking Half-Truths to Power may not necessarily be those most optimum for pursuing a form of pedagogical politics, the opportunity for which, I believe, is always present in these encounters. In a second mall scene with Amy and Jocelyn, we can glimpse another variation of Speaking Half-Truths to Power in which ignorance-as-power once again works its injury, even though comother Amy seems to be on surer footing with her interlocutor this time.

They were back at the same mall, days or weeks after the Emporium encounter, and this time they were at Macy's. Once again, Jocelyn was feeding Todd in a lounge and Amy carried Hannah into the shopping area to get something to drink. Once again, it was comother Amy who narrated the proceedings for me in stream-of-consciousness fashion:

> And so I had Hannah and I sat her down at the counter and I was trying to get my money out and the woman asked me, "So, how old is your baby?" You know, it's really kind of weird, you want to say things like "This is my baby but I'm not really the birth mom, but this is my baby." But I'm not saying anything. And then I said, "Yeah, yeah, she's three and a half months." And she said, "Oh, my baby's fifteen months and I remember when she was three and a half months old." And yet I'd be kind of thinking to myself, "Oh, should I say anything more or should I just walk away? Okay, just walk away." But it's odd because I sort of stop and think [to myself], Is this your baby? Yes this is my baby. But I'm not the birth mother!

Jocelyn's absence in this scene gave Amy more rhetorical room to maneuver than in their first encounter with the salesperson at the Emporium. With the absence of visible cues of biological maternity, Amy's range of strategic options expanded. She might have employed the full disclosure strategy, but instead decided to Speak Half-Truths to Power and walk away. Theoretically she could have passed as the birth mother, a third strategy discussed below. In fact, strictly on the level of visual cues and her response to the salesperson, she did pass in a sense, but with her words she did not represent herself directly as the birth mother. Rather, she omitted information that would have disabused the woman of her presumption that Amy was the birth mother.

Speaking Half-Truths to Power, as Amy did in this second mall scene, is not a particularly comfortable choice either. Partial disclosure is a form of dissembling, the product of which, like all things repressed, can return to haunt the dissembler. Rather than creating mere conversational awkwardness, Amy's self-censorship gave rise to a fleeting but palpable self-doubt about her relationship to her children. These observations highlight the ways in which an obfuscatory strategy employed in the face-to-face negotiation of a new social identity, without intending to mislead or misinform, can have the unintended boomerang effect of unsettling a newly developing personal identity. Not unlike the loss of control and autonomy

Eleanor felt in her encounter with the blood worker, Amy's partial disclosure strategy resulted in a kind of momentary confusion concerning her personal identity as a parent.

Playing It Straight

Passing as the birth mother, or "Playing It Straight," is a strategy chosen under duress. Like the closet, which removes lesbian sexual identity completely from view, passing as the birth mother constitutes the most repressive strategy available to comothers. In fact, Playing It Straight constitutes a double repression because it conceals not only lesbian identity but nonbiological parenthood as well. Individually, both categories garner precious little social approbation; combined, they are almost literally unthinkable. A comother can therefore avoid much social tension by passing as the birth mother, especially and perhaps precisely because she is compelled to do so by the particular setting she is in.

Melissa Goldstein, whose encounter with the five-year-old at her twins' preschool was described earlier, had proven an able and loving coparent to Amanda and Jeremy, as almost everyone in her closest adult circles knew—that is, everyone but her colleagues at work. Melissa was the financial director for a nonprofit housing organization, a place she described as progressive in principle but whose employees, she maintained, were actually quite socially conservative. She was "not out at all" to her subordinates, but at the time she took the job she knew she would have to inform them that she had kids. "I've known that I would have to take time off, stay home with them, things were going to come up." What's a coparent to do in a conservative work setting where professional relations with her staff depend upon her maintaining her respectability and credibility? Play it straight. Melissa recounted a particularly noteworthy episode of playing it straight in one of her many workplace performances as the twins' birth mother:

> I have their [kids'] pictures up at work, but they [staff] think I had them myself. One day they were asking me some question about the birth and I'm like, "Ah, yes!" They were asking me where my C-section scar is and I'm trying to remember where Linda's scar is; you don't really see it, it's not like a scar scar. And I'm thinking, now wait a minute, is it over here? I've gotten myself in some pickles.

Playing It Straight makes for uncomfortable moments, where comothers must spontaneously assess the likelihood that a false statement will lead to a tangled thicket of falsehoods so labyrinthine that one could not emerge from it with character intact. To avoid these pickles, as Melissa called them, or "in-deeperism" as Goffman terms it, comothers can mentally sidestep the pressure by making one simple note of the frequency with which they are likely to encounter a particular interlocutor. Eleanor, the comother who left the blood donation site in a hurry, chose to pass as birth mother Alana on a later occasion, when she was more experienced and prepared for the seemingly harmless ignorance whose coercive effects she now was able to anticipate with confidence. She also was able to make quick assessments about the probable frequency of contact she would have with her interlocutor.

> One time [at work] I was hiring an instructor. She was new and I knew I wasn't going to be dealing with her very much. And I said I'd been off because I was with my son. So she brought a baby present. She said, "Well, where's your son now?" And I said, "He's at home." And he was with Alana at the time. And I said, or something [vague] came out that he was with someone [at home]. She looked at me and said, "Oh, is it a full-time nanny?" And I said, "Yeah, it is."

Passing as the birth mother still leaves one feeling uneasy. Facing the ignorance of one's interlocutor occasions shame because the latter's refusal to look and to see—what Sedgwick would call her "privilege of unknowing"—whether by design or in effect, produces the secret about which the interlocutor then claims ignorance. Playing It Straight, politically regressive, time-honored, and sometimes lifesaving strategy that it is, protects oneself and one's family, but it does so at a psychological and social cost the magnitude of which we as a society are just beginning to understand.[13]

If nonbirth mothers in lesbian-coparent families regularly create and re-create their identity as parents through everyday, face-to-face interactions with strangers in the public arena, and these encounters are mediated by the complex of knowledge and ignorance governing disclosure of sexual identity, this same dynamic may be said to be at work for the entire family's presentation of group identity. Nonbirth mothers, as we have seen, bear a certain disproportionate share of the burden of educating uninformed individuals and groups in the public settings in which so many of their daily activities take place, but their efforts more often than not are supported by the descriptive practices of other family members.

Birth parents as well as children, through their words and deeds, join comothers in projecting an image of themselves as an intimate, familial group in public spaces and institutional settings. Their family descriptive practice is distinguished from that outlined by Gubrium and Holstein, again, however, due to the requirements of the closet. If, for Gubrium and Holstein, family discourse evokes an image of the familial that is itself an "ordered and recognizable set of articulations," and through this discourse organizes social interaction according to what the grammar defines as the familial, Sedgwick's epistemology of the closet is interwoven in the process.[14] While the descriptive practice of lesbian-coparent families is framed and facilitated by the preexisting grammar of the familial, their practice also challenges and reconfigures it.

FAMILISM, THE CLOSET, AND THE
PUBLIC SPHERE: MORE FAMILY "OUTINGS"

Many Bay Area mothers insisted that starting families had nothing to do with politics, which meant that their public activities by and large did not have particularly political meanings for them either. But for Pat Keating and her partner Sarah, both of whom had lost or were losing siblings to AIDS, there was no question that family and politics were inextricably linked. "If you are a lesbian couple having a child, you are doing something political. I don't care what anyone says about it. You are not just raising a family, you are doing something political," Pat told me with characteristic conviction. Whether or not Bay Area parents viewed what they did for and with their families as linked to gay identity and politics, their practices were indeed shaped by structural factors that ineluctably might be traced back to questions of particular knowledges, and politics, about sexual identity.

In their 1982 book *The Anti-Social Family,* Michelle Barrett and Mary McIntosh trenchantly criticized so-called profamily ideologies circulated by the increasingly powerful New Right, suggesting that these family ideologies, or "familism," ultimately served to shift attention away from the regressive policies of the Thatcher and Reagan regimes and to erode the gains made for women by second-wave feminism. The family values frenzy, which launched the third decade of its U.S. political career at the 1992 Republican convention, may in fact be a flare-up of the same familism that Barrett and McIntosh criticized as patently antisocial. The ideology holds that the family form most capable of meeting the emotional and material needs of children and adults, and most ideal for nurturing and socializing new members of society, is the family—in some versions sanctioned by God himself—composed of a married heterosexual couple and their biological children. This ideal combination of breadwinning husband, nurturing/caretaking wife, and children is held up as the standard against which all other family forms are adjudicated and usually deemed inadequate. Most people in the United States do not believe that this ideal type is in fact the statistical norm, as indeed it is not. Yet, as historian John Gillis has argued, the families we "live by" are different from the families we "live in" and have been since the bourgeois ideal was first invented.[15]

Lesbian-coparent families encounter this culturally diffuse yet deeply entrenched familism, one that naturalizes and normalizes the heterosexual conjugal family, in their everyday social interactions. The same familism that judges single-parent families deficient cannot even conceive of two-mother families in which one or both parents are biologically related to children. At the same time, these families face a generalized heteronormativity that includes a widely held but often unconscious assumption that all individuals are heterosexual unless proven otherwise. Together, familism and heteronormativity (what I will refer to simply as familism for semantic economy) form a cultural blind spot that lesbian-coparent families encounter and challenge through their descriptive practices.

Familism and the closet operate in tandem: the social repression of gay existence has enabled familism to flourish. By the same logic, the more visible gay people and gay kinship are, the more implausible familism appears. The appearance of gay kinship is at once a challenge to familism and an "outing" experience for family members. Comother Brenda Jacobson expressed this most succinctly: "My slogan is, it's easy to stay in the closet when you're single, but it's really hard with a family." In the same way that a nonbirth mother's information management concerning her relationship to her children always encompasses the potential for outing self and family, the physical presence of the entire family—two mothers and kids—sets the stage for a family formative (and performative) act. The act will be shaped invariably by the default assumption of heterosexuality inherent in familist perspectives. The character of the performances varies depending upon the setting: in family-based, institutional settings such as schools and day care centers; in more random public places such as restaurants and hospitals; in ad hoc group settings of short duration such as parenting classes; and, finally, in the workplace. Here we will look more closely at these different types of settings for the nature of the constraints they place on mothers' ability to become familiar in the community of strangers.

The Family-Based Institutional Setting

The family-based institutional setting is one in which, by virtue of mothers' parental status, they must have some minimal contact with extrafamilial others. The experience of Carrie, the blonde comother of three-year-old Polly, also fair-haired, and birth mother Serena, who is Latina, is instructive. Carrie and Serena alternated attending to Polly's day care depending on which parent's work schedule was the most flexible. For a number of months comother Carrie had been attending day care events and getting to know other parents as she dropped Polly off and picked her up from the school. The teachers and staff at the day care had been informed that Polly had two mothers, but other parents had not yet been disabused of their familist assumptions that Carrie was Polly's "mother"— that is, her only mother and her biological mother. On one occasion, birth mother Serena decided to attend a field trip sponsored by the day care, breaking the pattern of one mother (Carrie) appearing as the only mother, as invariably happens with two-mother families. The appearance of a second woman who clearly was responsible for and emotionally involved with Polly, but not the woman whom others assumed was *the* mother, gave rise to inquiries from parents who possessed no conceptual framework for understanding what they were observing. Serena and Carrie reflected on the situation:

> SERENA: I had not met all the mothers. I was in the pumpkin patch [field trip] with most of the mothers, and one mother looks up and she says, "Well, so, who are you? Are you Polly's mommie?" And I said, "Yes." She said, "Well who's that blonde lady?" And this mom was, you know, just kind of blurts this out and everybody

looks at me and I really at that moment didn't feel comfortable going into it. We haven't hidden it but we've just . . . the teachers all know.

CARRIE: The teachers have supposedly all read the file. But the other parents don't know.

SERENA: I'm planning to try to find a way, but I didn't, I was caught off guard by this kind of thing. And so I said, "Well she lives with us too." I didn't get into details. And I felt a little uncomfortable about it but it . . . but, you know, I'm like trying to eat my sandwich, Polly is in my lap, and she just kind of said, "Well, then who is that woman . . ." So I'm going to try to catch her at a later point and let her know. I want to be out about it and be comfortable.

CARRIE: Yeah, I didn't think about that, strategizing about how we would tell other parents, 'cause I could have said something to her earlier too.

As is apparent from Carrie and Serena's story, it is difficult for lesbian co-parents to anticipate exactly what pattern of interaction will trigger inquiries from strangers and new acquaintances. The family-based institutional setting, in which parents must interact with professionals, other parents, teachers, doctors, social workers, and so on, in fact is perhaps the most conducive for exiting the closet. Parents must interact with others on the basis of their status as parents, so they face a fait accompli regarding when, not whether, they come out. They do seem to derive some strength in numbers, however, when one parent isn't "caught off guard" while alone. At the same day care setting but at a time when Serena and Carrie were together, the dynamic changed, both in the way that they were perceived and in the way that they could present a unified front for their interlocutors:

CARRIE: Another mom figured it out when we both came.

SERENA: Right.

CARRIE: What did she say to you?

SERENA: Something like, "Are you Polly's mom, the biological mom?" And I said, at that point (with her I wasn't caught off guard as much), and so I said, "I'm her biological and Carrie's her . . . " and she finished the sentence, she said "adoptive mom." And I said, "Yeah." So she got it.

In these settings it is a great relief for mothers when people "get it" without their needing to explain in great detail. It is a relief because it becomes exhausting explaining the concept of two-mother families to the scores of individuals they come into contact with, but more specifically because, in this type of setting, the individuals parents are most likely to interact with usually have some form of power over them. One day care administrator in a small, ostensibly progressive community northeast of San Francisco where the day care options were limited did a phone interview with a prospective mother (birth mother Becky) and told her, "Yes, I would have a problem with that" and slammed down the phone. A hospital security guard in a major Bay Area city hospital refused to allow two mothers to enter the pediatric ward together to visit their sick child because "only parents" were allowed. As birth mother Eliza recounted, "We would say, 'Look, she doesn't have a dad, she has two moms.' But they were just uncomprehending, and we would argue and argue and argue. So then we would just go in one at a time. I would go in and say I was her mom, and then Gretchen would come later and they wouldn't even check . But if we came in at the same time, forget it." In Eliza and Gretchen's story, clearly there was no benefit to presenting a two-mother, unified front. Indeed, the personal and institutional familism of the security guards blinded them to the real, embodied, vocal presence of two women presenting themselves as parents, constituting their family through their actions and speech—all to no avail.

Then there was the ophthalmologist, evaluated by Bay Area mothers Olena and Resa to be their best hope for getting daughter Sara's congenital eye problems treated properly. Their concern, however, revolved around the institutional milieu from which this medical specialist had recently retired: the U.S. Navy. As Olena told it:

Sara was born with a congenital defect with both of her eyes, and suddenly we just wanted the best ophthalmologist. We didn't care [about anything else]. What we ended up with was somebody just out of the navy, he'd just been recruited at Pacific Presbyterian out of the navy, and we were just like, my God, this guy is going to think we're out of our minds; probably never met a lesbian in his life. And it made me realize that when you have children, you just, having children in general is just a whole process of letting go of your expectations of being able to control the environment, you know, or being able to pick what people they interact with, you just can't. We've had really good luck so far. He ended up being a wonderful doctor, but it really just struck me that, you know, we did all of our careful planning, screening, all the book said to do, and before you knew it, the most important person in her life was this guy from the navy. And you just, you know, you can't control much.

In all of these instances, parents' experiences of anticipated and actual ignorance concerning their families revealed the degree to which their efforts at presenting themselves as family took on an urgency and gravity commensurate with the institutional power they faced. When powerful people in their lives proved to be understanding or accepting, or when these individuals simply "got it" about the two-mother family, the relief from the anxiety and work of explaining could make couples downright giddy.

But this getting lucky should not imply that familism was not still present as a structuring force; these sites and persons were not "familism-free zones" that couples happened to stumble upon. Some individuals in institutional settings whom parents dealt with were simply more adept than others at perceiving the family relationships before them, often with split-second timing. Melissa Goldstein, the comother of twins Amanda and Jeremy from earlier in this chapter, recalled the first meeting with a new school principal that she and partner Linda attended together:

> We went to this school and met the principal last year and she was totally cool. I called and said, "I've got twins starting in September, I want to meet you, I want to tour the school," blah blah blah. The two of us showed up and she was . . . she looked at Linda and said, "Oh do you have kids starting as well?" And Linda kind of looked at me, and of course I hadn't said [on the telephone], "Hi, I'm a lesbian and my partner and I will be in tomorrow." So Linda kind of looks at me, and we're standing there in the office, I mean it's a madhouse because school's out, so all these kids and their parents are running around. And we're standing in there and Linda looks at me and she

looked at the woman—I didn't say anything—she [Linda] said, "Yes." So
then we walked into her office and then we just started talking to her about
the kids. And, she never missed a beat. She just kept, totally kept up with us,
and was really open and friendly. . . . When she took us on a tour of the
school, there was a parent volunteer in the library, she said, "These women
have twins starting in September." She was really great.

The not "missing a beat" meant that, in fact, there was the potential for
the Goffmanian interaction order to have broken down, with familism the
clear winner. That potential rupture was subverted, however, in this particular interaction. The principal's question to Linda, "Do you have kids
starting as well?" and the few seconds following it, represented the only
moments familism hovered in the air.

Likewise, in another couple's encounter with an important professional
in an institutional setting, the professional's assertive renunciation of the
familist moment proved indispensable to their entire interaction. Upon
hearing that their amniocentesis had come back "abnormal," Jamie Ruiz
and Marsha Holmes were referred to a genetic counselor at the hospital in
which Jamie was supposed to give birth in a few months' time. Overcome
by fear that they would be told the fetus was positive for Down's syn-
drome, the couple sat in the counselor's office, barely keeping their com-
posure. Marsha described what happened:

We were sitting very close together and Jamie was really upset and I was trying to be a shoulder to lean on, but upset too. Finally this woman just kind
of stopped after she started to discuss what these results meant, and she said,
"Are you two a couple?" I said, "Yeah." And she said, "I thought so by the
way you were acting, but I just wanted to check." And it was almost like she
shifted a gear and then she started to talk to us, about our family, instead of
to Jamie about her, the baby.

The genetic counselor in this interaction read their body language as well
as their affective states and verbally renounced the familist assumption
that the two women were merely friends. What is more—and this is the
crucial phenomenological point of individuals' "getting it" about lesbian-
coparent families—by "shifting gears" the counselor then treated them

like a family. In doing this, she completed what remained to be done interactionally for Marsha and Jamie to be constituted as a family. Marsha and Jamie's behavior together represented the performing end of the family formative act; the genetic counselor as receiver-audience in turn corroborated their performance, aligning her understanding and set of meanings with those of Marsha and Jamie, thereby bringing a family to life. In Gubrium and Holstein's words, "[T]he family materializes through usage [of family discourse]."[16] Out of the discursive traces of independently received knowledges about sexuality, intimacy and reproduction, together the three of them created a lesbian-coparent family where none had existed before.

In these cases in which individuals are significant and powerful in the lives of lesbian-coparent families by virtue of their service provider roles, when these individuals "get it" and communicate their acceptance, part of the power dynamic becomes neutralized, which may partly account for the sense of relief or satisfaction parents feel when this occurs. Recognition is not just a re-cognition, as in a rethinking. When employers recognize employee unions, whether by volition or compulsion, or when the state is under appeal to recognize same-sex marriage, recognition here is understood as an implementation or an enactment of what is recognized.[17] It is the same for lesbian-coparent families in their dealings with professionals and individuals in institutional settings whose recognition is critically connected to the success of families striving to get their needs met. Moreover, recognition in the sense of a rethinking indicates here the extent to which familism mediates these family formative acts and interactions. What is being "rethought" in this context is precisely the notion that families come in specified normative forms. The result of these recognitions is a radical refusal to ignore: no longer can the ideology of the normative family occupy center stage and sustain public credulity when that which society has been conditioned to disbelieve walks in the door of the principal's office, the genetic counselor's office, or the day care center.

In turn, this relates to considerations of geographic location and the ubiquity of familism. It is virtually an article of faith that large, urban environments are "as good as it gets" for living an openly gay lifestyle. Still, it is clear from the Bay Area mothers' encounters that even the most progressive, gay-friendly metropolitan and suburban areas cannot be said to be free of the familism and heteronormative assumptions common to less socially progressive regions. It is strongly suggestive of the sway familism holds over the public imaginary that a lesbian-coparent family would experience the awkwardness of an interaction in which a professional from the most reputable hospital in a Bay Area city struggled to "figure out" the relationships. Indeed, one couple recounted how even friends who were also in lesbian-coparent families let their long-standing familist notions render them temporarily insensitive. Coparents Angeline Bowen and Dana Engels, a couple exceptionally dedicated to having as open and egalitarian family relations as possible, described with dismay interactions they had had with friends and neighbors who failed to respect their family relationships:

DANA: Sometimes people forget even when they are people who've been in similar situations, couples with children! This woman who lives here . . .

ANGIE: Right, right, our downstairs neighbors who have a son and have got to have been through this whole thing and they still call Dana "the mommy." Or this other friend, who, sort of didn't invite me to the baby shower, didn't think it was as important for me to be at the baby shower, even though she'd just been pregnant and had a kid.

DANA: But to her credit, she called up and said, "What was I doing?" And "Had that happened to my lover it would have been really awkward." So what that says to me is that even us, even we who have been through all of this, are so preconditioned, that we have to be constantly guarding against our own homophobia, and, it's not even homophobia, it's like, thoughtlessness.

Public Space

It is interesting to compare parents' descriptions of their encounters with individuals in family-based institutional settings with their accounts of encounters with strangers in public places. Because the social stakes were lower with individuals whom parents did not need to know or develop a relationship with, they were more at ease with their presentations of family and sometimes even enjoyed the confusion they caused. This was true for encounters with strangers who both did and did not "get it." Parents conveyed considerably less anxiety as they discussed these interactions. This time their expressions ranged from bemusement to a kind of superior annoyance as they recalled encounters in, for example, restaurants. Comother Marsha Holmes, with a nearly shaved head and completely unshaven legs, explained:

> Sometimes we walk into a restaurant, say, a Sizzler, he [son Gary] likes the Sizzler, so when we go out for a slice of Americana, we go to the Sizzler. We'll walk in, and, if they [other patrons] don't think I'm his father 'cause they think I'm a man, then they're real curious, and they're kind of watching. And he [Gary] will be "wah, wah, wah," and so she'll [birth mother Jamie] pass him to me and he'll cling to me the same kind of way. So I'm always kind of watching and thinking, well, what do these people think? My perception of people watching us is that, a baby has a mother and that's it, you know. I'm always kind of curious, though.

And the mothers of Brian, Alana and Eleanor:

ELEANOR: But one time we were in a restaurant together and Alana was holding him for a long time, and then I was holding him for a long time, and a woman looked at both of us and asked, "Which of you is the mom?" So Alana said, quickly, "We both are." And so she went, "Oh."

ALANA: And she finished her salad.

ELEANOR: But then she looked over to us and said, "Which one of you is the biological, or, the birth mom?"

ALANA: She said, "the birth mom."

ELEANOR: So that was an appropriate thing to say . . .

ALANA: Yeah, she did real well. It just took her an entire salad to kind of get into it.

Just as nonbirth mothers face decisions about when and with whom to "tell it like it is," for the entire family, together as a unit out in public, parents have learned that inquiries from strangers are less important to their family identity than those of people in more formal institutional settings and relationships and thus that they have more leeway in their public performances. They can themselves be more curious—even critical—and less anxious about how they are being perceived.

On a continuum between interactions with total strangers in public places and with individuals on whose tolerance and acceptance parents depend, there is a midway situation or setting. The ad hoc group setting is a situation of short duration that includes, for example, birthing and parenting classes and children's playgroups. In parenting classes, prospective parents share a learning environment with other expectant parents, first as strangers, then as casual acquaintances. How important is it for lesbian co-parents to have their family status recognized in these types of settings?

According to Penny Cipolini and Megan Johnson, it mattered little that the individuals and couples in their breastfeeding class held for them no particular authority or even interest. Their experience of exclusion and invisibility resulting from the instructor's and other parents' familism was humiliating—and infuriating.

PENNY: We took a class at the hospital. And the instructor goes around the whole room, talking to the couples, and she's saying all of this stuff to "daddies."

MEGAN: She's congratulating the daddies for coming . . .

PENNY: And being supportive of their mates.

MEGAN: And this guy is missing a tennis game on TV and she was like, "Well we applaud you for coming because it is so important that the daddies be involved in helping the mother with breastfeeding." And, as nauseating as we found that just because we find that nauseating, it also excluded Penny. The woman kept saying, "Daddies, you do dah dah dah dah" and "mommies," meaning the breastfeeding mother. And they did not assume we were a couple.

PENNY: I mean there were people, there was a very Christian right couple that was sitting on one side of us that seemed to move further away. When Megan got up to go to the bathroom . . . at the end, the instructor gives a break, and all the pregnant women went into the bathroom and I stood out in the hallway waiting for Megan. And they'd come out and I felt like they'd walk around me like they were going to catch a disease. But finally by the end of the whole thing the instructor finally acknowledged . . . 'cause I was getting real irritated . . .

MEGAN: At the end the instructor says, "Thank you daddies for coming," and Penny's just livid. And the woman turns to her and she goes,

"And Penny, we'll make you an honorary half-daddy." So we had an evaluation and we wrote in there, "We are a couple . . . "

PENNY: "A lesbian couple."

MEGAN: "We're a lesbian couple and Penny is the other parent and she will be parenting our child."

PENNY: "Co-parenting."

MEGAN: "She will be co-parenting the child and we felt very invisible," or something like that, "unrecognized, that you insisted on calling everybody 'daddies' when Penny is obviously the other parent."

Megan and Penny indicated that they hadn't expected to be the only lesbian expectant parents in the class, and certainly the dynamic is completely different when there are other lesbians or more of all types of expectant parents. Their experience is instructive, however, on several counts. Professionals and service providers in the family business, even in the progressive Bay Area, still do not have linguistic categories or the sensitivity training for interacting with lesbian-coparent families. In the particular setting of this breastfeeding class, the instructor talked only to "daddies" and "mommies" and thus laid out the forms of address and lines of communication that categorically excluded Megan and Penny. In turn, this set the tone for how Megan and Penny would be treated by the others. Moreover, once this dynamic was set in motion, the couple's increasingly assertive attempts to convey their identity as expectant parents only led to greater heterosexist, indeed, homophobic reactions, as a sense of homosexual contagion was pressed into service, generating additional discomfort for Penny ("I felt like they'd walk around me like they were going to catch a disease").

An important effect of lesbian maternity is the way in which it insulates the birth parent from heterosexist opprobrium (where it is an issue) and simultaneously exposes nonbirth mothers to even greater levels of it. Prospective birth mothers become "good" lesbians vis-à-vis their non-pregnant partners, partly due to the valorization of biological motherhood and its association with heterosexual womanhood, and partly due to the absence of a socially recognized category of identity for nonbirth mothers, as we saw earlier in this chapter.

Finally, it is instructive to note the effects of interactions such as these in which couples most likely will never see those people again who started out as strangers to them but whose co-presence with them in a public educational setting, even for a few hours, creates lasting impressions. The participants in that class received more than an education on breastfeeding. Because Penny and Megan deemed this situation important enough for them not to pass as just friends, their insistence that they be recognized as coparents ultimately succeeded in removing a few blinders. (It turned out Penny and Megan had the same instructor for a subsequent class, and, apparently in response to their feedback from the first class, she framed her remarks and forms of address considerably more inclusively at the start of the new class.) Couples together gave each other support in these family performances, unlike the situation in which one parent was "put on the spot" or "caught off guard" in a face-to-face interaction when her partner was not with her.

The children's playgroup is another ad hoc situation of short duration that falls somewhere between institutional and random in the range of external settings in which families go about their business. Once again lesbian coparents face the choice of either educating people they most likely will not see again once the program is completed or allowing them to form whatever impressions they otherwise would. One factor that tips the scale in favor of more direct family formative (and educational) acts in these small, ad hoc group settings is the presence of a more permanent member of either parent's social network. When an individual from one network in a parent's social life enters the domain of the familial by way of a playgroup, for instance, this leads to still further "outings," as with Jocelyn and Amy and their decision to start their twins in a Gymboree class. Birth mother Jocelyn summarized this decision and the ramifications it would have in her work life: "I'm probably going to be out now [at work] because we're starting them [the twins] in Gymboree classes, and it just so happens it starts next week, but last Thursday was the open house and this guy that works at my work is in that class with his six-month-old. So I guess I'm going to be out at work."

The Workplace

From Jocelyn's remarks it is clear that work is another setting in which parents must educate people about dual-mother families sooner or later; it is not a question of if but when. This is so because the boundaries delineating work and family spheres as separate are routinely traversed by parents in general and mothers in particular. The dynamic for the Bay Area mothers was not the transposition of spheres described by Arlie Hochschild in *The Time Bind: When Work Becomes Home and Home Becomes Work* but more discrete but progressive incursions of family into the world of work and vice versa. Having children occasions the cross-border movements because people who would not ordinarily interact in places other than work, or who would otherwise feel disinclined to talk about their personal lives, come together in their talk about their kids and their family status. In their critique of the late cultural critic Christopher Lasch's assertion that the private domain of family is increasingly invaded and degraded by the "heartless" world of public affairs, Gubrium and Holstein suggested just the opposite: the family is more "an expanding domain of application . . . spreading well beyond what Lasch and others of similar opinion believe to be its proper domain—a particular version of the home."[18]

For lesbian mothers, however, their family outings at work involve coercion, just as there is a coercive element in some other institutional settings, as we saw earlier, in which parents must interact with professionals and others as parents, and as lesbian parents, to try to secure the quality of care and service they want for their children. In the work setting, though, the stakes involve the family's financial security, and mothers' disclosure of their sexual-identity-family status at work is a matter of rational, economic calculation. The ritual procedure of telling the boss of one's impending parenthood and asking for time off represents an immediate outing experience for prospective nonbirth mothers, for obvious reasons. Birth mothers, however, once again can pass as single (and therefore heterosexual) mothers if they choose. Overwhelmingly, for the Bay Area parents, their choice was to be out and supported as parents at their workplaces. Their disclosures in turn had the effect of providing employees with a common idiom through which they could communicate and come together and at the same time showed affirmation and support for the parent, as Belinda Tarpin, an office worker and birth mother recalled:

> Those first two days that I was back at the office I hardly got any work done because everybody wanted to see pictures of Cassie. So I was going around the company showing people pictures of Cassie (laughing). So there was a lot of support, and part of what was really neat was during the pregnancy and after Cassie was born, that a lot of the folks that had problems talking to me

before because it's like, well, what do we talk about besides the weather or business, we then had a common ground. We could talk about kids.

Perhaps most important, scores of people are being educated as a result of this spreading of the familial into the workplace. Consider, for example, the pedagogic staging of Shannon Cavner's coming-out speech at the financial services firm where she worked:

I wasn't exactly out. My boss knew. Some of the people knew. I work at the kind of place where you know some people, you meet people and you're close to them, but not other people. But it's not the kind of place where your personal life matters. You do what you do, and the emphasis is on what you do at work, not what you do away from work. Everybody knew I wasn't married. And so I decided I was going to tell everybody in my group that I was pregnant. But it was Ed, my boss's, idea to take us in the conference room, just because there were a lot of us. We couldn't fit in his office, that was really it more than any other reason. I work with all, at that point it was all guys in my group, there might have been one other woman. But I worked with all single men at the time. They're all very nice and all very well adjusted, very nice people. And so I told them that I was pregnant. And they were all happy and fine and then somebody said something about being raised by a single woman; there was some comment made. And I said, "Maybe I should mention, maybe I should state this just so people don't ask me a lot of questions about who the father is." And so I told everybody that I was gay and everything. They were all very good about it.

The timing of disclosure at the workplace can be tricky for some parents. They want to avoid premature announcements of their impending parenthood in the event that all is not well with the pregnancy, but when something does go wrong, they cannot rely on coworkers and bosses to be supportive and understanding because they have not yet been told. Co-mother Tori Avedon, an attorney in a civil litigation firm, described exactly this type of painful experience associated with not being out as an expectant lesbian parent:

She [partner Sally] was about eight weeks when they did the ultrasound, and I could only see one thing on the screen, and I said, "We're having two babies where's the other baby?" And the tech wouldn't say anything, and the doctor comes in, Mr. Gracious, "There's only one baby." We had two and half months of planning twins, and loving twins, and committed to twins. We went home and we were just grieving, just devastated. I was still not out at work. No one knew that I had married, that my partner was pregnant, that we'd just lost a baby. To us, we'd lost a baby. Horrible.

Closeted gay workers experience estrangement from coworkers beyond the usual level at times of personal loss or bereavement involving a partner. The loss of a fetus elicits similar feelings for an expectant parent who has not told or cannot tell her work colleagues of her lesbian identity and family status.

Like the other settings, the workplace is one in which the presentation of one's lesbian family status—as well as the audience's reception—is not altogether predictable. Still, most of the Bay Area women who were not already out at work felt confident enough to come out using their impending parenthood as the vehicle. This modus operandi worked for them because the act of bringing children into their lives had a humanizing effect on the way they were perceived and how they felt, as Cathy Lotti told me: "There's something about having children that really links you to every other person who has children. I really feel much more a part of the world."

What these family outings by the Bay Area mothers reveal about family formation in late-twentieth-century U.S. society is that family and kinship are and always have been symbolic systems, as anthropologist David Schneider observed over three decades ago.[19] That lesbian mothers are in the position to constitute their families discursively and interactionally, indeed that they must to overcome the orthodoxy of familism, points to the way in which the symbolic system that presents the heterosexual nuclear family as normative works its illusion with all the precision and intricacy of a finely tuned instrument. That kinship issues forth automatically and naturally from heterosexual procreation is a mystification that achieves its naturalness to the degree that its internal workings, its parts, its assembly process, labor, and the entire factory floor remain occluded. The normative heterosexual family at the center of familism has as its foundation the authority of heterosexual procreation. The biological facts of procreation, however, are not especially relevant in the maintenance of the illusion. The facts are subsumed within the cultural symbolism of the heterosexual-parent family. The biology, in other words, represents part of the inner workings that the illusion, the finished product, renders opaque.

Lesbian mothers' disclosures and family-formative interactions pierce this illusion, they reveal the tricks behind the magic, the labor in the commodity. In their interactions, they do this by forcing those with whom they interact to examine all of the received assumptions, all of the bits composed by conventional wisdom that have nourished the illusion. The idiom of homosexuality is the most powerful means through which this occurs. So long as relationships may be discursively recuperated back into the heterosexual family framework in some way—and familism is infinitely resilient on this point—the familist illusion is reinforced. By coming out, by (re)presenting themselves as family—sometimes by as "simple" an act as telling a colleague, "I'm pregnant"—lesbian coparents expose the entire machinery of familist ideology and, in so doing, institute new categories of kinship.

Lesbian-coparent families formed by donor insemination make a unique contribution to the reconfiguration of postindustrial kinship systems in ways other than those I have already described. At a social structural level, they create a network of latent kin relations that may or may not become activated, depending on the degree to which biogenetic relatedness signifies for them a fundamental, irrevocable human connection. In the same way that the bio-ontological credential carries extraordinary weight in parents' perceptions of their status in relation to their children at an intimate level (see Chapters 2 and 3), in mediating relations with families of origin (Chapter 5), and in the culture at large, at a structural level it may be activated in such a way that the very notion of extended family expands to include an unprecedented array of relatives. In the early 1990s, the British cultural anthropologist Marilyn Strathern presciently observed that the more procreative actors involved in bringing a new human being into the world, the more relatives one potentially has. "Potentially" is perhaps the most important idea here because the activation of this potential network of relatives is contingent on both knowledge of who shares a biogenetic connection with whom and whether that knowledge is acted on in a socially meaningful way by those who have that knowledge. The whole system, therefore, is epistemically based; it exists at the level of knowledge and awaits the human social acts of disclosure and recognition to make it manifest, to turn it into "reality."[1]

The key to the system for lesbian-coparent families formed through donor insemination is knowledge about the donor. The donor plays a relatively minor biological role in the process of family formation for lesbian couples, but socially and symbolically his position in their lives operates in important ways insofar as he represents a biogenetic link that mothers may choose to ignore or acknowledge as they go about "the primary task of establishing boundaries of the family's world," as Hess and Handel put it in their 1959 work *Family Worlds*. Ideas about the importance and influence of biogenetic relatedness shape the social practices of these families to such a degree that these ideas have themselves become a type of symbolic structure, subtly coercive in the way it frames the available options and decisions to be made about who is a relative and who is not. Hess and Handel wrote, "A family constitutes its own world, which is not to say it closes itself off from everything else, but that it determines what parts of the external world are admissible and how freely."[2] Sperm donors, donors' families, and children in one lesbian-coparent family who share a donor with those of another are all potential candidates considered by parents for inclusion in the lesbian-coparent family world. These people constitute the array of potential relatives in the latent kinship network in which the donor serves as a central link.

THE DONOR LINK

In Chapter 2 I described the choice intending lesbian parents make concerning the kind of donor they wish to have: known or anonymous, where the latter choice may be modified so that anonymity remains in effect only until a child turns eighteen. With known donors, I described how couples negotiate different relationships with them depending on the needs and wishes of the parties involved. I characterized the types of known donors and the relationships as either symbolic, flexibly defined, or quasi-multi-parenting arrangements. These relationships with known donors may be understood as something like first-order kinship relations where the donor is deliberately defined as linked to and known by the lesbian coparent family, whereas there is no such relationship with anonymous donors.

For all donor relationship types, however, the donor constitutes a link to other people that may or may not be socially activated. The potential network of kin relations that may be activated depending on whether couples choose to recognize and extend kinship status to them I will refer to as second-order kinship relations. In the case of known donors, second-order relations potentially include the donor's parents, grandparents, and siblings—that is, members of his family of origin—as well as his spouse or partner and any children he may have with that spouse, partner, or with anyone else. In the case of anonymous donors, there still exist second-order kinship relations, though at first glance it might seem impossible given that the donor's identity—and therefore his family or anyone he is connected to—would be unknown to mothers.

Before presenting the actual second-order kinship relationships recognized by the Bay Area mothers, to make the donor link more comprehensible, it seems useful to examine how the original donor choice structures the later second-order decisions and how the donor decision is itself determined by certain social factors.

The Donor Decision as Structured and Structuring

The initial known/anonymous decision concerning the donor may be understood as setting up or determining a stream of subsequent considerations that lesbian parents face in defining their families. The known/anonymous decision shapes the terrain of later options to such a degree it might best be understood as a structural determinant. However, the donor decision is itself structured by several factors, not the least of which involves the norms generated in both gay/lesbian communities and the larger culture concerning the desirability of a child's having access to knowledge concerning her or his genetic origins.

The decision to choose a known or anonymous donor is thus shaped by cultural norms having to do with the importance of knowing one's "blood" relatives but also by the actual availability of known or anonymous donors at the time of conception. With known donors, what counts is the availability of donors with mothers' desired characteristics and a willingness to negotiate the contractual terms of the relationship. Since the selection of known donors has mostly been left up to prospective mothers themselves, the process is less organized or influenced by institutional norms, whereas with anonymous donors, availability is determined almost exclusively by biomedical and fertility industry standards that select out and guarantee both a particular distribution and circulation of sperm.

With respect to distribution, industry standards have set the total number of families to which any single donor is allowed to make his reproductive contribution at ten, in a "catchment" area population of eight hundred thousand.[3] Since each family is allowed up to three children by the same donor, generally speaking, *any* ten families will share one donor whose maximum fertility rate will be thirty children for any catchment area. With respect to a particular circulation of sperm—meaning the particular mix of social characteristics associated with the donors—the type of donors available will depend once again on who is screened out and who is allowed to participate in a given facility's donor program.[4]

The availability of anonymous donors is also importantly determined by the choice that donors themselves make concerning whether they will agree to release their identity to the children resulting from the use of their sperm. The practical effect of the "yes" donor provision (which is the combination of institutionally organized anonymity with the option of future identity disclosure) is that the eligible pool of anonymous donors becomes substantially limited. For the Bay Area mothers, the availability of these "yes" anonymous donors utterly determined (and eclipsed) other features available in the supply of anonymous sperm. From the "yes" division of anonymous donors (that is, identity release when the child would turn eighteen) couples made selections on the basis of other features they might be interested in or wish to avoid: race and ethnicity, inheritable conditions, perceived athleticism, perceived intelligence, and so on. For example, one Bay Area couple wanted a Jewish donor who was willing to be known when the child turned eighteen. At the time they were ready to inseminate, the facility they were using had only one Jewish donor who was willing to be known, but he did not come into service for another three months,[5] three cycles of precious conceiving time that could not be wasted when a woman was already past her most fertile years. "So we went [to another sperm bank] thinking that maybe there were some Jews [donors] there that would want to be known. None of the Jews wanted to be known," Brenda Jacobson recalled.

Given the strong preference for "yes" donors, the logical end point of this winnowing process is that any particular matrix of one couple's preferences in a donor will match that of another couple. In concrete terms, this means that for any single donor, the chances that he will be selected by more than one lesbian couple during the time that he is in "active service" increase substantially once he has agreed to have his identity released in the future. Further, since the primary assisted-reproduction facilities used by lesbians in the Bay Area adhere to the standard of ten families per donor, this distribution together with the circulation of "yes" donors makes common donors among lesbian-coparent families not only possible but probable. The particular circulation and distribution of (anonymous) sperm produced by assisted-reproduction service standards thus work together to create a bio-reproductive economy of high demand for select male genetic material. In the particular case of lesbian families, then, there is a high likelihood that their children will have donors in common but that these donors will be anonymous to them.

If the known/anonymous donor decision is structured by a certain bio-reproductive economy, cultural norms about genetic origins, and the preferences of donors and recipients, the decision itself, once made, structures a subsequent set of considerations for couples—the decisions concerning second-order relations. The donor is thus a link potentially connecting a web of relationships; known donors generate considerations for couples that are different from those generated by anonymous donors, but they all ramify from the original known/anonymous donor decision.

Known-Donor Extended Relations

The second-order considerations stemming from a known-donor situation involve the donor's own family. If the donor is a symbolic father, a person known to mothers and their children as the person who "gave his seed," who is the donor's partner or spouse in relation to them? Who are the donor's other children, if he has any? The donor's parents and siblings? It is one thing to specify concretely the known donor's relationship to children and mothers; one line may be drawn as an initial boundary. But conditions arise when the relationship with the donor is such that his family may present themselves as persons who could be incorporated into the extended family of lesbian mothers and children. Thus mothers and children whose known donors are involved as parents, or are flexibly defined or symbolic, invariably negotiate, for example, whether the donor's parents are also "Grandma and Grandpa."

Let us consider examples of each type of known donor relationship.

Eliza Cohen, Gretchen Zindosa, and their preschool-aged daughter Rayna lived in a lower-middle-income suburb to the northeast of the Bay Area. Their donor was a friend of Eliza's whom she had worked with, along with his spouse, for a number of years in a foster care placement agency. Kyle, the donor, and his spouse, Laurie, had young daughters, Meredith and Lacey. It was important to Eliza and Gretchen that Rayna have someone she could point to concretely and label "dad." Kyle was not a parent to Rayna; he was someone who had helped to create her. But Kyle did have a relationship with Rayna. He thought she was "wonderful." He adored her. Birth mother Eliza reflected on the advantages of their relationship with Kyle: "It will be easier when she [Rayna] asks, 'Who's my dad?' It will be nice not to say, 'Oh, I don't know. He's, like, number 3060 or whatever.' It'll be nice to say, 'Well, he's a really nice man who was a friend of your ema's and your mama's.' "[6] Kyle was a symbolic father. He was Rayna's father *qua* progenitor and in name only. He did not "parent" Rayna, he bore no financial or other responsibility for her, he had two children with whom he had this type of relationship. Yet the fact that he was known to her and Rayna's mothers *and* had a relationship with them had given rise to the need for both families to decide where, if any, the boundaries between them lay and what the nature of those boundaries was.

The four adults decided that Kyle's biological paternity should be recognized in the eyes of the children, and thus *it* determined in no small way the connection among the children, and by extension, between the families. Eliza and Gretchen explained the decision and the outcome:

ELIZA: We decided that we were just going to be aboveboard with all of the kids, you know, whenever they ask, we tell them.

GRETCHEN: We thought we had a few years on that conversation, and then Meredith [Kyle's and Laurie's eldest daughter, three] kept asking, "Who's Rayna's daddy?"

ELIZA: "Who's Rayna's daddy?" She really knew, somehow. We had, in fact, signed an agreement so that we didn't have to lie to them, which seemed like a reasonable request. So she knows, they told her. And she [Meredith] was like, "Okay, so I have one and a half sisters . . . I have one and a half sisters."

GRETCHEN: Yeah, she says, "I love my sister Rayna."

ELIZA: She really loves Rayna, they're really sweet together actually.
          She adores her.

Through the biological connection among the children, which the parents chose to recognize contractually ("aboveboard" in Eliza's words) and "live out" socially, the two families were joined. The donor link gave rise to second-order or potential kinship relations that were then "activated."

Now it was not just Kyle and Laurie and their children who were incorporated into the everyday lives of Eliza, Gretchen, and Rayna as kin but Kyle's family of origin as well. "For Christmastime, Kyle's mom was around, so we had them over for dinner," Eliza recalled as if it were the most ordinary thing. So we have a progenitor but not a parent, a dad but not Dad, and family relations between two groups who have contractually and socially determined that the semiotic value of biological paternity counts for a great deal indeed.

Olena and Resa, and their two daughters Sarah and Shelly, mentioned in Chapter 2 as having a flexibly defined relationship with their donor, Rick, lived in an older, neglected part of the city. Altogether they earned less than $50,000 per year and shared their Victorian home, badly in need of structural repairs, with tenants both in their own apartment and in the other apartments of the building to help them with the mortgage. Rick, a good friend of Olena's for a number of years, lived in Michigan. He was not Sarah's and Shelly's legal father in that he had no de jure rights in them and was not named on their birth certificates. Olena was listed as a second legal parent on the elder daughter's (Sarah) birth certificate since she had adopted her, and adoption proceedings were under way at the time of our interview for coparent custody of baby Shelly.

Rick was an uncle figure to Sarah, even though she knew he had contributed to her conception and sometimes struggled to understand the symbolic and biological distinctions that her mothers encouraged. He was a socially significant male adult in her life whose relationship with her, her little sister, and her mothers was flexibly defined, depending on the needs and levels of understanding among them. The need for their daughters to have a symbolic father was not foremost in the family-defining priorities of Resa and Olena. Their relationship with Rick was driven by purely pragmatic considerations. For example, the three adults renegotiated

Rick's donor role for their second child, and Rick was available and amenable to changes in his status as determined by the children's interests. Such flexibility is precisely one reason many mothers choose known donors, although the search for such a donor is difficult.

One might expect that Olena's and Resa's family definition in relation to their known donor would stop at this first-order level of relatedness, especially since there was great geographic distance between them and Rick (and Rick's family). Yet neither Rick's nonlegal paternal status nor the geographic distance stopped Olena and Resa from asserting kinship ties with Rick's family! As they told the story of their visit to Michigan, it was clear the irony was not lost on them:

OLENA: We went to Detroit last spring. We met them [Rick's parents].

RESA: They only had just found out about it [Rick's donor role]. It really was not fair. They had only known a month or something. He just never told them. But they were very wonderful and nice.

OLENA: He was scared.

RESA: He was scared to tell them. And they did great. That's pretty great that they were willing to meet us. How that would have felt for them: "Here's your granddaughter. She's not yours." You know, just out of nowhere. I think it might have been very difficult for them. 'Cause they didn't go through the whole process of making the decision. You know, it wasn't their choice. So it was hard. And, that's one of the things about using known donors is that it has a, it's not just his decision, right, it's the decision of his brothers and sisters and parents. He's making a decision for the *whole extended family* on what their relationship would be with this child, which they might not agree with.

Resa's remarks are revealing of her view of biology—of Rick's biological paternity. While so much of the mothers' and Rick's relationship was based upon negotiation and collective definition, they seemed helpless before the power of biology to continue to define their family in this way when it came to second-order relations. While Rick himself was not exactly "Daddy" to Sarah and Shelly, Rick's parents were "Grandma and Grandpa," whose status as such even warranted a visit. Through his genetic contribution, Rick was suddenly making a kinship decision for his entire family of origin. This is the ideological work of biology. It was the discursive power of biological determinism that made Rick's genetic contribution so socially palpable that it no longer felt like a choice to extend the family boundary to include Rick's family and vice versa. Rick's biological paternity, originally and legally erased in the first-order relationship with him, returned to exert its power in second-order relations. As a note of comparison, many lesbian mother couples with known donors choose not to recognize the donor's family as related to them and thus allow biological paternity no legitimacy in their second-order extended-family decisions. For Resa and Olena, however, their relationship with their donor might be flexibly defined, but there seemed to be no flexibility in their connection with his family: blood was thicker than water and paper. Once again, then, the families were joined as a result of individuals' having chosen to ascribe social significance but no legal status to biogenetic events.

Natalie and Kim and their daughter Nikki lived in the East Bay in a quiet neighborhood with modest homes and simple landscaping. Their known donor, Mark, lived with his partner, Brad, in Los Angeles. When Natalie and Kim were trying to conceive, Mark would fly up to the Bay Area when Natalie was ovulating, and they would meet at the insemination clinic in San Francisco where the insemination would be coordinated. Natalie and Kim had always wanted a known donor and had pursued several leads before finding and reaching an understanding with Mark. Initially Natalie and Kim had wanted the donor to be a fully involved coparent. But then, according to Natalie, "We heard a lecture about coparenting [with a donor] and it sounded like, almost like you were setting up a divorce household. And it sounded so complicated and really hard for the kid that we just started thinking that maybe we really don't want this. So then we started looking for just a known donor who would see her sometimes or she would always know who it was." They found Mark through a mutual friend, and he had been involved in Nikki's life in ways that belied his nonlegal status. Mark and his partner Brad made financial contributions in support of Nikki. At his expense Mark flew up from L.A. and visited Nikki every month or two. Natalie and Kim consulted with Mark and Brad on the telephone about issues concerning their relationship, Nikki's welfare, her future, and the possibility of having a second child with Kim as the birth mother. In short, Natalie's and Kim's relationship with Mark and Brad was just shy of a fully multiparent arrangement—shy by a few hundred miles and the lack of desire on the part of Natalie and Kim for such an arrangement. But with a quasi-multiparent arrangement, where the first-order relationship was "tighter" and more intimate, it was but a small leap to incorporation of the donor's extended family into the mothers/children/donor family configuration. Natalie expressed the couple's view of this circumstance thoughtfully:

> Because Mark comes from a family of three boys and none of them have kids, his parents, when they found out that he had done this, were all excited as if [Nikki] was their grandchild. Well in a certain way she is, but, you know, it's all complicated, because her [Nikki's] grandparents are Kim's parents and my parents. But, Mark's parents are sort of her grandparents too. So they've seen her, they've been here, they came to her first birthday party. We've been to their house—last Christmas—in L.A., and we're probably going back down there again this Christmas. So, it's just complicated. I mean, legally, he has no rights at all and we've done that a thousand times over. We have all sorts of paperwork saying he has no parental rights and you know this and that. But emotionally, you know, we want him to be able to have a relationship with her, see her, and because we want that it's much more complicated. It just involves us continually talking with the two of them [Mark and Brad] about what works and what doesn't, and how often they can come. They just admitted recently they were fearful of us cutting them off, so they've been sort of walking on eggshells about certain things 'cause they feel like at any time we could just pull the plug 'cause we have all the legal rights. We have to say, you know, that we would never do that, no matter how much of an argument or whatever we're in with you, we're in this for the long run. We would not have chosen this situation if we didn't want to have her know you. The whole thing is that, this is, it's for her.

The quasi-multiparenting arrangement with Mark and Brad was different from flexibly defined or symbolic fatherhood in that Mark and Brad acted like and saw themselves as parents to Nikki. They were more involved as parents than the known donors in the families described above, and it was this involvement, more than Mark's biological paternity per se, that seemed to determine the extension of second-order family ties to his parents. Extending their family to include Mark's parents seemed less of a stretch than Olena's and Resa's recognition of Rick's parents as family because, in a context where none of the donors had legal status, Natalie's and

Kim's arrangement with Mark and Brad as social parents connected them through repeated intimate contact. In other words, social parenthood paved the way more smoothly toward extending kinship than did the more mechanical acknowledgment of biological paternity, even while the latter was powerfully compelling, as we saw with Olena and Resa, and with Eliza and Gretchen's perceived need to acknowledge in a contract the biological connection between their child and their donor's children.

No single arrangement is categorically better than another. In the variety of ways lesbian-coparent families work through their understandings of who should and should not be recognized as family, the point is that the known-donor choice presents this particular matrix of decisions regarding second-order family relations. The outcome often, but not always, results in the recognition and inclusion of the donor's family.

Anonymous-Donor Extended Relations

At first glance one might wonder how families can be extended through the donor when the donor is anonymous. If the donor is not known, neither he nor his relatives can be candidates for inclusion in the extended families of lesbian coparents and their children. However, the relations that can be recognized by mothers and stemming from the donor link are different—in kind—when the donor is anonymous than when the donor is known.

With anonymous donors, there is no first-order donor relationship, except in latent form. Mothers and children do not "relate" but are "related" to the anonymous donor in the *potential* recognition of the biological tie, which may occur for most of the Bay Area families with anonymous donors when children turn eighteen years old. The relationship is latent until activated, but it is there, residing in the knowledge of mothers and children that children may choose to know and therefore make explicit this biological connection.

It is because the relationship exists at the level of knowledge that second-order type relations are possible. First-order relations with the donor himself may be deferred indefinitely because the anonymous donor's name and whereabouts—his official identity—are not known. However, he has another identity, his identity as a donor. This is his sperm bank catalogue profile, or perhaps most precisely, his *sperm identity*. He is known unofficially to lesbian mothers and other insemination facility clients by his sperm identity: his donor number, willingness to be known or to remain anonymous, ethnicity, athleticism, intellectual interests, drug habits, favorite color, occupation, and so on. In short, he is known by the very selection criteria that prospective sperm recipients use in making their decision. Moreover, when it is recalled that the biogenetic economy as regulated by fertility industry standards and centers themselves is characterized by a scarce-product logic—high demand, rationed supply—it becomes clear that not only do recipients of anonymous sperm know very well the sperm identity of their donor, but the chances are very good that some will have selected the same donor.

These circumstances by themselves do not translate into second-order extended-family considerations. It is only when we add to the mix the factors of geographic proximity and community that donor-related, second-order-family considerations come to the fore. When the American College of Obstetricians and Gynecologists determined that gamete donors might provide their services for only ten families per catchment area of eight hundred thousand people, they were concerned about the probability of inadvertent consanguinity—genetic incest—and so determined that ten, and more recently twenty-five, was a "safe" number for avoiding recessive mutations "assuming assorted mating."[7] In other words, given the possibility of a brother and sister marrying and producing offspring as a result of their *not knowing* their first-degree genetic tie, an algorithm based on geography and population size was developed to determine its probability, and then the "safe" number was set. What the academy presumably did not and most likely could not factor into the algorithm is community and the fact that people's paths are more likely to cross when they belong to a particular cultural community *and* live in the same geographic region (catchment area).

Children in lesbian-coparent families with anonymous donors served by a local fertility facility are members of a community and even a subculture. They are members of local gay/lesbian communities and, within those, gay/lesbian family support groups. This does not present a problem for biomedical professionals concerned about inadvertent incest—which is the reason for the 10/800,000 formula in the first place—because it is unlikely that children in families who are closely connected socially will form heterosexual unions when they reach adulthood. Genetic incest concerns aside, it is more important for purposes of the present discussion that a lesbian and gay community and a lesbian and gay family support network are both located approximately in the catchment area served by the two primary gamete donation facilities and that consequently lesbian-coparent families with anonymous donors will not only *have donors in common* but *discover this fact by way of sharing information* about their donor's sperm identity. Through the sharing of knowledge of the donor's sperm identity within communities and parent support groups and networks, lesbian coparents learn of genetic ties their children share with children in other lesbian-coparent families.

And so they face second-order extended-family considerations resulting from the anonymous donor link: to recognize as extended family, or not, other lesbian-coparent families with whom the anonymous donor is shared. Of course, the anonymous donor is now simultaneously known and unknown. Knowledge about biogenetic relatedness that is officially suppressed seeps out informally to reveal a potential network of families connected by way of a common donor. Some of these families will choose to extend their family boundaries to include other lesbian-coparent families with the same donor, and some will not; but in either case, the donor himself, his social identity, his embodied being, will still be unknown to them.

Karen and Arlene, whom we met in Chapter 4 as an equal-sharing couple, had chosen a Chinese American donor from the catalogue of donors provided by the San Francisco sperm bank they used. They chose this particular donor because they were interested in someone with "intelligence, calmness, a positive personality and athletic ability." From their perusal of the donor profile catalogue, they gleaned that this particular donor might possess these qualities. They indicated that his race was not necessarily "an issue" either way for them, although it is easy to see that their inferences about the donor's personality and other qualities could be based on racial stereotypes.

Arlene and Karen were members of a gay/lesbian synagogue that sponsored community events and groups, some of which were organized specifically for gay and lesbian families. Karen recounted a story about their encounter with another lesbian-coparent family at one of these events that disturbed her greatly. They met a family in which the daughter looked just like Bobby. As Karen recalled, "I confirmed with the birth mother that she [the daughter] is, in fact, Bobby's half-sibling because her donor number is the same as Bobby's. It was easy to figure out because there were only two Chinese donors at the time that we were both inseminating. The kids are almost exactly the same age. So Bobby has a half-sister who's kind of like a twin."

Karen was disturbed, later in the conversation, when she learned that this couple did not want to acknowledge the biological connection between their daughter and Bobby. In fact, their entire interaction became strained, as Karen described it:

> Our preferences would have been to try to talk about how to handle the situation, and these parents were clearly not interested in broaching the subject. Under no circumstances was their daughter to find out that she was related to Bobby. This was strange for us because we are very open about everything in our lives and this couple's reaction to being linked to another family in this way was hurtful, at least to me. And the other part of this is that Bobby and their daughter will probably end up at the same school. It's all just very disturbing.

Through the specificity of the community these parents were members of, the logic of the anonymous-donor link and the sharing of information about the sperm identity of the donor, the officially anonymous donor became unofficially known, and the potential web of families was revealed. For Karen and Arlene, who had met at the 1987 Gay Pride Parade in San Francisco, the discovery was welcome, as they were interested in gay politics and community building generally and were equally open to the idea of extended kinship with other lesbian-coparent families.

Another family, Belinda and Caitlin and their daughter Cassie, were friends with another family whose daughter had the same donor as Cassie. They all lived in a community in northern California's wine country, about an hour and a half's drive north of San Francisco. They acknowledged their daughters' biological status as half-siblings. Belinda explained the situation:

> Yeah, even before they had her they asked us if it was okay for them to use the same donor. They figured out from our description of Cassie's donor profile that her donor was the same one that they had their eye on when they went to look at them. And since we're friends, they just asked us if we didn't

mind if they used the same donor. Of course, we thought it was great. And now we're all even closer now that their little girl is here and Cassie can know that she's her half-sister.

Belinda and Caitlin and Cassie lived in a small house on communally owned property where they were used to activating networks and sharing resources within both the lesbian and larger community of people there—most of whom had modest incomes and often struggled to pay bills. Given these circumstances, it made perfect sense that they would not think twice about sharing yet another resource, select sperm, and opening up their family boundaries to include another lesbian-coparent family.

Of the twenty-nine Bay Area families with anonymous donors, three mentioned circumstances in which they had learned of their sharing a donor with another family and wanted to acknowledge the connection. Others had not experienced this directly and so were not in the position to make a second-order extended-family decision. Some couples expressed their understanding of the potential web of families connected through the anonymous donor, but only indirectly, and in terms of the donor's future relationship with children rather than with families' relationships with one another. With a mixture of chagrin and amusement, several couples mentioned that anonymous donors willing to be known when a child reaches majority would have "ten eighteen-year-olds heading his way all at once saying, 'Hi Dad,' " to quote one mother. Some joked that the kids would be asking their newly discovered benefactors for college tuition.

Like the parents who didn't want to acknowledge their daughter's biological tie to Karen and Arlene's son, Bobby, only one Bay Area couple, Marjorie Rawlins and Sophie Mesner, expressed concern about who had control of the information about genetic links among children. This type of concern, I believe, sheds some light on just how powerful the discourse of biological or genetic determinism is, and more importantly, *knowledge about* biological ties. For knowledge about children's common biological ties through a shared donor, when exchanged between families, activates the latent structure by presenting second-order-level considerations for parents, which in turn may produce a manifest web of extended kin, depending on parents' actions.

What, then, is the concern? Why are some parents anxious about acknowledging extended kin stemming from a shared donor, to the point where they actively create tension in their interactions with other families? Marjorie and Sophie's views provide an answer:

MARJORIE: Something came up for us, we realized. Sophie had a far-off acquaintance or whatever, who started describing her sperm donor one day, and we realized that Zeke [son] is related to this kid. But *they* didn't know that Zeke was related to their kid. And we realized that that opened up a whole. . . . We don't describe our donor anymore, because we don't want that same thing to happen to us. We don't want somebody out there *who knows* that Zeke's related to their kid and *we don't know it.*

SOPHIE: And not vice versa.

MARJORIE: It's a very odd dynamic that's opened up.

It seems that what worries Marjorie and Sophie is not so much the implication of extended kin ties as the distribution of knowledge about the biogenetic relationships that exist "out there" among the children of anonymous-donor-inseminated lesbians. This appears to be another variant of the knowledge/power nexus for which, in a context in which couples have traded their official right to know for protection from kinship claims, the unequal distribution of knowledge comes as a surprise. The field of knowledge was supposed to have been leveled insofar as couples chose officially anonymous donors. Now, out of the blue, word comes of shared donors, of biologically related children. Information leaks through unofficial channels. The deal they thought they made has unraveled.

THE CIRCULATION OF KNOWLEDGE
IN THE AGE OF ASSISTED REPRODUCTION

To better understand this apparent role of knowledge in the kinship structure of lesbian-coparent families created through donor insemination, it is helpful to relate it to anthropological analyses of kinship systems more broadly. In his 1949 epic work *The Elementary Structures of Kinship,* the French structuralist Claude Lévi-Strauss laid out what he perceived were the underlying principles of kinship in primitive societies. Often relating them to their cultural counterparts in modern, complex societies, Lévi-Strauss insisted that above all these principles were the product of rules created and imposed by humans rather than arising out of biological imperatives. Complex sets of rules, of which the universal prohibition of incest is one, by their very presence and prevalence mark a point at which culture takes over from nature. That these rules govern kinship and not other forms of human relationship and activity—for example, economic activity—is significant, as it is through the extension of kin ties that human social life—society itself—begins to take shape.

Lévi-Strauss linked the universal prohibition of incest to the systems of exchange and reciprocity in primitive society analyzed by Marcel Mauss in his 1954 classic work on the gift. Lévi-Strauss described, for example, the ceremonial potlatch in which both material goods, in the way of foodstuffs, and gifts or items of wealth that have no use value but are valued for the wealth they signify are traded and often destroyed as ways of displaying and gaining status. In primitive societies, Lévi-Strauss argued, potlatches often have as their singular purpose one all-important trade: the offering of a daughter or sister in marriage to a male of another clan or kin group with whom social ties or alliance are desired. According to Lévi-Strauss, the exchange of women as valued objects in transactions negotiated by men, on behalf of male-headed kin groups, and for the social purpose of establishing social status and alliance is at the heart of the universal incest taboo. For it is through the rule of reciprocity and exogamous exchange that kinship systems are built and maintained. These complex systems emerging from the networks of kin groups that end up linked through these exchanges of women are hardly observable in their totality but must be mapped and derived from the logic of the rules, as in Lévi-Strauss's work.

Lévi-Strauss's study has been critiqued from many quarters, but Gayle Rubin's critique in her influential 1973 essay "The Traffic in Women: Notes toward a Political Economy of Sex" is of interest for present purposes.[8] Among other things, Rubin argued that although Lévi-Strauss was to be commended for emphasizing the gendered character of the exchanges, and for discussing relations between the sexes more generally at a time when sex and gender were all but ignored in most social science scholarship, he still failed to pursue the implications of his own insights.

Like Freud, whom Rubin also criticized for both similar and different reasons, Lévi-Strauss made startling and important observations about the social creation and role of sex and gender in both primitive and modern societies. Yet, like Freud, Lévi-Strauss would not or could not follow the implications of his own theorizing to their logical conclusions, perhaps because the risk of exposing the androcentrism of what would become Western canonical thought was too great.[9] For Rubin, the preemptively suppressed conclusions that might have been drawn from Lévi-Strauss's work involved the *other* system suggested by the exchange of women. Lévi-Strauss derived *kinship* systems from the rules governing the reciprocal exchange of women, with the emphasis on reciprocity. Reciprocity guaranteed alliance when the alternative was hostility and open aggression. Kinship and fraternity were mutually reinforcing and desirable outcomes of the exchange of women. The *other system* suggested by this, which Lévi-Strauss could not or refused to see, was of course patriarchy, or what Rubin termed "the sex/gender system."

Through a feminist lens, the emphasis of the reciprocal exchange of women focuses on the fact that it is women who are being exchanged, ever so reciprocally, by men. Not only are alliance and fraternity reinforcing of and by kinship networks, but their maintenance depends on the subjugation and traffic in women as valued objects. Fraternity and kinship depend first and foremost on the existence of the prior system—the sex/gender system—which first turns women into potlatch barter goods—gifts. Rubin referred to both the sex/gender system and its apparent, observable effects as a "political economy of sex."[10]

Elements of both Lévi-Strauss's and Rubin's analyses apply to the contemporary structure of the donor-extended kinship relations of lesbian-coparent families. As I have already outlined above, lesbian coparents whose children are conceived through donor insemination do depend upon both informal friendship and community networks and formal, rapidly institutionalizing markets for acquiring the precious liquid that will assist them in bringing children into their lives. Semen that has been screened and tested for potency and is preferably fresh is a commodity in a bio-reproductive economy for which there is greater demand than supply. This "liquid gold" is disembodied male product highly desired by women, who acquire it through various forms of monetary and negotiated transactions. It could therefore be argued that there has been a gender reversal of the traffic in women in the creation of kinship: the modern kinship economy consists of a circulation of male biogenetic product on be-half of woman-headed families. Women share donors, sometimes know-ingly, and form extended, second-order family ties—"alliances" in Lévi-Strauss's language. The erasure of biological paternity that occurs with officially anonymous sperm donation all but seals the fate of semen as a commodity whose exchange value derives almost exclusively from its use value to women who control their own reproduction. In short, there is a political economy of sex, but what is trafficked in is male, not female, and it results in a particular kinship structure that is unique to both the pres-ent age of assisted reproduction and the social location of its subjects.

These parallels to Rubin are instructive as they bring a feminist per-spective of Lévi-Strauss to bear upon the present discussion of the struc-ture of lesbian-coparent-family extended-kin relations.[11] The notion that the political economy of assisted reproduction for lesbians results in a gen-der reversal of the trader and the object traded tempts utopian impulses but is weak as a feminist argument that the sex/gender order is seriously threatened by lesbian appropriations of new reproductive technologies. Still, in reversing the relationship of women-as-valued-objects versus men's control of those objects—women of value, men of renown, as An-nette Weiner succinctly put it—lesbian "trafficking" in valued sperm for the creation of kinship returns control of at least one aspect of reproduc-tion to women.[12] Moreover, the erasure of paternity effected by anony-mous sperm donation brings to mind Engels's analysis of the discovery of biological paternity in various cultures as partly contributing to "the world historical defeat of the female sex."[13] Engels and others argued that the es-tablishment of paternity, along with the advent of private property, occa-sioned the overthrow of "mother right" in many cultures in which descent had been reckoned matrilineally.[14]

In the present case of lesbian mothers with anonymous donors, formal biological paternity has been disestablished. Censored from public record, and relegated to third-party, bureaucratic management, paternity in this context is a matter of classified information. If the "real" identity of the donor—the identity by which he is known to the sperm bank or physi-cian and presumably to the rest of the world—is legally suppressed for the parties for whom paternity is relevant, this is an erasure of father right, a relinquishment of male prerogative in children and in disposition of the now commodified "seed."[15] In one sense this constitutes one tiny reversal in Engels's "world historical defeat of the female sex."

When some lesbian mothers subsequently share donors' sperm identity with others and base second-order extended-kin decisions on that knowledge, they do not restore the status of father right, of paternity, so much as recuperate biology and genes as the basis for kinship. One might take a benign view of this as "socializing genetics"[16] or a more ominous appraisal that the revival of consanguinity and the genealogical grid works against the principle of choice for which gay kinship has held the most promise. In either case, what must be stressed is that while paternity is officially erased and biological consanguinity secondarily revived, all of this still exists epistemically, at the level of knowledge. When lesbian mothers share their donor's sperm identity, biological consanguinity is relegitimated in and by knowledge about it and exists as knowledge itself. Thus it is knowledge that is traded and trafficked in and serves as the currency in the constitution of lesbian kin networks.

The flow of knowledge and information in the reckoning of lesbian kinship via assisted reproduction is akin to the exchange of valuable objects (i.e., women) in nonmodern kinship systems. Lévi-Strauss emphasized reciprocal exchange (of women) as the currency on which not only kinship but society itself was based. The universal rule of exogamy, which forbade men from marrying their sisters and daughters and which was the same as the incest taboo, more importantly *exhorted* men to trade their sisters and daughters in marriage with another clan or kin group. This was the way alliances were built, hostilities were avoided, and the entire social group was stitched together; as an "admirable native saying" quoted by Lévi-Strauss put it, the rule of exogamy and the exchange of women in marriage "depicts the action of the needle for sewing roofs, which, weaving in and out, leads backwards and forwards the same liana, holding the straw together."[17] In the same way, the exchange of women in marriage wove together entire kinship systems.

Lévi-Strauss noted that in more complex societies, to which he consistently referred for comparative insights in his analysis of the "elementary structures" of kinship, rules of exogamy and endogamy were looser, based less upon a goal of developing kin alliances and more upon considerations of class, race/ethnicity, and social status more generally, and in some categories subject to state authority. (In the United States, the prohibition against same-sex marriage may be described as a rule of rigid gender exogamy, and interracial marriage, while legal, is socially disapproved due to an informal norm of racial endogamy.) The point is that in complex societies, for all but the very wealthy, marriage does not serve the function of building alliances between and among families as in less complex societies, especially given the relative ease with which marriages may be dissolved.

Such is the case in postmodern kinship arrangements in the United States today. However, assisted reproduction in family formation adds organization, once again, to this otherwise more fluid state. Technically assisted reproduction means that more self-conscious decision making determines human relatedness. Choosing a commercial gamete donor from a menu of options entails more explicit consideration of social and biological characteristics that the individuals creating families must manage. As "practical metaphysicians," to use the philosopher Charis Cussins's apt phrase, those who create families by new reproductive technologies are in the midst of developing in the postmodern era something like the exogamous marriage rules in premodern and nonmodern cultures analyzed by Lévi-Strauss: they impose organization and structure on processes in which the tendency has been more aleatory.[18] Here, however, the currency is not women traded in marriage; nor is it even sperm, rationed and distributed both commercially and "the underground way," as one Bay Area mother put it.[19] The currency is information and knowledge about biogenetic relatedness.

This explains why the "odd dynamic" described by Marjorie and Sophie earlier "opened up." In the context of officially suppressed knowledge of the sperm donor's social identity, the management of information regarding his sperm identity falls on the recipient couple. The rules and criteria established institutionally do not apply in the informal circulation of knowledge. Thus these practical metaphysicians become information brokers who must create the new rules governing their trade, when what is at stake is nothing less than the definition of their own families.

Chapter 8 | THE THEORETICAL FUTURE OF A CONSCIOUS FEMINIST KINSHIP

How does a society respond to a new social formation to which it has itself given birth? Does it become a "rejecting and rejected parent culture," to use Amy Agigian's evocative phrase, in its refusal to accommodate the needs of its own progeny?[1] Or does it cede to this generation and genre of kinship, ever so grudgingly, social, legal, moral, and political ground? Can it even recognize such a historic innovation as "its own," as the love-child of at least two modernist progenitors: techno-scientific advances in procreative knowledge (and their institutionalization in reproductive service organizations) and liberalizing developments in juridical opinion? Perhaps society is utterly ignorant of its own procreative role, and thus the new formation appears as an alien yet vaguely familiar entity, familiar in its alchemy of once-repressed, now reassembled elements—that is, non-normative sexualities and intimate associations of all but the heterosexual, male-privileging kind. More interesting still, if society's ruling institutions maintain their legitimacy and hegemony by means of repression, control, or absorption of oppositional Others, is it not inimical to their own projects to foster the growth of a family form that surely qualifies as their most queer and potentially subversive Other? How then ought we understand the relationship between institutions whose effective interest, from a critical theoretical perspective, is in maintaining heteropatriarchal dominance and their familial "offspring," who stand poised to challenge that paternal order?[2]

This concluding chapter addresses these questions, which, following the analysis in the preceding chapters of the ways in which lesbian-coparent families engage the world "on the ground," necessarily have wider-scale social and political implications. Yet these questions beg additional ones and presuppose others. For questioning how it is possible that a family form with great antipatriarchal potential has sprung to life and established itself within a volatile cultural context—one suffused with both politically reactionary and sexually liberalizing elements—presupposes that these families are viable and visible, that by their very existence or practices or both they challenge the contemporary gender order, and, perhaps most important, that powerful members of society view them as a threat to that order.

We have indeed seen in the preceding chapters how lesbian coparents, their children, and their kin are making themselves visible and viable in everyday life as lesbian mother families; that in their relationships with members of their families of origin and other relatives and with known donors and their kin, and in their interactions with casual acquaintances and strangers, they stand as living, breathing, loving, procreating evidence in defiance of compulsory heterosexuality, confronting directly the ideology of the naturalness and rightness of the heterosexual-parent family. Moreover, we have seen, in their internal family relations and their parenting and labor practices, the enormous (if inconclusive) potential for the undoing of gender: the delinking of gender from power and forms of inequality within nuclear families. In sum, we have glimpsed the very real changes occurring "on the ground" as these families engage in the sociohistoric business of institutionalizing a new set of arrangements by which, to recall Gayle Rubin, "the biological raw material of human sex and procreation is shaped by human, social intervention and satisfied in a conventional manner."[3] Only here the biological requirements are satisfied in a most unconventional manner for a society historically prone to favor rigid gender categories and heterosexual unions.

To influence everyday attitudes, worldviews, and habits of mind through the presentation of unconventional arrangements, and through progressive familial practices, speaks to lesbian mothers' capacity to define the social contexts relevant to their lives, to their desire to lay claim to the communities that support them, and to their relations within milieus in which their trials and triumphs play out. We have yet to consider fully, however, how societal institutions may respond to and shape the future of these families' existence and social welfare. What the future holds for lesbian-coparent families in fact depends upon the institutions—biomedical technology and law—that have facilitated their formation and growth in the first place, as we saw in Chapter 1. Their future also turns on the extent to which institutional and political elites view lesbian-mother families as harmless or dangerous. In what follows I consider the broader feminist theoretical implications for women, reproduction, kinship, and lesbian-coparent families as they are likely to continue to be shaped by two of the most formidable, elite male–controlled institutions in the developed world: the juridical and biomedical establishments. I highlight both a progressive vision of what would be needed for promoting social justice and well-being for woman-headed families and a critical theoretical assessment of the likely effects of biomedical technologies of procreation on all families.

FEMINIST JURISPRUDENCE AND
THE ETHOS OF MATERNAL CARE

Families headed by women range from single-, dual-, and multiple-mother families to heterosexual-parent families that are woman directed or centered, and in the aggregate are diverse in terms of sexuality, class, race, religion, and so on. Feminist theories of necessary changes in law and jurisprudence thus must attempt to account for both identity and difference among such familial relations. Feminist theory of course has long struggled with this problem in other areas such as work, history and social movements, and formulations of the subject of feminism per se.[4] Those theorizing the subject of a feminist family jurisprudence encounter problems of definition and of articulating principles that account for diversity without losing sight of what makes their efforts necessary: the lacunae and biases in masculinist legal doctrine and practice that discourage, discriminate against, marginalize, and otherwise try to suppress woman-determined families.

Agigian points out, for example, that because lesbians must still fight for basic civil liberties and rights already enjoyed by heterosexual women (equal protection, the right to marry) liberal approaches to legal change will benefit lesbians and their families more immediately and crucially than radical approaches, though the latter might be more ideal in the long term.[5] The theoretical approach to feminist family jurisprudence must account for these differences in sociostructural location and life situation in a way that does not deny their reality, or abridge any existing rights, guarantees, and protections, but provides a framework for sexual-familial justice that makes differences in such existing rights, guarantees, and protections unnecessary.

One proposal involves changing the formal definition of family to a functional one. According to the legal scholar Martha Minow, a functional definition would mean that any group of individuals who acted like a family could and should be treated as one under the law. "Someone who has taken care of the child on a daily basis, is known to the child as a parent, and has provided love and financial support" is a functional parent.[6] Those who entered into such functional relations would be treated equally under the law, but exiting those same relations would be more difficult, since, as Minow argues, there are a variety of ways and arrangements by which families are created, but there should be few ways of severing familial ties (and thus obligations) once they have been established. The most obvious critique of this approach is that it grants courts so much definitional discretion that it cannot provide lesbian and alternative families basic protections, such as protection from antigay discrimination by the courts themselves. Justices could easily "find" behaviors that were not "familial," effectively substituting formal definitions for functional ones. Also, under Minow's proposal, family members would always lack secure knowledge of their legal status, a status that would in fact remain ambiguous due to the definition's imprecision, and thus its purpose would be defeated.

Another approach that applies especially to families created via assisted procreation is a contractual model whereby all parties to the procreative endeavor formalize their intentions in contracts. Any questions about familial standing or status would be referable to and enforceable through the contract. This contract model is already used by lesbian-coparent families and single inseminating women, but once again individual courts have wide latitude in determining, for example, which interpretations of family are in the best interests of the child and thus the extent to which they will be guided by the contracts.

In her vision of a more just family jurisprudence for unconventional and woman-headed families, legal scholar Nancy Polikoff has offered perhaps one of the strongest statements criticizing the deeply masculinist biases and privilege embedded in contemporary family jurisprudence in the United States. In her 1996 article "The Deliberate Construction of Families without Fathers: Is It an Option for Lesbian and Heterosexual Mothers?" Polikoff set forth a premise that would be incendiary if not blasphemous to neopatriarchal academic and public discourse about the family but that speaks to the lived reality of a growing number of women and their families.[7] Echoing the words of many of the mothers we heard from in Chapter 2, Polikoff wrote: "I start this paper with the premise that it is no tragedy either on a national scale or in an individual family, for children to be raised without fathers. Children raised without love and guidance, without shelter, nutrition, and health care, without meaningful education, without physical safety in their homes and on their streets—that is tragic."[8] Polikoff systematically discusses the legal barriers and penalties faced by women raising children without legal fathers, concluding that

> [s]tatutory and doctrinal impediments to legal validation of families without fathers constitute more than a rejection of private family ordering. [As] long as [the state] demands that every child have a legal father, [it] furthers rhetoric that a father belongs at the head of every household as the ultimate authority figure. Professor Martha Fineman observes that "the success of single mothers would be a blow to traditional masculinity." *Legal validation* of single mothers would be an even greater blow. . . . By validating such families, the decisions implicitly demand that society look elsewhere for a solution to the real problems facing today's children.[9]

Polikoff's proposal for legally validating families without fathers is a framework she refers to as "equitable parenthood."[10] This framework has the benefit of retaining elements of formal definitions of family (which have broader legal force) and flexible elements contained in functional definitions of family. Under equitable parenthood, the status and role of parents are legally privileged, but the number and gender of parents are unrestricted. This moves formal family definitions away from requiring that children have one male and one female parent, thus legally legitimating single-parent families and those with same-sex parents. And to stress the relationship and obligations of parents to children, Polikoff recommends that biological mothers be privileged such that, in the case of lesbian-coparent families, nonbiological mothers gain parental status only if they act as a parent to the child and in a context in which the biological mother intends that they develop a parental relationship with the child. Polikoff provides for this control on the part of biological mothers to guard against the dangers of excess discretion and flexibility in functional definitions.

This latter privileging of biological parenthood carries the same penalties for nonbiological mothers as does the present system insofar as a nonbiological mother's relationship with a child may be legally terminated at the discretion of the biological mother. Such discretion seems cruel in contexts in which nonbiological mothers have fully parented and loved children, children who may then suffer the loss of their second parent as a result of their biological mother's decision to end her own and their relationship with the comother. This same disadvantage potentially inheres in yet another feminist family re-envisioning, one that, by most standards, stands as the boldest, perhaps most radical, and for this reason politically least feasible conceptualization but that nonetheless bears serious scrutiny as an "ideal type," a model of legal and social accommodation of families grossly disserved by existing policies and jurisprudence.

In her account of the failures of the present system to offer justice to women and their families, the legal scholar Martha Fineman explicates two premises currently guiding family law that she believes must be abolished: the "equality" presumed (by the law) to exist between women and men who are parents, and a normative emphasis on the conjugal-sexual pair of adults as the basic unit of families. In her 1995 book entitled *The Neutered Mother, the Sexual Family, and Other Twentieth Century Tragedies,* Fineman demonstrates through detailed discussion of case law and feminist legal theory how a presumption of gender neutrality on the part of courts, a presumption that feminists have themselves inspired through earlier reform efforts to secure equal treatment under the law, in fact

results in unrealistic, punitive responses that are harmful to mothers and children. Custody policy at divorce reflects the determination that parents are assumed equally entitled to custody regardless of the "mothering" they did (or did not do) during the marriage. Gender neutrality has substantive implications and signals a change in orientation in which caretaking is devalued and biological and economic connection are deemed of paramount importance.[11]

In addition to the gender neutrality presumption currently guiding custody law, Fineman criticizes the emphasis on the sexual-conjugal relationship underlying definitions of family generally used in contemporary family law. Fineman asks why the (heterosexual) lovers of mothers ought to be expected to coparent when the sexual relationship between adults is the least stable and permanent of all intimate bonds. For Fineman, this horizontal sexual tie between adults as the central unit in family formation reduces children to objects of parental manipulation when the conjugal relationship goes awry. Instead, it is the vertical intimacy between mother and child that most needs protection and preservation because it is this tie that most accurately embodies (and reveals) the fundamental basis of familial relations: dependency. Young children are dependent on caretaking adults; older adults are dependent on caretaking (adult) children; and all caretakers are dependent on the community or the state at some level.

The idea that caretakers can provide breadwinning *and* meet the noneconomic needs of dependents mystifies what Fineman calls the "derivative dependency" resulting from the caretaker's need for external resources to fulfill the caretaking role.[12] Fineman confirms that the state currently protects and subsidizes an idealized family form, the white, middle-class, heterosexually married nuclear family, but that the rhetoric casting this family's performance as successful "contributes to a mythology in which the construct of the 'independent' family masks the universal and inevitable nature of dependency." All families that deviate from the state-sanctioned norm, especially and most obviously single-mother and woman-headed families, are thus penalized and vilified. So too is their dependency construed, not as arising out of the nurturing work they do, but as the "shameful product of a dysfunctional nonconformity."[13]

To adequately address the stultifying and inhumane effects of the presumptions of gender neutrality and sexual-conjugal integrity under current family law (and Fineman is clear that the law is necessary but insufficient for achieving the kind of societal change she envisions), she proposes two radical, admittedly utopian re-visions: ending marriage as a legal category and instituting the "nurturing unit" of mother/child as the basic family unit.

The elimination of the legal status of marriage would mean that the interactions of all adult sexual "affiliates" would be governed by the same rules that regulate all adult nonsexual interactions under contract, property, tort, and criminal law. People could still engage in "ceremonious" marriage, but unions of this sort would have no legal meaning or consequences. Contracts concerning property and other aspects of sexual relationships are already widely used, Fineman points out, so the elimination of the legal status of marriage is not so far from practice as it might at first appear.

The benefits, however, would be significant. The most important benefit of the abolition of marriage as a legal category would be realized in the dissolution of the state's interest in preserving marriage as an institution. With the abolition of a state-preferred model of intimacy, all voluntary, adult sexual relationships would be permitted and equal; "nothing prohibited, nothing privileged."[14] Children could not be treated differentially according to the marital status of their parents; the concept of marital property would be no more, as would obligations for spousal support during and after termination of the relationship. Fineman joins left opponents of gay marriage in this proposal with the assertion that, rather than attempting to analogize more sexual relationships to the marital norm, which in turn creates ever more sexual "deviants," the elimination altogether of legal marriage "render[s] all sexual relationships equal with each other and all relationships equal with the sexual." Here is Anthony Giddens's "plastic sexuality" completely unfettered and realized.[15]

This proposal works in concert with Fineman's other, equally radical and politically infeasible (but nonetheless theoretically important) one: the instantiation of the caretaker-dependent relationship, symbolized by the mother-child dyad, as the basic unit of family. Fineman states that "[i]t is necessary to give new content to the concept of family in order to provide a protected space for nurturing and caretaking." By designating the mother/child vertical relationship the signifier of the nurturing function of family, Fineman substitutes the content of the state-supported but private, patriarchal family with the intimate relations most in need of protection and support. "The new family line," she writes, "drawn around dependency, would mark the boundaries of the concept of family privacy" and would designate the set of intimate relations that would become the beneficiaries of "a redistribution or reallocation of social and economic subsidies now given to the natural family that allow it to function 'independently' within society."[16]

Fineman's re-envisioning, as she and many other scholars imply, directly addresses the current lived social reality of woman-headed families. Given the dissonance between familial change and nostalgic efforts to idealize and preserve the patriarchal model, which I discussed in Chapter 1, Fineman's vision reveals the specifically and wholly ideological character of those conservative definitional efforts. For, under Fineman's program,

> Instead of being a society where our ideals and our ideology (the private, natural family) are out of sync with the real lives of many of our citizens, we would become a society that recognized and accepted the inevitability of dependency. We would face, value, and therefore subsidize, caretaking and caretakers. . . . What would unsubjugated motherhood look like? Unsupervised motherhood, as a social institution, recognized as performing a valuable societal role, would be given privacy (without paternity), subsidy (without strings), space (to make mistakes).[17]

Fineman emphasizes that the mother-child unit functions as both symbol and reality and that these are flexible, malleable, and changing. Symbolically, the mother-child dyad represents a specific practice of social and emotional responsibility, where "mothers" may in fact be men who wish to mother (nurture) while those women who are biological mothers but who do not or cannot mother may in fact be legally deprived of their children; the "child" in the metaphor stands for all persons in positions of "inevitable dependency," including those who are ill, elderly, disabled, and of course children. The reality of who actually does the lion's share of nurturing and caretaking in society, of course, is what genders the mother in the mother-child concept.[18] But Fineman's emphasis on the mother-child nurturing unit accommodates all forms of caretaking relationships; thus gay fathers who nurture their children, who are socially and emotionally responsible for the well-being and care of their children, would be protected and supported by the state under Fineman's proposal. So too would those same gay men be supported when they cared for loved ones, say, suffering from AIDS.

By invoking the ethos of care as a principle of human intimacy to be socially encouraged, protected, supported, and emphasized as primary, Fineman's vision does for family law and jurisprudence—and the definition of the familial in society more generally—what Sara Ruddick's *Maternal Thinking* did for peace politics. Fineman's proposal is an advance over Polikoff's, in my view, to the extent that it does not formally privilege biological parenthood as a built-in mechanism for retaining the legal status of parenthood. In Polikoff's version, where lesbian-coparent families are concerned, it is the biological mother's prerogative to determine whether the comother will be regarded and will become a legal second parent—enacted contractually. Maternity is privileged over mothering. For Fineman, biology matters less than care, even though biological mothers are implied as the referent of the mother-child nurturing unit; and since in her vision mothers who wished to care for their children would be supported, those who were unable to due to lack of resources would be distinguished from those who were unwilling and thus would be protected from class-discriminatory custody decisions.[19]

Fineman's vision is utopian, as she acknowledges, because it theorizes what is necessary for ideological and structural change, change that is needed to undo, if not transform, "existing punitive and parsimonious social policies."[20] Though it is extremely unlikely that these changes will occur anytime soon, Fineman's analysis offers a basis for gauging the level of (elite, patriarchal) ideological repression that currently stands in the way and is likely to emerge in proportion to the "progress" all families make toward an ethic of care and the emancipation of sexuality. To put it differently, Fineman's vision demystifies the haze of legal formalism and state repression deployed against alternative families by making us conscious of what our collective id has been trying to express: sexuality and parenting are decoupled, perhaps permanently, and our social and legal conventions need to be updated to account for this reality.

ROMANCING THE GENE:
FAMILY, KINSHIP, AND THE
TECHNOLOGICAL DISPERSION OF PROCREATION

Fineman's acuity alerts us to the changes in law, social policy, and vision necessary to reflect the lived reality of family diversity under the new conditions. It is now important to consider the implications for lesbian-coparent families (and other family types under the new conditions) of the increasing technologization and commercialization of procreation. It is clear how donor insemination facilitated the emergence and growth of lesbian-coparent families, but the implications for their future must be understood in the context of who will control the (new) means of procreation, what types of procreation will be allowed, and how the resulting offspring and families will be socially valued.

If the development and widespread use of contraceptive techniques initially facilitated the separation of (hetero)sexuality from baby making and thus parenting, now procreative technologies sustain that separation for growing numbers of heterosexual couples who are deemed infertile, single heterosexual women wishing to become mothers without male partners, and of course lesbians and gay men wishing to become parents. The complex of reproductive service organizations, research institutions, biomedical technology, and pharmaceutical companies (which market fertility drugs used for superovulating women's ovaries for collecting ova) all compose the expanding field of procreative technologies that depend, for their existence, on baby making that does not occur exclusively through heterosexual intercourse. Infertility is the watchword and focal point in this world of assisted reproduction, in which the economic interests and research investments by biomedical science must generate returns sufficient to propel profits and development forward into an unspecified future. It is a happy coincidence (and most likely a precondition) for the field of assisted reproduction that many women are increasingly deferring childbearing, since conception and pregnancy are more difficult to achieve among older women. It is impossible to know how much of this phenomenon is itself a function of the development of procreative technologies that need and therefore may create "infertile" women and couples.

This point, however, is illuminated by the fact that lesbians who require quite minimal assistance having mostly to do with procuring and injecting semen are "found" to have infertility problems by virtue of having not conceived within a defined number of insemination attempts. That defined number of attempts, signaling the moment for researching the infertility question, is established by reproductive service organizational norms and often coincides with the average number of insemination attempts before conception is achieved. Increasingly, however, that defined number of attempts has been lowered, so that, by some reproductive medical standards, a finding of "infertility" and the call for greater technical intervention follow a rather limited amount of unassisted or low-assistance procreative effort.[21] In other words, commodified, biomedical technological assistance becomes more "necessary" as the definition of infertility, determined substantially by these organizations (and disseminated throughout mass culture by means of aggressive marketing and storytelling), self-interestedly specifies reproductive conditions requiring assistance.[22]

Very few procreative efforts in the developed world will be construed as *not* needing some biomedical technological assistance according to this logic. This principle is already in full operation in the process following conception, with the normative use of ultrasound, amniocentesis, other forms of genetic screening of the fetus (genetic counseling for parents), and all manner of fetal monitoring, imaging, and surveillance. All of this makes the fetus a specular object of surveillance and a person (preindividuated?) endowed with rights and privileges independent of and often surpassing those of the woman whose womb the fetus inhabits.[23]

What is left of reproduction, now that not only are sexuality, procreation, and parenting separated from one another, but procreation is increasingly falling under the management of biomedical experts? What is left of procreation that is not, to paraphrase Habermas's formulation, precolonized by the system? The future of the meaning of kinship itself, in addition to that of particular family types, including lesbian-coparent families, will depend greatly on the interaction between intending parents and the powerful commodity logic of the biomedical establishment, which is partly nourished and expanded through the field of assisted reproduction.

In keeping with her earlier incisive studies of kinship in both Euro-American and Melanesian contexts, the feminist cultural anthropologist Marilyn Strathern has provided one of the most penetrating analyses of the likely effects on family and kinship resulting from assisted-reproduction technologies. Her 1995 article "Displacing Knowledge: Technology and the Consequences for Kinship" offers predictive "extrapolations" of current procreative knowledge and practice and their likely effect on how North American and northern European cultures will understand family, kinship, reproduction, and personal identity. Since Euro-American kinship systems are those most affected by the new reproductive technologies, Strathern's analysis is developed with these systems in mind. She thus sets up her argument by stating, "If one of the distinctive characteristics of this system were the value placed on procreation and thus on parentage in the definition of kin relations, it is likely to be responsive to changes in procreative practice."[24]

Strathern's projections of the changes are twofold, and she characterizes them as displacements or separations: the (nuclear) family will be displaced by kinship relations that will have expanded as a result of the technological dispersion of procreation; and procreation itself will be separated or displaced from reproduction, where the latter is understood as a "copying" or transmitting of one's personal characteristics (personal identity) in the body and person of a child.

The first displacement, of family by and from kinship, is not meant to suggest that the family will disappear; rather, it will, in a sense, recede in relation to the multiplication of kin ties that may be possible as a consequence of procreative technologies. With assisted procreation (as we saw in the previous chapter), the number of procreative actors and relations increases to include, in addition to the intending parents, gamete donors, medical technicians, and all other persons involved in "assisting" the procreative endeavor. Procreation, which was once thought to be an act of biological reproduction occurring between two intending (or nonintending) parents, becomes dispersed as the number and roles of persons involved multiply. Thus Strathern writes,

> The new actors associated with reproductive medicine create a field of relationships that does not overlap in any simple way with familial ones. . . . The child is "produced" by the couple who want it, but the kinship is dispersed.
> . . . Dispersed kinship is constituted in dispersed conception; it includes those who "produce" the child with assistance as well as those who assist. As a consequence, there thus exists a field of procreators whose relationship to one another and to the product of conception is contained in the act of conception itself and not in the family as such.[25]

Particularly important for the way in which dispersed procreation will have the projected effect of there being "more to kinship than family life"[26] is the way in which gamete donors are at once stripped of any familial rights in the child and thereby removed from the immediate family, but in that very distancing of procreators lies the possibility that "distant" kin ties exist—ties that ultimately count, as we saw in the preceding chapter, because what is foundational to the procreative act is the idea of the transfer of biogenetic substance to the product of conception. This clearly may be seen in the fact that, among the Bay Area families, only one of thirty-four couples had chosen a donor who would be anonymous to the children "for life." Most others reserved the right for their child/ren to know their donors once they reached eighteen. Mothers worried a great deal about their children knowing to whom they were kin.

We also see Strathern's dispersion (and proliferation) of kinship—as a result of the dispersion of procreation—in the donor-extended kin ties from Chapter 7. Not only was kinship increased directly through known donors to include donors' families, but it increased indirectly via anonymous donors whose sperm identity was shared both literally and figuratively by different families, who then chose whether to use the knowledge of the shared donor to expand their kin ties with one another. We saw how this decision to activate the latent (biogenetic) kin ties based on asymmetrical knowledge of those ties produced some anxiety for mothers. Strathern suggests that what is happening is a displacement of one kind of knowledge for another: the more explicit it becomes that biogenetic substance has been the implicit cultural foundation of kinship, the more one's choice in activating it, in acknowledging it, may seem fatalistic. There is no going back once the biogenetic connection has been revealed, made explicit. For Strathern, making explicit what was previously implicit sets off an "irreversible process": "The implicit can never be recovered and there is no returning to old assumptions; displacement becomes radical."[27]

The biogenetic basis of kinship as a symbolic system has always meant that one can trace out kinship from an act of procreation, usually by way of the conjugal, nuclear family. Consider, for example, the U.S. mass media treatment of the revelation that DNA matches between Thomas Jefferson's "legitimate" offspring and those of his slave Sally Hemings were "confirmed scientifically" and reported in the journal *Nature* in early 1999. The finding was interpreted in the popular press by observers and academics as proving, once and for all, that a "procreative act" had occurred between Jefferson and Hemings. From there, from the evidence of shared DNA, came the wholesale retroactive mapping of Jefferson's lineage. The

New York Times produced a Jefferson-Hemings family tree, complete with photos of living descendants. Jefferson's kin could now more fully be accounted for with the truth of his paternity scientifically established.[28]

For Strathern, however, with the procreative act dispersed and removed from the family, genitors and biogenetic "relatives" will have sloughed off all pretense of the familial and will appear in all their bald genetic aspect. It comes as a little frightening for parents who must make a choice, who must expose the biogenetic foundation of kinship as a choice, to then do so. But the separation of the procreative act from the family means that the biogenetic basis of family and kinship becomes more visible as a symbol—that is, when the referent transforms itself from flesh-and-blood substance to information about that substance, information about the body from which it was alienated. And in this way the dispersion of procreation can create a dispersion and multiplication of kinship that transcend both the immediate family and extended-family members.

In addition to the notion that the dispersion of procreation creates a dispersion of kinship, Strathern notes a second effect of conceptive technologies—the separation of procreation from reproduction—which has a paradoxical or confounding effect on the first one just described. If the first one stands to increase and disperse kinship, the effect of the separation of procreation from reproduction will have a suppressive consequence for kinship, or rather, for the social activation of biogenetic kin ties. Strathern states this paradox as " '[M]ore' kinship does not necessarily lead to 'more' relatives."[29]

Strathern reasons that if we understand Euro-American views of reproduction as copying, duplication, or transmission of personal traits and characteristics in the child who embodies them, dispersed procreation means that the notion of a direct transmission of genetic traits from parents to children no longer will be tenable.

> [R]apidly increasing knowledge about the complexity of genetic make-up displaces any simple reckoning of traits being passed down through family lines. If primitive knowledge of the inheritance of characteristics is being displaced by knowledge about genetic mapping, then the simple idea that one person passed on a characteristic to another, like a piece of property, may become displaced by a sense of the complex way in which elements combine.[30]

What the child, the product of reproduction, becomes is a unique constellation of genetic traits in his or her own right, a constellation that has
very little to do with who is parenting the child, or even who the procreators are.

> It would seem the more we know about this constellation, the less we shall in
> fact need to know about the relationships. . . . Since family histories were
> used to make inferences about genetic disposition, kinship genealogies were
> medically important for tracing the "inheritance" of genetic defects. Nowa-
> days it is possible to imagine direct access to the genome itself. If "there is no
> essential difference between reading the genes by a patient's description of
> their symptoms and family history *and reading them directly*" (Brenner
> 1991:37) then all one need know is what genes one has. . . . [T]he genome is
> connected to the possibility of genetic mapping, of documenting the indi-
> viduality of the body that will be the object of the new parents' concerns.[31]

In this way do the origins and social identity of the genetic material become irrelevant. Thus reproduction as an intergenerational transmission
of personal traits loses what is distinctly duplicative about it, in favor of
the production of a unique genetic constellation whose integrity and dis-
similarity from others provide the basis for individuality. Personal identity
may thus become based on genetic identity, where genes, because we will
have greater, unmediated access to them, eliminate the need for using kinship as their proxy. Strathern observes, "[I]dentity may or may not be located with reference to specific other persons."[32]

For Strathern, the result is that, if we no longer need kinship genealo-
gies for inferring genetic inheritance, and if genetic identity becomes autonomous from familial and kinship relations, it may be possible, finally,
to define kinship and family in nongenetic ways. Strathern muses, "Would
it follow, then, that Euro-American kin constructs would come to seem
more like those of (say) the people of Melanesia, who never held a genetic
theory of reproduction?"[33] It is not likely, Strathern concludes, because
"the substantial and bodily part of the person will continue to be regarded
as constituted in his or her genetic make-up, and that is exactly what does
not depend on a reproductive tie with the parent." This means, finally,
that what we make of family and kinship will depend on how we as a society activate and value such relationships (as opposed to, say, valuing chil-

dren as techno-institutional products with their assemblages of designer genes).

Strathern's final statement concerning the paradoxical nature of the effects of the displacement of family and kinship and the separation of procreation from reproduction explains how they have mostly to do with knowledge, displacements of knowledge, although all of these displacements will have and do have material effects—especially in the bodies of the "cyborg babies" themselves. Strathern maintains, "On the one hand, knowledge is about biological process, and the more we know about the process the more (it would seem) we know about what makes kinship. On the other hand, while the procreative act is constitutive of kinship in a biogenetic sense, making that knowledge explicit makes more not less evident the fact that the social relationship is contingent."[34] But it is not just that the social relationship is shown to be contingent, for eliminating kinship as a proxy or symbol for biological process has the additional effect of showing that the fusion of the two was always a social, epistemic construct.

CONCLUSION

What, then, is the likely effect of procreative technologies for the future of lesbian-coparent families and other types of families? And what, more broadly speaking, might be said about the conditions that will herald the next generation of children living with lesbian parents? It could well be that more and more intending lesbian coparents will achieve conception by way of high-tech procreation, with all its trappings, including customized genetic selection made possible by the fact that sperm banks and assisted-reproduction organizations are functioning more like gene brokerages. The more intending lesbian parents participate in the techno-commodification of procreation, the more likely they are to experience the effects Strathern projected—and those they have already experienced as described in Chapter 7.[35]

But Strathern's analysis does not apply only to those parties who seek assistance in their procreative efforts, for culturally the effects are expressed primarily in and through knowledge—the dissemination of knowledge locally, societally, and cross-culturally. What we collectively know about reproductive biological process will come to have very little to do with what we know about family and kinship, and this knowledge will (and does) circulate throughout society, not just among those who are starting families via biotechnical assistance and experience it directly for themselves.[36] Still, as Strathern argues, and as Corrine Hayden has argued with respect to lesbian-coparent families per se, it is what people do with the knowledge of biological process and genetic relationship that will be important for the kinds of familial and kinship relations that are created and sustained.[37]

As we have seen, late-twentieth-century lesbian coparents take bio-genetic connection very seriously, partly because they must if they are to have any legal basis for claiming parental status and retaining custody of their children. Sociojuridical coercion then plays some part in this need to privilege biogenetic relatedness. On another strictly discursive level, however, as Hayden observed, the "asymmetry" introduced between lesbian coparents resulting from one partner's parturition and biogenetic connection to a child is seen by them as somehow fatal, even though by mothers' own actions they demonstrate that it is perfectly socially contingent. The practice of "tying in" the nonbiological mother via strategic use of surnames, feeding and infant care practices, second-parent adoption, choosing a donor whose physical features seem to match those of the non-biological mother—in all these ways and more, mothers make an equivalence out of what they perceive to be less legitimate bases of kin connection with what they perceive to be *the* foundation of kin connection: shared biogenetic substance. This is trading in symbols, where a quantity of symbolic practices compensates for, is rendered commensurate with, the supreme symbol of biogenetic substance.

Thus the more biogenetic substance and relatedness remain foundational to lesbian coparents' ways of thinking about what makes family and kinship, even when these are made explicit in the form of knowledge *about* the identity of the donor, for example, the greater the likelihood that Strathern's effects will play out for the coparents: increased and dispersed kinship (as mothers activate lines of connection dispersed among procreative actors, as we have already seen) and the paradoxical emphasis on a child as a unique genetic creature with diffuse ties to distant kin, all of which have little or nothing to do with his or her embodied genetic integrity and personal identity. The possibilities for creating designer children, via stratified reproduction in which the genetic material of those persons deemed endowed with the most desirable features will be increasingly in demand in the genetic marketplace, already exist and are manifested, for intending lesbian parents, in the menu of sperm offerings from which they make a selection. If one menu doesn't appeal, another set of offerings may be found on the Web. And so on.

On one hand, then, intentional lesbian-coparent families both manifest and use as a resource a degree of elevated consciousness that will be and is brought to bear on family formation and practice. The greater the explicitness of intention and knowledge in the creation of familial relationships, in turn the more likely are practices to be informed by values that are more explicit. As we have seen, through the public practices of lesbian-coparent families, no longer will it be possible for heterosexual procreation to be understood as singularly foundational to family and kinship. Inside these families, conscious attention to issues that had the potential to militate against egalitarian parenting and labor practices appeared to facilitate conflict resolution. Likewise, with mothers' families of origin—a term that is likely quickly to become anachronistic given Strathern's analysis—mothers actively sought and found ways to provide generational continuity amidst the threat of rupture along gay/straight lines. In short, it would seem that the deliberateness and consciousness with which lesbian-coparent families come into being have promising implications for the normalizing and transformative role these families play as they alter cultural understandings of kinship.

On the other hand, within a society that is ever-rationalizing, where knowledge and culture increasingly follow the commodity form, is it really possible to speak of a transformative, "conscious" kinship? The production of cyborg babies through biotechnically assisted procreation is indicative of the level at which a biomedical-industrial complex has colonized the lifeworld and replicates that lifeworld in its own image. As Sarah Franklin has noted, postmodern procreation, with its substitution of technology for nature as supplying "the facts of life," follows the "post-Enlightenment Baconian prerogative" in that "science fathers itself."[38] Is it not the case, then, that a more conscious kinship, an understanding of familial formation and relations that draws on more explicit knowledge, might more aptly and ominously be seen as one that grounds itself in the certain logic of rational science and the unlimited possibility offered by "free" markets? Conscious kinship might then, after all, be a euphemism for rationalized and commodified kinship—reification in Lukács's formulation.

If we take, however, the possibility that Strathern holds out for the place of practice in the definition of familial relations, through their internal and external practices lesbian-coparent families are positioned to undo much of what has been foundational to twentieth-century ways of thinking about kinship: the linkages of gender and power, heterosexuality and procreation, and heterosexuality and family. Perhaps most importantly, they provide a model of intimate connection that rigorously opposes the violence that is done both within and in the name of the patriarchal family.

The Study Design, Method, and Participants

I chose to study families headed by same-sex parents in the Bay Area primarily because this region boasts one of the highest concentrations of gay people in the United States, many of whom are politically organized and socially active, participate in diverse subcultures and communities, reside in geographically differentiated urban and nonurban locales, and choose to create and sustain families and kinship networks of their own. There are, of course, no reliable estimates available for either the Bay Area or, for that matter, the United States, enumerating people with gay, lesbian, bisexual, or otherwise queer sexual orientations because general probability surveys of household composition have routinely excluded questions concerning sexual orientation; because gay and lesbian couples may not legally marry, so that survey data concerning marital status have consistently excluded same-sex domestic partnerships; and because the question of how to define g/l/b/t identity for counting purposes continues to be the subject of epistemological debate and disagreement.[1] Scholars and researchers of gay culture and populations now generally acknowledge the problems associated with sampling gay and lesbian populations or determining their distribution along social or economic lines, as Donovan has summarized: "Students of homosexuality concede that identification is practically impossible due to the hidden nature of the homosexual population. Instead of drawing samples randomly from a complete universe, we are obliged to take them from the most accessible sources."[2]

For the same reasons, it is difficult to know how many families in the United States, and in the Bay Area, are headed by same-sex couples or how many children have gay, lesbian, or bisexual parents. A 1990 estimate has placed the number of children raised in lesbian or gay households in the United States between eight and ten million, while an earlier estimate placed the number at six million.[3] The former report also estimated that there are "approximately three million gay men and lesbians" who are parents, an estimate corresponding to those from separate studies around the same time, in which the number of lesbian mothers was estimated at 2 million, while the number of gay fathers was estimated as ranging from 1.1 to 2.3 million.[4] The number of lesbians who have children through donor insemination as opposed to those raising children from previous heterosexual relationships is also uncertain, but clinicians and researchers, including those who have conducted studies in the Bay Area, believe that it is "substantial and increasing."[5]

Clearly it is impossible to know exact figures for gay-parent families, and as some researchers believe, the level of social intolerance of homosexuality still results in an overall "negative net bias" of self-reports of gay experience and identity, suggesting that the estimates of gay-parent families may also be below the actual number.[6] These difficulties in ascertaining reliable population estimates directly affect whether the results of studies of smaller samples of gay-parent families, such as this one, may be understood as reflecting the general population of such families. Despite these limitations and difficulties, for this research I chose to interview and observe a sample of families in the larger Bay Area precisely because the Bay Area is home to so many gay and lesbian people who have created families by incorporating children into their lives, and the prospects for learning about their experience and lifeworlds through intensive interviewing and observation were considerable.

In the East Bay, for example, on any given day, one can step inside a supermarket and see a gay-father couple standing in the checkout line with their child. Or if one is strolling down the streets in Berkeley during the weekend, whether on Telegraph Avenue, the "gourmet ghetto" of North Berkeley, or the bustling sidewalk just outside the downtown YMCA, it is in fact almost difficult not to spot at least one lesbian couple enjoying some leisure time with their child or children. Of course, one must be sensitized to apprehending these relationships as same-sex-parent families, and this relates to another reason I chose the Bay Area for this study: even in the most socially tolerant, progressive, gay-populated regions, the viability of these families is assured only to the degree that they are recognized and may function with some measure of social support. Precisely because the Bay Area is one of the most progressive, gay-supportive regions in the United States, one would expect that conditions would be near-ideal for gay-parent families to thrive, as indeed many do. Given this favorable environment for gay-parent families, researchers may assess their practices and challenges, their interactions with others, their relationships with institutions, in short, their daily lives, in the *best* of circumstances. Documenting the process whereby a new, markedly non-normative familial form becomes instituted in the most favorable circumstances allows us to understand the ways in which these circumstances facilitate or impede its progress. In sum, the Bay Area offers a glimpse of the "ideal-typical" situation as a window onto the social change that may be effected by and through these families as they serve as the index or advance guard of postmodern kinship arrangements.

WHY LESBIAN-COPARENT FAMILIES?

If the experiences and practices of same-sex-parent families would provide insight into the dynamics that may be different or may change when the gender composition of parents is the same, gay-cofather families could provide valuable and rich information equal to that supplied by lesbian-comother families. However, I chose to study dual-mother families for a number of reasons.

My interest in studying families with same-sex parents first arose in relation to my feminist analysis of gender inequality as emanating from, and constituting relations within, families headed by heterosexual couples. I agreed with feminist theorists, sociologists, and other observers of Western modernity, especially with second-wave feminists whose critiques of the patriarchal family were particularly trenchant, that the sexual division of labor within heterosexual-parent nuclear families is a major source of gendered power. The question I initially posed to myself then went something like "Are families headed by same-sex parents more egalitarian?" For if gender could, in a sense, be "controlled for," inequality emanating from gendered relations between parents, especially their division of labor, might disappear, and the specific practices by which same-sex parents accomplished familial labor might be enormously instructive.

But since gendered divisions of labor within modern heterosexual-parent families have been tied to assumptions about the biological imperatives of a birth mother's caregiving and nurturing, assumptions that then have justified a whole range of sex-typed labor assignments between husbands and wives, it seemed crucial that same-sex-parent families in which at least one partner had given birth within the couple relationship be the focus. Thus I limited the selection criteria to dual-mother families in which at least one partner had given birth to a child that the couple had planned and were currently raising together in a residence they considered their home. Same-sex couples, men or women, who had originally adopted or fostered children, rather than those with biological children, presumably would not face the same types of family labor decisions raised by the maternity of one of the parents. Likewise, because conventional paternity has required considerably less psychological and emotional involvement (and at least historically has not been normatively associated with nurturance), gay-cofather families in which one partner had contributed genetic material as a biological parent would not quite capture the constellation of factors relevant to familial divisions of labor based on the parturition and breastfeeding capacity of one parent.[7]

Since not only the division of material labor but the psychodynamics and affective relations in (heterosexual parent) families all contribute to what was once called the phenomenology of families, gendered power and inequality arise in and through interpersonal familial relations that are structured by the gendered subject positions of parents and children, especially those of parents. But again, since those gendered subject positions themselves arise, in part, within affective, psychodynamic parent-child relations involving emotionally (and ideologically) charged biological processes, lesbian-coparent families in which one parent has given birth present a significant departure from the opposite-sex-parent model, since both parents have been "socialized" as women.[8]

For these reasons having to do with the sources of gender inequality within families, I chose to study lesbian-coparent, nuclear-type families and sought a purposive or "theoretical" sample that would not include couples with children from previous heterosexual relationships or marriages. Another, more pragmatic than conceptual reason I chose lesbian-coparent families was that at the time I initiated this project there were far fewer gay male couples creating families of their own, either through adoption or through contracting with women functioning as ovum donors and gestational service providers. In either case, these families still would not quite serve my theoretical sampling objectives.

Theoretically, studying lesbian-coparent families for ascertaining the egalitarian potential of a same-sex parental configuration would mean that a comparison with contemporary heterosexual-parent families was at least implicit in such an inquiry. However, with this research, I was not interested in making an explicit comparison, as would be relevant to a controlled, experimental or survey research study whereby results and outcomes could be assessed quantitatively or replicated scientifically, as is standard in the physical sciences and much of behavioral science. Rather, my approach proceeded first from what Michael Burawoy has referred to as the "hermeneutic" dimension of social science, with a complementary emphasis on the "scientific" or explanatory dimension. In his articulation of the value of participant observation as a "paradigmatic" way of studying the social world, Burawoy wrote:

> Situated at the crossroads of the humanities and natural sciences, social science combines both understanding and explanation. Understanding is achieved by virtual or actual participation in social situations, through a real or constructed dialogue between participant and observer, or what we call the *hermeneutic* dimension of social science. Explanation, on the other hand, is the achievement of an observer or outsider and concerns the dialogue between theory and data, or what we call the *scientific* dimension.[9]

With this research I sought to learn about and understand the everyday lifeworlds of lesbian couples and their children on their own terms, as they experienced and made sense of them, without explicit reference to heterosexual-parent families, though an implicit comparison obtains throughout. With this aim, and especially since so little is actually known or understood about this new family form, one wants to cast a wide net in terms of the type of data collected but also to engage with participants in a fairly intensive, intimate way.

At the same time, the question of egalitarianism central to the original goals of this inquiry necessitated an examination of these families' division of labor—a well-developed, "macro" concept already "operationalized" in various time-study approaches—as well as their interpersonal dynamics around parenting. Both of these latter issues relate to existing theories of gender inequality and the reproduction of gender (via the reproduction of mothering) and are therefore concerned with explanation in the sense of Burawoy's "scientific" dimension. It was important, then, that I study a sufficient number of families that would allow me to identify patterns I could analyze across the group as a whole, and to derive some provisional generalizations about them, but that would not compromise the rich, textured data that may be elicited in participant observation research. So, to achieve Buroway's twin objectives of understanding and explanation, I needed also to achieve some balance between breadth and depth with the data I collected.

Finally, studying lesbian-coparent families (as opposed to other same-sex-parent families) by interviews and engaged observation (as opposed to survey, questionnaire, or quantitative data research) suited my own feminist epistemological orientation and intellectual interests. Feminist researchers have thoroughly critiqued masculinist and other biases of the so-called objective or neutral stance of the researcher, claiming that any suspension of personal, political, or even scientific goals or views is not only not possible but not particularly desirable or intellectually ethical when the researcher engages interactively with living human subjects. My epistemological stance is to value and foreground the lived experience, thoughts, words, deeds, memories, and feelings of human beings, as these elements crucially constitute the substance of social life. The depths of psychic life that may find expression and play out between lovers in a conversation with a third party, or other instances of what Peter Winch called nondiscursive knowledge, are more likely to emerge in intensive, intimate interview and observational settings.[10]

For all of these reasons, from the narratives of women who were theoretically and structurally positioned to experience egalitarian relations in the families they had created, I wanted to learn whether something like this might in fact be occurring and to understand what it might mean for them. But since I also wanted to understand their experiences as families in the extrafamilial social contexts in which they conducted the business of their daily lives, the inquiry went beyond questions about "who did what" among their myriad household chores and child care responsibilities or how they might engage in nongendered parenting. Indeed, an entire world opens up when a researcher steps outside preconceived analytical frameworks and attempts to grasp the sensual fullness and surprise elements of lives marked by increasing cultural complexity and changing forms of consciousness.

METHOD: INTENSIVE
INTERVIEWS AND ENGAGED OBSERVATION

To interview and observe their families, I contacted the thirty-four lesbian-coparent couples who make up the Bay Area families in a number of ways. I located three couples initially through personal referrals and contacts. Four couples agreed to become participants when I met them at an event organized by a lesbian parent support group in San Francisco. Twenty-six couples became participants by responding to a letter I sent to an anonymous selection of clients from the database of a San Francisco sperm bank and insemination clinic. The clinic staff selected client names from couples self-identified as lesbian who had used any of its services at any time and for whom a live birth had resulted. Upon receiving the letter, the recipients contacted me if they wanted to participate in the study. One final couple joined the study after a couple from the sperm bank list told them about it.

Studies of gay and lesbian people, for all the reasons I stated earlier, tend to use "convenience" samples rather than random, probability samples, and participant self-selection poses certain limitations about how generalizable results may be. In this case, for example, those couples who were most eager to talk about their families and thus self-selected presumably could bias the results overall to reflect that enthusiasm. My use of different recruitment methods reduced this problem somewhat, but I also attempted to overcome it with the manner in which I represented my study to prospective participants and in the interview questions themselves. In my letter to the sperm bank clients, for example, I indicated that I was interested in learning about many aspects of their lives, particularly the changes in their couple and family lives once they had their children. Among the aspects I listed in the letter, I specifically mentioned household work, but nowhere did I allude to egalitarianism as an explicit topic. Also, many couples told me that they were interested in participating in the study upon reading my letter because they were assured (and relieved) that I did not have a deviance or pathological perspective of their families. My impression is that if there is a self-selection bias, that bias may be in favor of couples who were in fact *tired* of legitimating and proving the "wholesomeness" of their families and who perhaps felt that they could be more relaxed and candid in interviews where they were not being "judged." Indeed, most if not all of these couples had been or were going to be subjected to intense state scrutiny through a home study, which is necessary for second-parent adoptions. Also, even sympathetic researchers whose aim is to explicitly compare gay parenting to heterosexual parenting for purposes of establishing the fitness of gay parents necessarily proceed from a presumption of gay parental deficiency or pathology that then must be disproved.

Since a primary line of inquiry did involve parents' division of labor, I generated an open-ended interview guide in which the most specifically focused questions revolved around household chores, child care responsibilities, and paid work schedules and earnings. I placed (and asked) these division-of-labor questions about midway through the interview guide, for I structured the interviews such that couples could begin by narrating chronologically how they met, how and when they decided to start their families, and so on. In the interviews the division-of-labor questions thus grew out of a narrative of their lives together that they were already constructing, and in this way I tried to deemphasize this topic even while I asked the most pointed questions in this regard.[11]

Over nine months in 1994, I interviewed and observed these thirty-four couples with their children in their homes, which were located in counties as far south as Santa Cruz County, as far north as the Sonoma County wine country, and as far northeast as Yolo County near Sacramento. Of course, Silicon Valley's Santa Clara County to the southeast of the Bay Area was also well represented. But exactly half of all families in this study resided in either Alameda County or San Francisco County, which comprise Oakland and Berkeley in the East Bay and the City of San Francisco proper, respectively.

Formal interviews lasted from two to three hours and included both parents together, except for three couples with whom I was able to conduct both separate and joint interviews. These latter couples were those I became acquainted with earlier in the process, when I was exploring in preliminary fashion some of the topics I would later refine for the more systematic interviews. I spent more time with these families than I did with those I interviewed later. For example, I joined one of these families on two different excursions to a small, local public playground. I spent more time with three others as a result of having originally met them while they were picnicking at a family event in Golden Gate Park in the city. And although the later interviews and observation sessions became more routine, it was very common for couples to invite me to share meals with them, and in this way I was still able to get a sense of the rhythms and rituals of their domestic life and engage in fairly intimate conversation with them.

There are both limitations and advantages to interviewing couples together. Since I wanted to interview enough couples to reach a "saturation" point in the field, as it is called (whereby with each new family I interviewed I learned fewer and fewer "new" or different bits of information until I eventually stopped interviewing), I chose to conduct only joint interviews with each remaining couple.[12] My experience with the earlier couples in separate and joint interviews was that they spoke remarkably candidly in the joint interviews, expressing conflict and disagreement openly (as did the couples throughout), and I learned relatively little more from separate interviews, with the exception of one family.[13]

The limitations of interviewing couples together thus revolve around how candid individual partners feel they can be. On the other hand, intensive joint interviews and observation sessions can allow couples to relax into their usual, interpersonal dynamics, while the closeness and intensity of the situation do not permit them to stage a sustained front.[14] For the specific issue of household labor, in the interviews themselves I included questions that required factual answers. In this way, partners could affirm or correct their responses to questions concerning time spent on the job, commuting, feeding children, shopping, vacuuming, and so forth in each other's presence. By asking "how" questions I was able to elicit factual responses and thus attempt some triangulation among the type of responses I received and among the participants themselves.

THE FAMILIES: THEIR CHARACTERISTICS AS A GROUP

In accordance with my selection criteria, all but two of the couples I interviewed had planned, conceived, and were currently coparenting children in a nuclear-type family arrangement. One of the two couples whom I interviewed but did not include in this analysis had separated and were no longer living together as partners. Another couple, whom I have included here, came together after one of the partners had already had twins from a previous lesbian relationship that ended shortly after the twins were born, and the biological mother had solo-parented for about a year before meeting her current partner. But both mothers in this family considered themselves mutual coparents to the twins, and at the time of our interview they were trying to come up with money for the second-parent adoption in Santa Clara County (which had just raised its fees to the highest level among all the Bay Area counties), and the comother had plans to bear their next child.

All of the couples included in this study considered themselves partners for life, although one-third of them said they either "would not" or "probably would not" get married if same-sex marriage were to be legalized in the United States.[15] Yet with respect to legal guardianship and custody of children, all of the mothers I interviewed were very clear that nonbirth mothers should be legally recognized as second parents. Thus all of the couples residing in counties where second-parent adoptions had been granted to lesbian comothers had thought about, planned, initiated, or completed the adoption process at the time of our interview.

In terms of racial, ethnic, cultural, and national identity, of the sixty-eight women I interviewed, forty-six, or two-thirds, were of western European-Anglo descent; thirteen, or almost 20 percent, claimed a Jewish ethnic heritage; three women identified as Japanese or Japanese American; three identified as Latina; two claimed Filipino roots; and one mother hailed from Australia. The lack of racial-ethnic diversity in studies of gay or lesbian populations that use convenience samples is emblematic of the problems associated with convenience samples more generally. Since the pattern of convenience sampling among lesbian populations has been one in which whites persistently outnumber all other racial-ethnic categories, it is not clear whether this represents sampling bias or the actual proportions of racial-ethnic groups—including whites—within gay and lesbian communities. It is particularly difficult to assess racial-ethnic diversity among the population of gay and lesbian families. Conducting a very similar study among lesbian-coparent families in the New York metropolitan area, for example, Renate Reimann produced a sample in which 90 percent of the mothers were of Anglo-European descent. In terms of racial-ethnic diversity, then, the women in this study are similar to those in other studies of lesbians and lesbian mothers, and for most of them, their experiences must be understood as race-advantaged.[16]

Also, the women in this study, like those in other studies, including Reimann's, were high earning and well educated. In 1994, fifteen families had a combined family income of over $100,000 per year; twelve had a combined income between $50,000 and $100,000; and six families made less than $50,000 per year, with only three falling below the national median income for dual-earner families in the early 1990s.[17]

The two factors that most likely bias this sample, like Reimann's, in favor of higher earners have to do with geographic residence and the expense of starting families. First, families represented in this sample all live within a one-hundred-mile radius of San Francisco, where the environment is generally gay supportive, as I described at the beginning of this appendix, and where medically certified and legally protected alternative reproductive services for lesbians are available. Recruiting participants in the Bay Area meant that I necessarily drew people from the wealthiest counties in California: for example, the average per capita income for San Francisco County in 1993 was $32,777.[18] In fact, San Jose, Oakland, and San Francisco ranked third, fourteenth, and sixteenth, respectively, among all metropolitan regions in the United States for selected measures of income in 1989, according to a 1994 publication of annual metro, city, and county data in the United States.[19] Thus, for example, median U.S. household income in 1989 was $30,056, while for Silicon Valley's San Jose metropole that figure was $48,115; the figure for Oakland was $40,620 and for San Francisco was $40,493. To use another measure, 11.4 percent of San Jose's,

10.5 percent of San Francisco's, and 8.1 percent of Oakland's households reported incomes over $100,000. These figures begin to shed light on the high earnings of the mothers in this study.

Second, when we consider the costs involved with the procurement of sperm, insemination services, consulting, and other related services before the prospective birth mother even becomes pregnant, all of which is not, in any case, covered by insurance, lesbian couples are faced with *preconception* expenses running anywhere from $1,000 to $10,000, sometimes higher, depending on the number of attempts necessary to become pregnant and the difficulties encountered along the way. Even if couples are inseminating at home, if they wish to have donor semen screened for STDs (including HIV) and potency, they must employ the services of a licensed physician, sperm bank, or medical laboratory. The implication is that lower-income lesbians may bypass these institutional routes altogether (as was the practice before professional alternative insemination services became available to lesbians) and assume some risks that are otherwise much diminished by reproductive service organizations. It may be the case, then, that the more institutionalized, high-tech, and commercialized these services become, the more economic resources—even cultural capital—will be required for lesbian couples to legally and medically protect their family planning, and the less likely lower-income couples will be to have access to them.

About half of the women I interviewed said they worked in upper management or professional positions; one-third worked in semiprofessional, administrative, sales, or social service positions; and the remainder worked in skilled, unskilled, and service labor positions—a distribution of occupations similar to that found in a 1986 study by Lynch and Reilly. Four mothers were seeking full-time employment at the time of our interview. The high levels of education attained by the women I interviewed were also consistent with those noted by Lynch and Reilly: all of the women were high school graduates; ten had completed "some college" courses or had graduated from technical or certificate-granting schools; twenty-three (about 34 percent) had earned baccalaureate degrees; thirty (44 percent) held a master's degree; and twelve (about 18 percent) had obtained a medical, law, or other doctoral degree.

Seven families of the thirty-four had two children, and the remainder, thus far, had one child. In only one of the seven families with two children were both parents birth mothers. Twenty-one of the twenty-seven couples in families with single children were either thinking about or planning their second child. In twelve of these families, the partner who had not given birth the first time was planning to become pregnant with the second child, using the same donor as the first. Seven were planning for the birth mother of the first child to have their second child as well, and two families were considering adopting a second child. In all of the families, male children outnumbered female children by about three to two, for a total of twenty-three boys and seventeen girls, and at the time of the interview, the children ranged in age from three months to eight years. Also at the time of our interview, in 1994, their mothers ranged in age from twenty-eight to fifty-two years.

A TELLING OF THEIR LIVES: A NOTE
ON REPRESENTATION AND REALITY

In her important study of white women's ideas about race and racism, Ruth Frankenberg noted that "an interview is not the telling of a life." "An interview," she wrote, "is not, in any simple sense, the telling of a life so much as it is an incomplete story angled toward my questions and each woman's ever-changing sense of self and how the world works."[20] Frankenberg's remarks highlight the quality of an interview for the partiality, silences, and what the ethnomethodologist Harold Garfinkel called the "indexicality" of meaning embodied in it.[21] An interview may not be *the* telling of a life, but surely it is *a* telling of a life—one that occurs at a particular moment in time and that is indeed colored by the prompts of the interviewer, the mood and assumptions of the person or persons interviewed as well as those of the interviewer, and the particular meanings produced within the context of the interview and projected by all parties to it.

The nature of the "data" produced by an interview shifts depending on the procedures involved in transforming the data into text. The lived experience of people remembering, recounting, and voicing their past and present experience as well as their observations is necessarily technologized so as to be preserved and then represented by the researcher and author of the text. In this case, I conducted all of the interviews, listened carefully to all of the tapes countless times, transcribed them, and categorized the participants' words and accounts mostly according to the topics that now roughly make up each of Chapters 2 through 7. The "data" began as the embodied experience of persons sharing stories and opinions about their lives with a researcher who prompted these tellings and who guided their general direction. The status of the data at this point depended entirely on the trust established between myself and the women who so generously gave of their time, space, and emotional lives.

Here the power dynamics between researcher and subject(s) can become most acute, and I attempted to overcome some of this hierarchical, subject-object structural dynamic by adopting a dialogical mode of interaction with the participants, as so many proponents of feminist research methods and reflexive social science have advocated and debated.[22] As is standard research practice, I also assured participants that their identity would remain anonymous and confidential and that they could stop the interviews, turn off the tape recorder, or decline to respond to any of my promptings. No one actually exercised any of these latter options except for the children: the babies, toddlers, preschoolers, and school-aged kids who needed their mothers were quite indifferent to the demands of tape-recorded interview sessions and interrupted the interviews as their needs required! For the mothers, any hesitancy to respond almost always had to do with a judgment or opinion they wanted to offer but that concerned them, as they did not wish to offend some imagined audience. But rather than censoring themselves, they qualified their statements with such provisos as, "I know this is on tape but . . . " or "I think I can say this . . . "

I invited participants to ask questions of me, about the research, about my intentions—though it was not always easy to offer a satisfying account of what I was after, since, as with any long-term research project, often the key questions changed in my mind, or took different forms, and were revised the more time I spent "in the field." In *The Coming Crisis of Western Sociology,* in reference to reflexive sociology and what he took to be its historical mission, Alvin Gouldner wrote that it would "*transform* the sociologist, to penetrate deeply into his daily life and work, enriching them with new sensitivities, and to raise the sociologist's self-awareness to a new historical level."[23] In the interviews, especially during moments in which the direction of questioning was reversed and I had to reexamine and represent my motivations anew, I more fully apprehended how my personal assumptions and identifications were changing in ways similar to what

Gouldner advocated. I began this project believing (and representing to my informants) that this was mostly an intellectual, sociological question I was investigating, as indeed it was. But as I became more involved in the interview process, and as I met more people, I realized the extent to which unconscious motivations and elements were at stake. At first I had thought that my own experience of a rigidly patriarchal family was chief among the personal psychological reasons I chose to research dual-mother families, and this, again, was and is still true. As the research continued, I seriously examined my own heterosexual training and came round to the belief, first formalized by Freud, that most of us, including myself, are originally and always potentially polymorphous perverse, that is, sexually pluralistic—or, to use the term currently in fashion, "poly-amorous." Compulsory heterosexuality was a type of violence done to me and most people, against whatever inclinations to the contrary they and I might have had.

It was also during the moments of deep emotional exchange with my informants that I came to more fully appreciate the power dynamics of interrogative situations per se, even when the conversations are structured dialogically and with great care and respect for all participants.[24] During the interviews, I did not assume a neutral or disinterested stance, as some researchers have advocated, nor did I consciously misrepresent my stakes or interests in the project. Likewise, social scientists assume that research subjects in interviews do not willfully intend to misrepresent but that they do not want their words to be taken out of context or appropriated in a way that is disrespectful to them. But the procedures by which even the most respectful, meticulous, and sensitive researcher/writers turn interview data into text can do violence to the original context and meaning from which the data emerged. In his introduction to *Writing Culture,* James Clifford wrote: "The raw material of oral history consists not just in factual statements, but is pre-eminently an expression and representation of culture, and therefore includes not only literal narratives, but also the dimensions of memory, ideology and subconscious desires."[25]

In the writing of other people's (partial) telling of their lives, much happens to the raw material Clifford describes. In the end, what is the status of data first generated from a telling of a life by members and speakers of the group under study, then "captured" on tape, only to be transferred to another memory machine, where it is manipulated according to the priorities and categories of, in the last instance, the author of the text? To put it most directly, the data presented in the ethnographic chapters of this book consist in the representations of participants that I have analyzed, interpreted, edited, and re-represented. The debates concerning what might be called the verisimilitude of such data have to do with the degree to which representation and reality may be understood as one and the same thing, as mutually constitutive, or as completely absorbed within representation alone. Harold Garfinkel thought that accounts and reality are best understood as mutually constitutive of one another, while postmodernists view representations as social facts in and of themselves.[26]

My approach to this question as it concerns the narratives of the subjects of this book is to view their perceptions and subjective experience, as they have made sense of them and expressed them, as constituting a reality that is significant and palpable, for them, for the people who share their lives or interact with them, and, in turn, for sociohistorical process. The richness and fullness of that reality is necessarily subjected to a synthesizing process that transforms it into text. But textualization does not necessarily reify the living material embodied in interview narratives. For, as Frankenberg wrote, the interview narratives-as-texts themselves are "self-reflexive, and they confirm as well as contradict other accounts of the social world outside of the project. In a wider sense, they intersect with other local and global histories."[27]

The accounts I have analyzed in the ethnographic chapters do provide a window into a reality constituted by both contradictory and enduring sets of social relations, whose verisimilitude might be evaluated in relation to the broader social context I have presented in Chapter 1, and to the discourses about kinship and family, gender and sexuality, and power and inequality generated by and referenced within this work.

NOTES

INTRODUCTION

1. See Gilman ([1898] 1998) and Firestone (1970).

2. See, for example, Wittig's collection of essays *The Straight Mind* ([1982] 1992), the eponymous essay in particular; de Beauvoir's *The Second Sex* ([1952] 1989); and Le Guin's *Left Hand of Darkness* (1969).

3. See Connell (1995, 79).

4. For the view that families were headed toward equality in the United States and the United Kingdom, see Blumstein and Schwartz (1983) and Young and Willmott (1973). For a summary of the status of gender equality as mediated through the family in continental Europe, see Segal (1983).

5. Summarizing the results of several studies conducted in the 1980s, Faith Elliot (1996) wrote, "On the one hand, women believe that they should assume only those occupational commitments that mesh with their family responsibilities and search for work accordingly and, on the other hand, employers and male employees have clear ideas of what is appropriate work for women and structure their employment opportunities accordingly" (29). The gendered patterns of horizontal and vertical labor market segregation, as

Eliot also noted, result in women's concentration in lower-paying, typical "women's" occupations, which are something of an extension of their familial roles and are located at the lower ends of occupational hierarchies.

6.   Contemporary critics of fatherless families consider them a scourge and feel that social policies should be coercing men who abandon or neglect their families into taking responsibility for them. I address some of these concerns in Chapter 1.

7.   Even in Sweden, where welfare policies are generous and work-and-family balance is vigorously encouraged by the state, men who become fathers and who are specifically targeted for economic incentives to stay home with their children following a birth or adoption do not do so in significant numbers. See Hoem and Hoem (1988) for the policy initiatives undertaken by the Swedish government. Recently, however, a Norwegian report estimated that 70 percent of eligible fathers took advantage of the "fathers' quota": four weeks of paid leave offered to new fathers that is lost if fathers do not use it (Cancian 1999).

8.   This point is illuminated by Teresa de Lauretis's work on the connection between individual private fantasy and public filmic representations of reversals and transformations of desire, which effectively rework the oedipal drama. See especially chap. 3 in *The Practice of Love* (1994). Also, the point is not lost on the ideologists of the religious and political right, who seem to understand that those groups who control the discourse and iconography of the family will most influence public opinion in favor of their views, even when these bear little resemblance to the actual lived experiences of individuals and their families.

9.   Chodorow (1978, 38).

10.   In unfriendly, conservative analyses of the potential effect of gay parenting upon children's development and well-being, the issue of parents' sexuality occupies a central position. These analyses begin with the premise that same-sex love, intimacy, eroticism, and desire are socially undesirable and morally indefensible. Thus they treat gay parents' sexuality as inherently harmful to children, either because, in their view, all forms of gay parental sexual behavior and

intimacy are equivalent to (heterosexual) extramarital sexual behavior or because gay parents are more likely to raise gay children—which again, within a homophobic worldview, represents
an undesirable outcome. For these specific arguments about the
harm of gay parents' sexuality for their children, see Wardle (1997).

11. For the formulation of "the creation of a relevance" upon reproductive biology, see Connell (1987, 287); for the comment about
gender as a "particular historical response," see Connell (1987,
286). It should be noted that Connell clearly sees "historical response" as something that is continuously re-created through practice rather than mechanically carried forward or reproduced over
time. Rubin's (1975) well-known formulation may be found in her
"Traffic in Women" (165).

12. Connell (1987, 286–87).

13. See Rivers (1998, 18).

14. Of course, dual-father families with two male incomes would be
the most economically advantaged.

15. Connell (1987, 290).

16. I invite the reader to consult the appendix for my thoughts about
the subjective investments—personal, intellectual, and political—
I have brought to this project throughout the course of research
and writing.

17. Hochschild (1989).

I. THE EMERGENCE OF LESBIAN-
COPARENT FAMILIES IN POSTMODERN SOCIETY

1. By now the debates concerning the term that best characterizes the
contemporary epoch are well known. The signs vary in the stress
they place on the contemporary period's difference from or
identity with various Western conceptions of modernity. For example, *postmodern* (Harvey 1989; Jameson 1984, 1990; Lyotard
1984) signals a demonstrable rupture from modernity, while *radicalized modernity* (Giddens 1990) connotes an intensification of
modern processes and tendencies. Throughout this text I will use
postmodern not so much to signal a position in the debates as to use

a term that signifies identifiable, substantial change over the last three decades, especially, for present purposes and as I discuss in this chapter, in the way that sexuality, reproduction, family, and kinship have become disaggregated and reshuffled, producing new genres of "recombinant" families in a protean fashion that is itself a hallmark of the contemporary period.

2. See the excellent anthology edited by Alan Wolfe, *America at Century's End* (1991), for a wide-ranging set of essays, mostly by sociologists, that address changes in American social life and institutions—including the domains of intimacy and community—over the last half of the twentieth century.

3. Since the implications for the reproduction and/or maintenance of gender inequality are substantial, and in particular since gendered power relations within families have depended greatly on the ideological justification that the sexual division of labor is tied to biological imperatives, the choice of lesbian-coparent families in which at least one has given birth to the child/ren allows for the best assessment of the changes that might be effected by families headed by gay or lesbian parents. I explain this decision to focus on lesbian-coparent families (as opposed to gay-cofather families) in greater detail in the methodological appendix, which describes the study design, the methodology, and the families who participated in this research.

4. On the New Right ideological backlash and organizational infrastructure, see, for example, Francis (1982), Gordon and Hunter (1977), and Petchesky (1981).

5. Marshner (1982, 1). For a more overtly antifeminist manifesto penned in the late 1970s by perhaps the most powerful right-wing woman leader, Phyllis Schlafly, see *The Power of the Positive Woman* (1977). In addition to Gordon and Hunter (1977) and Petchesky (1981), for feminist and scholarly analyses of profamily and New Right ideology and organizing in the 1970s and 1980s, see Brady and Tedin (1976), Conover and Gray (1983), Harding (1981), and Klatch (1987). For a more centrist, if right-of-center, social science treatment of family politics at this time, see Berger and Berger (1983).

6.   In her collection of essays *In the Name of the Family* (1996), feminist sociologist Judith Stacey offers an in-depth cultural and political analysis of family values discourse in the 1990s. On the more recent debates about "fatherless families"—perhaps the more accurate term would be crisis of masculinity(ies)—see the collection *Lost Fathers* (1998), edited by Cynthia Daniels, which includes essays by scholars from various nonaligned positions in the academic version of family values politics. In that collection, Stacey's piece "Dada-ism in the 1990's: Getting Past Baby Talk about Fatherlessness" examines the claims that fatherless families cause a host of social problems, pointing out that the concept itself collapses a number of different parenting and familial constellations and that the conclusions drawn from "fatherlessness" analyses are too monolithic to be meaningful. This piece also assesses recent reassertions of neopatriarchal ideology by overt polemicists and social scientists alike.

7.   Lyotard (1984, xxiv).

8.   For this discussion my focus will primarily include North American and European "developed" countries for the reason that these societies constitute the culture context most relevant to and populated by "alternative" families.

9.   Castells (1997, 136).

10. Castells (1997, 138).

11. Castells (1997, 137).

12. See Dornbusch and Strober (1988); Elliot (1996); Stacey (1990); Thorne (1992).

13. Elliot (1996, 12).

14. See Chester (1985) and Scanzoni et al. (1989).

15. See Weeks (1986, 1989).

16. In the late spring and early summer months of 1999, almost daily jubilant reports of dramatically lower welfare rolls across the United States filled mainstream press pages and airwaves. The caseload decreases resulted from the 1996 repeal of the federal public assistance guarantees for needy families. Since single mothers and their children make up most of those now former welfare recipients—

America's "disappeared," as the late Senator Paul Wellstone termed them—it seems politicians and policy makers can now, with impunity if not public approval, legislatively engineer the erasure of families deemed undesirable and undeserving from public assistance and consciousness.

17. See Bravemann (1996) for an excellent review and discussion of the historiographies.

18. D'Emilio (1983), the chapter "Capitalism and Gay Identity."

19. See, for example, Haraven (1983) and Tilly and Scott (1975).

20. D'Emilio (1983, 104).

21. D'Emilio (1983, 104, 105).

22. Berman (1988, 54). See also Ferguson (1982).

23. See Faderman (1991, esp. 97, 148, 336 n. 20).

24. Faderman (1991, 74–75, 98).

25. See Harry (1983).

26. Connell (1987, 36).

27. Rich (1980); Altman (1979, 47).

28. Cited in Rivers (1998, 11).

29. Marcuse (1955); Lorde (1992).

30. See Benkov (1994).

31. Bozett (1987); Lewin (1993).

32. Lewin (1993, 192).

33. For a strongly worded critique of lesbian mothering as "redomestication" of lesbians, see Robson (1994). For Lewin's resistance-versus-assimilation formulation, see Lewin (1994).

34. Pollack and Vaughn (1987).

35. Polikoff (1987, 52, 54).

36. The high court remanded the case to the state, requiring state attorneys to show a compelling state interest in banning same-sex marriage. Because the case relied on Hawaii's constitutional guarantees under its Equal Rights Amendment, some of the arguments made by attorneys for the plaintiffs concerned gender-based equal rights, which in turn made reference to the antiracist 1967 decision in *Loving v. Virginia* overturning that state's anti-miscegenation

law. See Wolfson (1994–95) for the legal strategy used and a description of the case.

37. Polikoff (1993, 1549–50).

38. Hunter (1991); Wolfson (1994–95); Mohr (1994, 48); Kaplan (1997, 219).

39. This is very similar to Mohr's (1994) argument about marriage, in which he suggests that a truly "social marriage" would run counter to the principles that "legally define and create marriage and so preclude examination of it" (48, 49).

40. See Fineman (1995) for a critique of this emphasis on conjugality in U.S. family law and culture.

41. Among Weston's (1991) study participants, few were parents at the time, though many were considering becoming parents. As a theoretically informed, finely nuanced empirical study, Weston's work has done much to bring theory and practice together, considering carefully the opinions and family life representations of her informants. The fact that parenting was not particularly central in her analysis, or rather occupied one place among many dimensions of "chosen families," speaks to the pluralist, antihierarchical perspective informing it. Study of gay parenting seems crucial for understanding whether alternative models of reproduction, parenting, and adult-child familial life might qualitatively change the very social context and institutions by which normative (heteropatriarchal) sexuality and gender are currently produced and maintained. My project focus here, then, is quite different from that of Weston's study.

42. For studies on the North American and European emergence of gay-parent families that, taken together, signal a type of macro-level, collective movement, see, for example, Arnup (1995), Bozett (1987), Griffin and Mulholland (1997), and Patterson (1995).

43. I use this term advisedly, as the diversity of families ostensibly captured by it is immense. See Allen and Demo (1995) for an illuminating discussion of the difficulty involved in identifying a selection principle or criterion for defining gay families, a difficulty inherent in classificatory projects around sexuality, as the politics of sexual identity inevitably turns on such attempts at definition.

On this latter point, Sedgwick offered perhaps the paradigmatic queer-theoretical argument in her *Epistemology of the Closet* (1990).

44. The Boston Women's Health Book Collective's 1992 edition of *Our Bodies, Ourselves* describes the procedure. On the 1978 Feminist Self-Insemination Group, see Klein (1984).

45. For an excellent review of some of this history, see Agigian (1998), to whose research and insights presented in her doctoral dissertation on lesbians' use of alternative insemination I am greatly indebted. Agigian has argued that assisted-procreation organizations serving lesbians (e.g., the Sperm Bank of Oakland, Pacific Reproductive Services, and Rainbow Flag Health Services, all in the Bay Area), though their semen "banking" and insemination services are functionally no different from medicalized alternative insemination, may be distinguished as providing procreative options for women who wish to become mothers rather than as "treating" a medical problem, "infertility." According to their philosophy, there is nothing particularly medical about the service, but nonphysician insemination is illegal in twenty-three states in the United States, according to Agigian, and most facilities are therefore compelled to have a physician on site. Medicalized alternative insemination, however, as Agigian shows persuasively, is controlled predominantly by male physicians and the male-dominated medical establishment, which preside over the domain of "infertility treatment." The interest in promoting and preserving male-headed nuclear families is a key, if tacit, objective in medicalized alternative insemination.

46. Information management about the donor becomes an issue for lesbian-coparent families both when they are selecting a donor and later when their definitions of their own families change. Chapter 2 presents parents' practices and experiences with the first concern; Chapter 7, the second.

47. Judging from the wide range of ancillary services they provide, from information regarding their parenting support groups, breastfeeding classes, seminars, workshops, donor-recipient matching services (for parties who wish to be known and/or to coparent), and community outreach Web sites, these services stand in stark contrast to

the more clandestine medical model procedure for heterosexual married couples, where a woman is inseminated by a physician in her or his office using the anonymous sperm the physician has procured from a bank. In such situations, the "treatment" is for the husband's infertility, but because the husband will be the legal father, the use of purchased anonymous semen is kept secret, and thus is the husband's infertility and biological nonpaternity hidden.

48. Agigian (1998, 41).

49. In the United States, according to a 1988 Congressional report, one in five women who requested insemination in 1987 was refused, usually for nonmedical reasons (U.S. Congress 1988, 9, cited in Agigian 1998, 87). Three years earlier, an article in a leading infertility journal, *Journal of Reproductive Medicine*, had explored ethical considerations of inseminating "single women," a category under which the authors included lesbians. Titled "The Single Woman and Artificial Insemination by Donor," the article reported on physicians' objections to such inseminations, including the objection that a "a lesbian mother may influence the child to become homosexual" (Strong and Schinfeld 1984, cited in Agigian 1998). While the implicit judgment here is unequivocally eugenicist and homophobic, as it assumes that the creation of a baby who would grow up to be gay should be "feared and prevented," as Agigian observes, the "homophobia implicit in this stance is assumed to be so normative as to require no comment" (89). For other accounts of the discrimination women have experienced in their pursuit of medicalized aid, see Hornstein (1984) and Klein (1984).

50. Excellent discussions of the broader social implications and legal issues involved in legal gay marriage may be found in Hunter (1991), Sherman (1992), Stacey (1996), Sullivan (1997), and Wolfson (1994–95). As this book went to print, the prospects for a protracted political battle over same-sex marriage had become greater as a result of the Supreme Court's anti-antisodomy decision in 2003. Both progay marriage and antigay marriage sides are mobilizing and preparing strategy.

51. Hunter ([1991] 1997, 299).

52. Bartlett and Kennedy (1991, 2).

53. See the National Gay and Lesbian Task Force (NGLTF) Web site map "Specific Anti-Same-Sex Marriage Laws in the U.S." for the thirty-seven states with laws on the books as of November 2002, retrieved November 2002 from www.ngltf.org. For information concerning the status of marriage laws and pending legal cases, as well as historical data, see the Lambda Legal Web site at www .lambdalegal.org.

54. See Graff (1999) for an excellent review and analysis of the status of same-sex marriage in various countries, including the United States.

55. Jacobs (1999).

56. The options for families in these situations are coercive and impossible: couples may move to Canada, which is one of ten countries that grants immigration rights to same-sex partners; they are forced to split up when the one partner is deported; or they continue residing in their homes and communities under the constant threat of deportation (Jacobs 1999).

57. Feminist legal scholar Martha Fineman (1995) has argued for the abolition of formal definitions of family in favor of functional ones such as that used in this case. I discuss Fineman's proposal in detail in the concluding chapter of this book.

58. For fascinating discussions of the metaphysical issues involved in the negotiation of techno-parenthood, see Cussins (1998) and Novaes (1989).

59. There is an analogy to abortion provision that might be drawn here, in both the pre– and the post–*Roe v. Wade* situation in the United States, where women's actual access to abortion depended (and increasingly depends) on the social and moral commitment of "doctors of conscience" to provide the service and on women's resources to travel often considerable distance to the provider's clinic. Carole Joffe's book *Doctors of Conscience: The Struggle to Provide Abortion before and after* Roe v. Wade (1995) offers a definitive, compelling account of the stakes involved for those doctors who refused and continue to refuse to collaborate in the denial of women's reproductive freedom. To my knowledge there is no so-

cial study to date that examines the motivations of judges who defy popular and dominant legal opinion in recognizing the status and rights of gay parents. Nor, for that matter, have there been studies of pastors who risk sanction or excommunication for performing same-sex marriage rites, as the 1999 case of a United Methodist pastor brings to mind (Neibuhr 1999).

60. These are not necessarily "binding" precedents in the sense that judges hearing later cases are compelled to follow such rulings. The decisions made in these cases are extremely discretionary and cannot be taken as a categorical or legal fact that applies to all prospective petitioners. The source for these data is National Center for Lesbian Rights [NCLR], "Fact Sheet: Second Parent Adoption," retrieved September 2002 from www.nclrights.org/publications.

61. In the case of parental separation, courts throughout the country continue to have on their dockets cases where nonadoptive, nonbiological mothers who have separated from their lesbian partners have appealed for visitation rights (NCLR 1997b). Those decisions that have not been sealed and are thus a matter of public record have been mixed, depending on county and state recognition of second-parent adoptions. For example, some jurisdictions grant standing to nonbiological mothers to pursue claims for visitation apparently in lieu of granting second-parent adoptions, while others that do grant the latter often rule against nonbiological mothers who apparently have not availed themselves of the second-parent adoption option (NCLR 1997a).

As for extended-family members challenging lesbian comothers for custody of their children, it is not clear whether an adoptive comother's status and rights would be upheld when, for example, a biological mother can lose custody of her child to her own parents, as in the famous Sharon Bottoms case. In this highly publicized legal battle, which began in 1994, a Virginia trial court removed Sharon Bottoms's two-year-old son from her custody due to the judge's belief that her lesbianism was "immoral" and "illegal." In April 1995, the Virginia state supreme court upheld the ruling (Minter 1996). Here again we see the conservative (if not reactionary) element of the law vanquishing all progressive potential, and there is no reason to expect that second-parent adoptions, though the number of state and county jurisdictions granting them may be on the rise, will be upheld in the face of custody challenges from "blood" relatives who exploit the homophobia of judges.

As a potential harbinger of a future in which high-tech reproduction and family law innovation work in tandem to provide a form of legal prophylaxis for alternative families, in February 1999, a San Francisco lesbian couple intending to become parents did two things toward this end. With biomedical-technical assistance, they manipulated conception such that both women were biogenetically related to their child, and they secured a San Francisco county judge ruling that the prenatal parenting agreement they drew up that laid out their parenting intentions was legally valid and enforceable. Thus both expecting parents, before the birth of their child, had absolute standing and status as legal parents. I discuss in greater depth this way of legally defining families through such contracts in Chapter 8.

62.   See Harvard Law Review (1990, 139).

63.   It should be noted that this is one of the clearest examples of the medico-juridical system's interest in privileging and preserving the patriarchal family, as it actively discriminates against women choosing to create families without men.

2. BECOMING PARENTS: BABY MAKING
IN THE AGE OF ASSISTED PROCREATION

1.   See Meeker (1999) for an informative review of the archive. For a fascinating history of gay culture and politics in the Bay Area from the Gold Rush days to the mid-1990s, see Stryker and Van Buskirk (1996). This work makes excellent use of the materials from the archives of the Gay and Lesbian Historical Society, including a running visual history displaying numerous photographs, artifacts, artwork, and pamphlets complementary to the narrative.

2.   Stryker and Van Buskirk (1996, 26). Hay died in 2003, a few months before this book went to press.

3. See the chapter in Stryker and Van Buskirk (1996) on the first half of the 1990s as marking the turn to *queer* as the master signifier of non-normative sexualities and gender displays in cultural practice and politics (117–53). In particular, the authors argue that the 1990s witnessed the emergence of the first major transgender movements along with the more diffuse academic and grassroots deployments of "queer" as a unifying category.

4. All names of participants are pseudonyms, as are the names of anything that, in conjunction with other information, I thought might permit the identities of the participants to be discerned. All ages listed are participants' ages in 1994.

5. Franklin (1997) provides an analytically nuanced if ethnographically wrenching account of British women and couples undergoing in vitro fertilization (IVF), presenting their story of psychic and emotional anxiety around becoming pregnant—an anxiety that was itself produced by the ideology and procedures associated with IVF. Franklin refers to IVF as a "hope technology."

6. See Cussins (1998) for a nuanced account of the ways race, ethnicity, class, and kinship interpenetrate in heterosexual couples' constructions of their ontological status as parents when the "natural" procreative path is displaced and assisted by medical technology.

7. Twenty-seven couples had one child at the time of our interview. Of these, twenty-one were either thinking about or planning their second child. In twelve of these twenty-one families, the partner who had not given birth the first time was hoping to become pregnant with the second child, using the same donor as the first. Seven others were planning for the birth mother of the first child to have their second child as well, and two families were considering adopting a second child.

8. See Chapter 1.

9. Martin (1993, 24).

10. Note that we are not speaking here of agreements made within the purview of the law per se, a subject I discuss in the final chapter. Parents who choose known donors legally are not protected like those with anonymous donors, who are protected de facto as a group. Insofar as they draft individual contracts with known

donors, these contracts may or may not be adjudicated as binding or in their favor if challenged.

11. This is not to make a generalization that most couples in the population of lesbian-coparent families choose this option, since the Bay Area group is not representative. Nonetheless, given the multifaceted recruitment method, described in the appendix, it is notable that the preference for anonymity and the use of an institutional third party (sperm bank or physician) did not vary according to recruitment procedure.

12. This is precisely Eve Sedgwick's point about how ignorance functions socially and often gets deployed strategically. In her *Epistemology of the Closet* (1990), she recounts a case of "an ingenious and patiently instructive orchestration of ignorance" in which the U.S. Justice Department ruled, in June 1986, that an employer might freely fire persons with AIDS to the extent that the employer could claim to be ignorant of the medical fact that there was no known health danger in the workplace from the disease (5 n. 7).

13. Again, see Franklin (1997).

14. See Coltrane (1996), Risman and Johnson-Sumerford (1998), and Schwartz (1995).

3. BEING PARENTS: THE END OF
OEDIPUS AND THE EXPANSION OF INTIMACY

1. Some quantitative studies of lesbian mothers ascertained the status of biological or nonbiological mother before administering questionnaires and surveys (see, e.g., Patterson 1995). The research motivation for this was to gauge the involvement in child care and home care on the basis of traditional maternal versus nonmaternal "roles" as compared to heterosexual-parent roles. I felt that it was better to conduct the interviews "blind" to this status, as much could be learned about how mothers themselves defined the biological exigencies of early infant care when they were not preassigned to these statuses.

2. Connell (1987, 111–16, 112).

3. See Dinnerstein (1976), Benjamin (1988), and Mitchell (1974).

4.   For Chodorow's subsequent affirmations of her claims in *The Re-production of Mothering* (1978), see Chodorow (1994, 82–84) and Chodorow (1995, 522). On African American families and the ways in which Chodorow's theory cannot and does not account for them, see Collins (1992) and Carothers (1990). The character typology observation is from Connell (1987, 201). Adrienne Rich's observations are in "Compulsory Heterosexuality and Lesbian Existence" (1980, 9).

5.   Chodorow (1978, 30).

6.   In a 1994 review of studies of heterosexual-parent couples in which fathers assumed at least equal or greater primary care of infants, Radin noted the possible determining factors for fathers who chose to do this. Those factors, summarized from five studies, including two U.S. studies, one Australian, one Swedish, and one Israeli, included parents' perceptions of the fathering they had experienced as children. Men were either compensating for negative relationships with their own fathers or replicating what felt to them to have been positive ones, while women with "good" though somewhat distant relationships with their fathers had chosen male partners who wanted to be more involved parents. The other factors included coercive financial situations, such as men's unemployment, and voluntary arrangements, such as women's pursuit of careers and employment. Interestingly, the researchers studying the Israeli parenting arrangements found that children of Israeli fathers—who proved to be the most nurturing and the least "typically" masculinist and who treated sons and daughters the most similarly, as compared to other primary caregiving fathers, who still sex-typed their children—characterized daughters as more androgynous, while both daughters and sons exhibited empathetic orientations to others and what psychologists refer to as an "internal locus of control," or a sense of self-confidence, directedness, and competence. See Radin (1994). Radin, who conducted the studies of primary parenting fathers in the United States (and was a co-investigator in the Israeli study), hypothesized that the "partial" gender role reversal of fathers and mothers would shed light on whether gender *roles* or gender *identity* was the most salient fac-

tor in differential outcomes for children. Without defining gender roles or gender identity, her distinction seemed to turn on whether the "role" of primary caretaker mattered more than the gendered style of parenting (masculinist or feminine, translating roughly as stimulating but punitive and nurturing, respectively). The Israeli fathers seemed to demonstrate that men who engage in more nurturing, less typically masculinist parenting behavior provide the key ingredient for the most beneficial outcomes for children, whereas American primary-caregiving fathers were still viewed by children and parents alike as more "punitive" and strict than mothers. Thus the gender *identity* element, according to Radin's distinction, seems to be more important than the "role reversal." This, I think, begins to get at the crux of the matter concerning which aspects of gender determine an unequal division of parenting labor in heterosexual-parent families. I address this later in this chapter in the discussion of the absence of paternal masculinity in lesbian-coparent families.

7. Mothering is something that, theoretically, anyone can do in that it involves consistent, attentive, nonarbitrary caregiving. Thus Chodorow's and my usage of *mothering* is not intended to mean that it is something only women can do. See, in chap. 4 of Chodorow (1978), "A Note on Exclusive Mothering," 73–76. See also Ruddick (1989) for a social-philosophical treatment of how the extension of the principle of "maternal thinking" to wider social relations potentially provides an ethical basis for social change. The practice of shared primary caregiving by lesbian coparents was also reported by Reimann (1998) in a dissertation study very similar to the research I am presenting here.

8. Nina and Emily were the only parents I talked with who expressed this perspective that the biological mother had to get up without assistance from the other parent. As we saw in the earlier examples, there are any number of creative ways to break down the nursing experience into activities in which both partners can participate.

9. The other couples explained that they differentiated themselves (or were planning to) as "mama" and "mommy," or some variation. Other mothers deferred to whatever forms of address their children

decided worked best. Molly England and Jolene Tyson, the youngest couple among the Bay Area mothers at thirty and twenty-eight respectively, explained their open-ended perspective on how their daughter Sid would refer to them:

MOLLY: Right now I'm "mama," and she's "mom." It kind of sounds like that's what it is. And then we decided that when [Sid] gets to whatever age and she wants to call us something else, as long as it's not derogatory, that's fine. I mean, if she says, "I don't feel comfortable with this, I'd rather call you guys this," or whatever, we'll let her make that decision. We're not going to be . . .

JOLENE: Rigid.

10. The family-structural fact here is that the Bay Area families included only those in which there was only one birth mother at the time, or each partner's pregnancies had been or were going to be staggered. I know of some couples in which both partners gave birth around the same time. Presumably their "breastfeeding nexus" issues would be quite different, if they had any at all (other than the problem of two ultra-exhausted mothers).

11. In her doctoral dissertation research, Steckel (1985) compared the object relations of ten planned lesbian families and ten matched heterosexual-parent families to ascertain differences in the separation-individuation processes of the children. Her research design and participant recruitment method, however, established in advance the primacy of the birth mother over the nonbirth mother among the lesbian couples. Also, birth mothers in about half of the lesbian couples either were with different partners or had not sustained a lover relationship with the original parent-partner, leading the author to refer to these families as not "intact." Labeling the lesbian birth mothers and the heterosexual mothers as "the mothers" and the lesbian nonbirth mothers and fathers as "other than mothers," Steckel analytically, and I think not inconsequentially, ensured that the lesbian birth mothers retained the status of primary parent, comparable to the heterosexual mothers, even though

all of the lesbian nonbirth mothers participated in caregiving to a far greater degree than did most of the heterosexual fathers. Steckel's assumptions, and findings, thus differ from those presented here as a result of her a priori acceptance of the biological credential and primacy of the birth parent.

12. Chodorow (1978, 109).

13. Even with a sensitive, feminist father's strong desire to share primary parenting, a heterosexual mother in such circumstances may still feel protective or defensive of her maternal relationship with her child and may feel threatened by the father's "incursion" into her space. For an exceptionally candid, poignant examination of such a relationship, see Balbus (1998, esp. 188–89). Ehrensaft (1987) also demonstrated how heterosexual mothers, in the most optimum circumstances, feel threatened or uncomfortable with male partners' adoption of significant parenting activities and behavior.

14. Chodorow (1978, 109, 107).

15. See note 11.

16. See Steckel (1985, 91).

17. Mitchell (1996, 347).

18. Steckel (1985, 193).

19. Chodorow (1978, 218).

20. Steckel (1985, 109–10).

21. Steckel (1985, 191).

22. Chodorow (1978, 78).

23. Chodorow (1978, 70, 71).

24. Chodorow (1978, 121).

25. Chodorow (1978, 125).

26. Chodorow (1978, 113).

27. Chodorow (1978, 113, 176).

28. Freud ([1925] 1961).

29. Chodorow (1978, 176).

30. Chodorow (1978, 176).

31. This accords with other studies demonstrating that, compared to the exposure that children of single heterosexual mothers have to

adult men, children of lesbian mothers have more contact with young and adult men precisely because mothers want to provide children, especially boys, with "gender role models." Lesbian mothers are far more likely to seek out and sustain relationships with men than are single heterosexual mothers. The difference for lesbian mothers is that in these relationships they have no sexual stakes and no personal stakes other than friendship. See Kirkpatrick, Smith, and Roy (1981) and Kirkpatrick (1987) for the findings that lesbian mothers are more concerned than heterosexual mothers that their children have opportunities for good relationships with adult men and that lesbian mothers, especially those in committed couple relationships, reported having more adult male family friends and including male relatives more often in their children's activities than did heterosexual mothers. An interesting finding from one study of lesbian parents whose children were first born into and raised in heterosexual marriages was that the lesbian mothers had more contact with the fathers of their children than divorced heterosexual mothers did. See Golombok, Spencer, and Rutter (1983).

32.   The same could be said for heterosexual-parent families in which fathers are primary-caregiving parents *and* exhibit a consistent nurturing and empathic interpersonal style. Radin's (1994) review of studies of primary-caregiving fathers, especially the Israeli study, demonstrates that fathers doing primary caregiving—because they develop a regular, emotional relationship with children—offer a "realistic," embodied version of masculinity, in which oedipal and abstract masculine elements are marginal. In Chodorow's perspective, it is the absence of *personal* relationships with men as men, rather than as abstract paternal figures, that encourages (especially sons') idealization of masculinity, a fantasy process drawing on the most culturally available sources and representations of masculinity—usually in concert with paternal masculinity.

33.   Of course, it may not be taken for granted that either condition prevails always and everywhere for lesbian coparents. The burgeoning therapeutic literature and availability of services for lesbian- and gay-parent families affirm that, like the psychodynamics in any family or intimate group, those of the lesbian-coparent

family need care and attention. What I am suggesting, however, is that, according to the terms of psychoanalysis itself and on the evidence from empirical studies, lesbian-couple relationships tend to be more emotionally satisfying for both partners than are heterosexual relationships and that this has developmental consequences for children.

34.   Chodorow (1978, 218).

4. UNDOING THE GENDER DIVISION OF LABOR

1.   The distinction I am making here corresponds to the one Juliet Mitchell (1974) makes between production, reproduction, and psychodynamics as the primary analytic domains of family. Following Connell (1987) more closely than Mitchell, my use of the category "material labor" combines Mitchell's "production" and "reproduction," while "cathexis" is equivalent to her "psychodynamics."

2.   On women's lower social status as a result of their domestic caregiving, see, for example, Chafetz (1988). Hartmann (1981) rearticulated the Marxist-feminist perspective formulated by Engels (1972).

3.   Weitzman (1985) presented the startling statistic that after divorce women and children experience a decline in their standard of living of about 70 percent, while men experience an increase in theirs of about 40 percent. The validity of Weitzman's figures has since been refuted, but the general direction of the changes in standard of living for postdivorce women, children, and men remains accurate.

4.   See, for example, Hochschild (1989), Huber (1988), and Kamo (1988).

5.   On housework, see Baxter (1992) and Coleman (1988). Mainardi (1970), Hartmann (1981), and more recently Greer (1999) present especially critical analyses.

6.   See Coltrane (1989, 1990) and Risman and Johnson-Sumerford (1998).

7. Berardo, Shehan, and Leslie (1987), Berk (1985), Ferree (1991), and Hiller and Philliber (1986).

8. In the most recent study of egalitarian practices among heterosexual parent-couples, that of Risman and Johnson-Sumerford (1998), the recruitment procedure winnowed a field of seventy-five prospective family participants who indicated they share paid work and family work equitably down to a sample of fifteen families. The couples in these families were then analyzed as "postgender"—as they, according to the study's authors, both perceived that gender did not organize their allocation of breadwinning and family responsibilities and demonstrated in "actual" measures of household labor that this was a reasonable perception. For other studies in which heterosexual couples claimed and actively sought to be egalitarian, even though their efforts were not evaluated as entirely successful, see Blaisure and Allen (1995) and Ehrensaft (1987).

9. Some researchers and lesbian feminist writers have suggested that lesbian couple relations, in general, are more egalitarian than heterosexual relations, both theoretically and experientially. See, for example, Jay and Young (1979), Ettore (1980), Blumstein and Schwartz (1983), and Nichols (1987). Most forms of inequality or unequal power are associated with differences in "relative resources" and relationship involvement between partners (Caldwell and Peplau 1984) or with matters of intimacy, as Lynch and Reilly (1986) found. Some suggest that lesbian couples without children share work and household responsibilities relatively equitably due to their strong beliefs in fairness, as we heard from Natalie and Kim in the preceding chapter concerning their relationship with daughter Melanie; due to couples' perception of the desirability of independence, as Blumstein and Schwartz (1983) and Clunis and Green (1988), found; and due to relatively infrequent butch-femme "role playing" by couples when deciding domestic responsibilities—as found by Caldwell and Peplau (1984) and Lynch and Reilly (1986). Though Christopher Carrington (1995) found the gay male couples in his study falling into gendered roles in their family provisioning and entertaining practices, Lawrence Kurdek

(1993) found that compared to both gay male couples and hetero-sexual couples, partners in lesbian couples were equally likely to do household labor, following what he termed an "equality pattern," rather than a "balance pattern" (gay male couples) or a "segregation pattern" (heterosexual couples). Whether these patterns of labor equality among lesbian couples persist when children enter the picture, when couples become coparents in nuclear-type families, has remained largely unexplored until very recently. Valory Mitchell (1996) found in a group of thirty-two women with children under the age of ten that, along a measure of fifty-seven different household, decision-making, and child care tasks and time items, on average, "the distribution of work, influence and time was never more than one-quarter of a point from exact equality" (350). Renate Reimann (1998) reported similar findings in her group of twenty-five lesbian-coparent couples.

10. See Berk (1985, 165).

11. Berk (1985, 204).

12. I want to be clear about the distinction between the claim I am making here that no special significance is attached to the birth mother with respect to work and the claim I made in Chapters 2 and 3 that birth mothers seem to possess a bio-ontological "credential" compared to their partners. In the latter case, mothers did seem to impute a special, privileged status to birth mothers on the basis of their biological connection to children, much of which is culturally and legally derived and reinforced (except in cases like Baby M, where male and class privilege trump that of biological relatedness). Given that biological relatedness is generally privileged in our culture and thus may be taken up or deployed as meaningful by individuals for any number of situations, why should lesbian coparents see it—that is, maternity—as significant in their parent-child relations and not in their allocation of labor? In the former, parents accepted a definition of the birth mother as having a special relation to the child and, being fair-minded, attempted to compensate for this apparent disparity between partners by "tying in" the nonbirth mother. In the latter, a birth mother's "specialness" apparently did not translate into skills or knowledge that qualified

her over the nonbirth mother to do particular tasks. The distinction, therefore, seems to lie in "being" and "doing": that is, birth mothers *are* something special due to their maternity, and this must be compensated in the name of fairness between partners, while at the same time they needn't *do* anything special on account of who they *are* or their connection to children. Let us compare to the heterosexual case: mothers are in a sense special for giving birth, and they are emotionally "closer" to children, but this is "compensated for" by father's paternity. However, because of who she is and her relationship to the child, she is seen as uniquely qualified to do certain tasks.

13. Since I interviewed and observed parents and children together in all but three families, the question arises as to whether the mothers were not telling a happier story than I might have heard had I talked with each partner individually. As I describe in the appendix, to reduce the potential effects of this methodological limitation, in the interviews, in addition to open-ended questions where partners could describe their own views and feelings on the subject, I asked questions specifically requiring factual answers. Partners could affirm or correct their responses to questions concerning such items as time spent on the job, meal preparation, children's day care arrangements, shopping, and so forth in each other's presence.

14. Hochschild (1997).

15. This egalitarianism is similar to that reported by Blumstein and Schwartz's (1983) and Kurdek's (1993) lesbian couples who did not have children and Reimann's (1998) couples with children.

16. On work, men, and gender identity, see again Berk (1985), Hochschild (1989), Holmstrom (1972), and Rubin (1976).

17. See, for example, Coontz (1992) and May (1988).

18. Friedan (1963).

19. See, for example, Parsons and Bales (1955).

20. As I describe in the appendix, I interviewed more than once, and separately, three couples earlier in the course of the field research. Clara and Madeline and their children were one family with whom I spent more time and consequently learned of more inti-

mate details of their lives, especially from Madeline, as she and I and the children spent time together on two occasions without Clara.

21. Although Brenda was close to completing the second-parent adoption process, she was alone among nonbirth mothers in this study in her "campaign" to persuade Marilyn to let Michael have her surname. Not only was she unsuccessful, but the fact that she had to lobby Marilyn points to a departure from the practice of most couples of doing everything possible to "tie in" the nonbirth mother, and it indicates to me some deeper process of inequality at work.

22. See Hochschild (1989, 277–78).

23. I am reminded here of a grim story reported by a news organization in the early 1990s of a husband whose routine had not included taking his infant to day care but who, in "helping" his wife, agreed to do it one summer day and left the house on his way to work with baby secured in the back seat of his car. The husband ran errands and then went to work, forgetting about his baby in the back seat. With the summer heat having reached record levels, the consequence of his "forgetting" was tragic.

24. See Chapter 1 for a review of their positions on gay marriage and family. See also Stacey (1996, chap. 5).

25. Baca Zinn (1990) presents a compelling analysis of normative and deviant family structures in relation to racial identity.

5. TRUTH AND RECONCILIATION: FAMILIES OF ORIGIN COME AROUND AND COME OUT

1. See Weston (1991, 3).

2. Weston (1991, 73).

3. Weston's (1991) study did include some gay parents (nine of eighty people interviewed), some of whom were biological parents. In her chapter "Parenting in the Age of AIDS," she explored the reintroduction of the biogenetic element in gay "chosen" families via the lesbian baby boom and situated the implications as setting up a healthy tension in the blood/choice binary. *Genealogical grid* is a

term used by anthropologists for describing kinship systems that may be mapped in terms of biogenetic relations. The use of the genealogical grid as an underlying assumption and method for analyzing kinship systems has been rigorously critiqued among anthropologists: see, for example, Schneider (1968) and more recently feminists such as Yanagisako and Collier (1987) and Franklin (1997). These disciplinary critiques are crucially important for revealing how scholars themselves reflexively import biologically essentialist understandings into their analyses that often blind them to alternative interpretations. Biologically based understandings of family *are* hegemonic in U.S. society generally. My view is that this needs to be recognized while at the same time criticized and denaturalized.

4. See especially chaps. 3 and 4 in Weston (1991).

5. Weston (1991, 51).

6. Weston (1991, 62).

7. See Mendola (1980, 107).

8. Weston (1991, 196).

9. On the cultural significance of family photographs and their display, see Hirsch (1981) and David Halle's sociological analysis in his *Inside Culture* (1993, chap. 3).

10. On class and taste, see Bourdieu (1984).

11. On the concept of kinwork, see Stack and Burton (1993).

12. Penny had also worked on the "lesbian issue" by sending her parents materials on Parents and Friends of Lesbian and Gays (PFLAG), among other things, and had begun to view her parents as being "in process."

13. Weston (1991) suggests that the idea of gay people as set apart from the human species on account of a nonprocreative sexuality is deeply rooted in the culture and that gay kinship works against this species-difference essentialism by showing gay people as fully social persons "capable of laying claim to families" (204–5).

14. Weston (1991, 37–38).

15. Weston (1991) found among her study participants that parents and caregivers were typically seen as the emotional focus and con-

cern of their decision to come out. Siblings were seen to be "open" and easier to disclose sexual identity to, whereas biological parents, as well as caretakers in place of biological parents (i.e., social parents) were, in Weston's words, the "emotional epicenter" (53). Works with helpful psychological analyses of parents' relations with gay and lesbian children include Griffin, Wirth, and Wirth (1986), Muller (1987), Myers (1982), and Rafkin (1987).

16.   For an excellent review of the definitional issues revolving around gay kinship, see Allen and Demo (1995).

17.   Stacey (1996, 108).

18.   See note 3.

19.   The story of the wall of photos in Penny Cipolini's parents' home is significant here for what it conveys about the role of public exposure and revelation versus private acceptance of gay family members. The vestibule of the home is often defined as public space, since residents greet strangers, acquaintances, and friends there. The wall of photos in the Cipolini home in particular represented the domain where the private is made public, as Penny's partner Megan suggested: "So they [Penny's parents] do it [acknowledge baby Kathleen] privately. But they won't do it publicly. To a point of no pictures in their home. That's considered public."

20.   This analysis of relations with the families of origin is based on the representations of the lesbian mothers I interviewed and does not reflect the opinions or observations of the relatives themselves. Concerning the role of public acknowledgment in the construction of gay kinship, see Chapter 6. Chapter 6 provides more in-depth analyses of the ways in which disclosure decisions and strategies structure the manner in which lesbian-coparent families themselves "come into social existence" in the public sphere.

21.   See Chapters 1 and 8.

22.   In Griffin, Wirth, and Wirth's (1986) collection of interviews with parents who were members of PFLAG, several people alluded to fears of contagion, contamination, and taint early in their process of understanding their children's gayness. When parents viewed their children's gay sexuality as a problem, and a problem of the child, not of society—a typical initial and often enduring reac-

tion—the impulse to contain and occlude it was palpable. See especially chap. 5.

23. Weston (1991, 40).

24. Griffin, Wirth, and Wirth (1986, 106).

25. Weston (1991, 52).

26. Cooley ([1902] 1964, 184).

27. Lorca ([1929] 1998, 111).

28. Weston (1991, 53). That siblings are more automatically accepting and understanding than parents of a family member's gay identity is a perception yet to be documented but nonetheless widely held. In the case of Japanese American families, another perception prevails: that later generations of Japanese Americans—for example, the Sansei and Yonsei versus the Issei and Nissei—are more progressive and therefore more predisposed to accepting cultural innovations, including behavior transgressive of traditional familial and sexual norms. For excellent overviews of Japanese American family life, see Glenn (1986), Takagi (1994), and Yanagisako (1987).

6. BECOMING FAMILIAR IN THE COMMUNITY OF STRANGERS

1. Gubrium and Holstein (1990, 26–28); Pirandello (1922).

2. In this chapter I use the term *comother* interchangeably with *nonbirth mother* and *nonbiological mother* because this chapter analyzes in detail the social position of the nonbiological mother and I think it important that she be referred to with a more positive term than that which the negative prefix *non-* creates in the terms *nonbirth* and *nonbiological*. All of these terms are problematic in that they can be interpreted as reflecting a status hierarchy between parents: for example, by virtue of having given birth, the one partner is privileged in the birth/nonbirth or *bio-/nonbio-* distinction, and *co-*, as in *comother*, can suggest being not the main subject but an adjunct, rather than a more neutral meaning, as in *co-chair*. I use the terms in this chapter strictly to distinguish the two parents from each other to the extent that this distinction is relevant to the

issues under discussion. My usages are not intended to reflect a hierarchical view of the parents.

3. Miller (1988), quoted in Sedgwick (1990, 67).

4. See Stein (1997, chap. 5, esp. 133–34).

5. Stein (1997, p. 133).

6. Goffman (1963, 13).

7. Goffman (1963, 88).

8. Gubrium and Holstein (1990, 160).

9. Gubrium and Holstein (1990, 58–66).

10. Women in slave families in the American South adopted a kinship and survival practice referred to by anthropologists and historians as "fictive kin," in which girls and women who were not related to children by blood became second or "other" mothers when biological mothers were separated from children or otherwise could not care for them alone. See White (1985). Carol Stack used the term *fictive kin* to describe the designation of friends and non-blood-related people as kin among the families she wrote about in her pathbreaking 1974 ethnography of a black community in the early 1970s. Collins (1992) used *othermother* to refer to a woman fulfilling the primary mother role with children with whom she was blood kin but not the birth mother as presented in her research findings on African American mothers. The term *social parenthood* is used more and more to designate a wider variety of nonbiological relationships of care and nurturance of children. Weston's (1991) concept of chosen families is yet another way to blur the distinction of biological and social kin, especially with respect to gay and lesbian families. While all of these categories of fictive kin and social parenthood reflect similar cultural practices, lesbian co-mothers formalize their relationships with their children through second-parent adoptions (where this is possible) or through other mechanisms such as employee health benefits and through social interactions in which they become *real parents* rather than fictive kin in the sense described above.

11. See both Sedgwick (1990) and Sedgwick (1988, 102–24).

12. Segwick (1990, 8).

13. The research findings on attempted and successful suicides by gay and lesbian youth as compared to nongay youth are becoming more conclusive that homophobic oppression can now count as one of its consequences the self-inflicted loss of life among a generation who should be expected to be forming their own families in the new millennium. Instead, more and more are taking their own lives. See Remafedi (1994) for a summary of the research on gay and lesbian youth suicide.

14. Gubrium and Holstein (1990, 159).

15. Gillis (1996).

16. Gubrium and Holstein (1990, 159).

17. For an account of how recognition, as a Western idea, came to be understood as an affirmation of honor, then of dignity, then of the inherent equality of the entity so recognized, and how modern political philosophical projects ought to approach it, especially concerning issues of nationalism, identity, and culture, see Taylor (1994, 25–73).

18. Hochschild (1997), Gubrium and Holstein (1990, 160). See also Lasch (1979).

19. Schneider (1968).

7. THE STRUCTURE OF
DONOR-EXTENDED KINSHIP

1. See Strathern (1995); also Berger and Luckmann (1967).

2. Hess and Handel (1959, 43).

3. Kathy Fleck, Coordinator, Practice Committee, American Society for Reproductive Medicine, personal communication, May 3, 1998. *Catchment* refers to the geographic area in which gamete recipients reside for any given gamete donation facility. The number of ten families per donor per catchment area of eight hundred thousand is likely to increase to twenty-five as a matter of industry policy based upon a revised opinion of the American College of Obstetricians and Gynecologists (1997).

4. Some facilities in the recent past have discriminated against gay men from becoming (anonymous) donors with the rationale that their HIV risk was too great and could not be adequately or safely managed by the facilities.

5. Donors may be accepted into insemination programs upon an initial successful screening, but before their sperm is actually used they must be retested for HIV and STDs, and their own schedules must be coordinated with the needs of the facility managing the donor program and its clients.

6. *Ema* is Hebrew for *mommy*.

7. American College of Obstetricians and Gynecologists (1997).

8. For other critiques see, for example, Schneider (1984).

9. Teresa de Lauretis (1994, chap. 1) suggests something similar with respect to what she and others have referred to as Freud's "doctrinal inconsistencies."

10. Rubin preferred the terms *sex/gender system* and *political economy of sex* to *patriarchy* because she sought to encompass a broader class of phenomena and processes than the term *patriarchy* would indicate.

11. See also Strathern (1988).

12. Weiner (1976).

13. Engels (1972, 120).

14. It could be protested that references to premodern societies and kinship systems are anachronistic, yet many feminist scholars, including anthropologists, are revisiting theories of kinship in light of the development of new reproductive technologies, a subject I discuss more in the following chapter. For a fascinating discussion of the importance of the discovery of physiological paternity, not only for premodern peoples but for anthropologists attempting to understand it, see Franklin (1997, chap. 1).

15. Rothman (1989) lays out the importance of distinguishing rights in children as property resulting from the genetic contribution of the parent and rights resulting from social parenthood based upon nurture and care. She suggests that working mothers who hire nannies and other child care providers with whom children develop

close ties become more like fathers who have rights in children as a prerogative of having contributed genetic material (and of providing financially for the family).

16. See Cussins (1998).

17. Lévi-Strauss (1969, 479).

18. Cussins (1998).

19. The analogy of the distribution of sperm as the valued object of exchange is appropriate only in the context of lesbian rather than more general family formation via assisted reproduction. For example, one could argue that the commodification and traffic in oocytes in the creation of offspring mostly for white, middle-class, male-headed heterosexual families offsets any feminist gains from lesbian appropriations of sperm. For a compelling, dystopic view of such a scenario, see Raymond (1993) and Corea (1984).

8. THE THEORETICAL FUTURE
OF A CONSCIOUS FEMINIST KINSHIP

1. Agigian (1998).

2. Any doubt as to the interests—if not by intent, in effect—of continued male dominance in especially techno-scientific fields of knowledge may be laid to rest by reports such as that in the *New York Times* (Goldberg, 1999) in which the president and other high-ranking administrators at MIT admitted to pervasive "but unintentional" bias and discrimination against women (faculty) scientists in hiring, promotion, compensation, and distribution of research funds and lab resources.

3. Rubin (1975, 165).

4. For feminist theory on the identity/difference problem as it concerns work, see, for example, Scott (1990); as it concerns history and social movements, see Bacchi (1990); and as it concerns the subject of feminism itself, see hooks (1994), Riley (1988), Di Stefano (1990), and Young (1990).

5. Agigian (1998, 204).

6. Minow (1991, 274).

7. Neopatriarchal academic advocates include Blankenhorn (1995) and Popenoe (1996).

8. Polikoff (1996, 375).

9. Polikoff (1996, 393–94).

10. See Polikoff (1990).

11. Fineman (1995, 70, 71).

12. Fineman (1995, 8).

13. Fineman (1995, 227).

14. Fineman (1995, 230).

15. Fineman (1995, 230). See Ettelbrick (1989) for an argument against gay marriage from a left perspective. In *The Transformation of Intimacy* (1992) the British social theorist Anthony Giddens observed that because sexuality has become increasingly delinked from its historically reproductive and conventional functions and modes of expression, it is likely to continue on this path, especially as globalization promotes cross-cultural deregulation.

16. Fineman (1995, 231, 232).

17. Fineman (1995, 233).

18. It is here that Fineman's (1995) program *potentially* privileges biological mothers because the actually existing referent of the nurturing unit of mother-child as symbol is most often biological mothers and the children they have borne.

19. I am reminded here of a case reported in the news media in the late 1990s in which a black child had been in the care of a white, foster-parent couple because the child's biological mother had been drug addicted. The foster parents petitioned for permanent custody, but the judge ruled in favor of the biological mother, who was recovering from her addiction. Here biological maternity was decisive; but I imagine that in Fineman's (1995) conceptualization the biological mother would still retain custody, even though the child had been *cared* for by the white couple, because her desire to care for her child would have been recognized and supported by the state, with all the economic assistance and social services that would entail.

20. Fineman (1995, 232).

21. In 1994, the average number of attempts before successful conception, used as a fertility standard and reported to inseminating women by Bay Area assisted-reproduction organizations, was six months. Now women who do not get pregnant after only *two months* are considered to have entered the infertility zone, thus requiring additional intervention and technical services (personal communication with Laura Mamo, a researcher of Bay Area reproductive service organizations and their use by lesbians, May 2001). Whether or not inseminating lesbians choose to view the institutional standard as establishing the infertility line and therefore seek additional intervention and services (ranging from a switch in donors to intrauterine insemination to laparoscopy, superovulation, and in vitro fertilization), the movement of the infertility line from six months to two months is indicative of the general direction in which procreative services are advancing as they commercialize. See Mamo (2002).

22. See also Franklin (1997) on this.

23. See Petchesky (1987), Rapp (1990), Raymond (1993), and Taylor (1998).

24. Strathern (1995, 350).

25. Strathern (1995, 352).

26. Strathern (1995, 351).

27. Strathern (1995, 347).

28. See Williams (1998) for a necessary corrective to the sanitized view of the relationship between Jefferson and Hemings as based on love or affection, a view that has dominated public discussion on the topic and is notable only for the ideological work it performs in dressing up relations of domination. What has also gone unremarked in public discussions of this matter is the way in which scientific evidence of biogenetic relatedness, in the form of DNA testing, counts as the definitive proof, the definitive truth, of kinship reckoning.

29. Strathern (1995, 353).

30. Strathern (1995, 356).

31. Strathern (1995, 356–59).

32. Strathern (1995, 357).

33. Strathern (1995, 359).

34. Strathern (1995, 360). On cyborg babies, see Davis-Floyd and Dumit (1998).

35. In her dissertation research, Mamo (2002) interviewed a small number of lesbians planning to get pregnant; of twenty-six, seventeen had attempted demedicalized, at-home insemination first. Of these, four were able to conceive without "technical assistance," while thirteen went on to achieve pregnancies using more high-tech procedures and assistance.

36. The implications of Strathern's analysis have much to do with the cyborgification project initiated by Haraway (1985) as the basis of a new technohumanism or posthumanism.

37. See Hayden (1995).

38. Franklin (1995, 335).

APPENDIX. FAMILIES BY THE BAY: THE
STUDY DESIGN, METHOD, AND PARTICIPANTS

1. The difficulties in measuring the "gay" portion of any population are legion and complex. The exclusion of sexual orientation categories and the marital status problem on household and census survey questionnaires are emblematic of the deeper problems associated with the validity of what is being measured, and indeed with the epistemological assumptions of the researcher(s). For example, the debates about what sexual orientation even is, about whether sexuality and sexual object choice are biologically based, socially constructed, or some combination thereof, are unlikely to resolve to yield some fixed measurable trait, behavior, self-reported desire, or fantasy life. Futhermore, survey designs and data are often manipulated to favor a political agenda or personally desired outcome. For an excellent discussion of these issues and a review of Kinsey as well as studies from the late 1980s and early 1990s measuring a range of same-sex affectional and erotic behaviors, self-reported encounters, and identifications, see Gonsiorek and Weinrich (1991).

2. Donovan (1992, 28).

3. The estimate of between eight and ten million comes from Harvard Law Review (1990); the six million figure is from Schulenberg (1985).

4. Quote from Harvard Law Review (1990, 119); the estimate of two million lesbian mothers is from DiLapi (1989); the figure for gay fathers is from Bozett (1987).

5. See Allen and Demo (1995), Gottman (1990), and Patterson (1992).

6. On negative net bias, see Fay et al. (1989) and Gonsiorek and Weinrich (1991). Again, it must be emphasized that estimates are subject to criticism for their reliability and validity depending on the purpose for which the data are collected and presented. Gonsiorek and Weinrich (1991) describe how researchers with a conservative bias or even right-wing agenda tend to produce or report population estimates that are lower than those of other studies because lower estimates of the gay population will make the proportion of people with HIV or AIDS, for example, appear disproportionately homosexual. In fact, one conservative legal scholar, Lynn Wardle (1997), has done exactly this, seizing upon the lowest estimates of gay/lesbian/bisexual persons and/or behavior and then citing high morbidity and mortality rates for gay men and lesbians as an argument against gay parenting. Wardle cites a study on the negative effects of gay parenting on children by Paul Cameron, a conservative academic psychologist who was in fact expelled from the American Psychological Association on grounds of professional misconduct for reporting false results (Gonsiorek and Weinrich 1991).

7. For exactly these reasons, however, normative meanings of paternity stand to be radically reworked by gay-cofather families. See Lacquer (1992) for a feminist historical analysis and reading of paternity from the perspective of a heterosexual father.

8. On the phenomenological study of interior family processes, see Laing and Esterson (1964) and Laing (1965).

9. Burawoy (1991, 5).

10. See Winch (1958).

11. Instead of using the interviews to collect factual, socioeconomic, and demographic information from couples, before the interviews began I asked them about their income, employment, education, length of relationship, religious affiliation, racial, ethnic, cultural or national identity, age, and similar information about their children and their children's donors and recorded their answers on a data template I had created for this purpose.

12. Strauss and Corbin (1990), authors of *Basics of Qualitative Research: Grounded Theory Procedures and Techniques,* wrote that saturation occurs when "(1) no new or relevant data seem to emerge regarding a category; (2) the category development is dense, insofar as all of the paradigm elements are accounted for, along with variation and process; (3) the relationships between categories are well established and validated" (188).

13. This family had a history of one partner, the nonbiological parent, expressing sustained hostility toward the other partner as a result of the former's lack of interest in parenting at the outset. I learned of the depth of the painful feelings involved from a separate interview with the biological mother. Since this couple had adopted a rigid division of labor, typed according to birth mother/nonbirth mother, whereby the birth mother was completely economically dependent on her partner, I present their situation in detail in Chapter 4 and list them among the very few families with such strict divisions and practices.

14. See Allan (1980) concerning the staging of particular impressions by family research subjects.

15. This wariness toward de jure marriage suggests that even as contemporary gay and lesbian marriage campaigns attempt to divest marriage of heterosexual privilege, some still view it as either irrelevant to their lives or as serving conservative, heterosexist, or patriarchal interests.

16. See Reimann (1998).

17. Annual median income for all family types, according to a 1992 census data report, was $36,812, while that for dual-earner families was $45,779 (U.S. Bureau of the Census 1992).

18. See California State Department of Finance (1995).

19.   See Slater and Hall (1994, p. xxxiv).

20.   Frankenberg (1993, 41).

21.   Garfinkel (1967).

22.   Of course, the debates concerning the postmodern, textual turn in anthropology are related to calls for reflexivity in sociology, though they differ in their view of the location of power in the research process and the ontological status of the material generated by ethnographic/field research. See Bourdieu and Wacquant (1992, esp. 36–46) for a review of some of the formulations of reflexivity in sociology, including Gouldner's (1970) early call for a thorough accounting of the political position of academics and sociologists as occupying a structural position of power vis-à-vis research subjects. Clifford and Marcus may be understood as inaugurating the postmodern turn in anthropology by highlighting the "crisis of representation" and the politics of ethnographic research and writing in their well-known edited collection *Writing Culture* (1986). Feminists, of course, have criticized and responded to these works for their exclusion of feminist methodological insights. For these critiques as well as ongoing debates and developments in feminist research practice, see, for example, Balsamo (1990), Gordon (1988), Harding (1987), Mascia-Lees et al. (1989), Smith (1987), Stacey (1988), Visweswaran (1994), Wolf (1996), and Yeatman (1994).

23.   Gouldner (1970, 489).

24.   See Chapter 6 for comothers' stories of being questioned about who they are in relation to their children. The power dynamics of interrogation, even the most innocent questioning by well-meaning strangers, are illuminated by their experiences.

25.   Clifford (1986, 7).

26.   Garfinkel (1967); an example of the postmodernist position is Rabinow (1986).

27.   Frankenberg (1993, 42).

Agigian, Amy. 1998. "Contradictory Conceptions: Lesbian Alternative Insemination." Ph.D. diss., Brandeis University.

Allan, G. 1980. "A Note on Interviewing Spouses Together." *Journal of Marriage and the Family* 42:205–10.

Allen, Katherine R., and David H. Demo. 1995. "The Families of Lesbians and Gay Men: A New Frontier in Family Research." *Journal of Marriage and the Family* 57 (February): 111–27.

Altman, Dennis. 1979. *Coming out in the Seventies.* Sidney: Wild and Woolley.

American College of Obstetricians and Gynecologists. 1997. *Committee Opinion,* no. 192. Washington, D.C.: American College of Obstetricians and Gynecologists.

Arnup, Katherine, ed. 1995. *Lesbian Parenting.* Charlottetown, Canada: Gynergybooks.

Atwood, Margaret. 2003. *Oryx and Crake.* New York: Nan A. Talese.

Baca Zinn, Maxine. 1990. "Family, Feminism and Race in America." *Gender and Society* 4:68–92.

Bacchi, Carol Lee. 1990. *Same Difference: Feminism and Sexual Difference.* St. Leonards, Australia: Allen and Unwin.

Balbus, Issac. 1998. *Emotional Rescue: The Theory and Practice of a Feminist Father.* New York: Routledge.

Balsamo, Anne. 1990. "Rethinking Ethnography: A Work for the Feminist Imagination." *Studies in Symbolic Interaction* 11:45–57.

Barrett, Michele, and Mary McIntosh. 1982. *The Anti-Social Family.* London: Verso.

Bartlett, Katherine T., and Rosanne Kennedy. 1991. *Feminist Legal Theory: Readings in Law and Gender.* Boulder, Colo.: Westview Press.

Baxter, Janeen. 1992. "Power Attitudes and Time: The Domestic Division of Labor." *Journal of Comparative Family Studies* 23:165–82.

Bellah, R., R. Madsen, W. Sullivan, A. Swidler, and S. Tipton. 1985. *Habits of the Heart: Individualism and Commitment in American Life.* New York: Harper and Row.

Benjamin, Jessica. 1988. *The Bonds of Love: Psychoanalysis, Feminism, and the Problem of Domination.* New York: Pantheon Books.

Benkov, Laura. 1994. *Reinventing the Family.* New York: Crown.

Berardo, D., C. Shehan, and G. Leslie. 1987. "A Residue of Tradition: Jobs, Careers, and Spouse's Time in Housework." *Journal of Marriage and the Family* 49:381–90.

Berger, Brigitte, and Peter L. Berger. 1983. *The War over the Family.* Garden City, N.Y.: Anchor/Doubleday.

Berger, Peter L., and Thomas Luckmann. 1967. *The Social Construction of Reality.* Garden City, N.Y.: Anchor.

Berk, Sarah Fenstermaker. 1985. *The Gender Factory: The Apportionment of Work in American Households.* New York: Plenum Press.

Berke, Richard L. 1998. "Chasing the Polls on Gay Rights." *New York Times,* August 2, A3.

Berman, Marshall. 1988. *All That Is Solid Melts into Air: The Experience of Modernity.* New York: Penguin Books.

Blaisure, K. R., and K. R. Allen. 1995. "Feminists and the Ideology and Practice of Marital Equality." *Journal of Marriage and the Family* 57:5–19.

Blankenhorn, David. 1995. *Fatherless America: Confronting Our Most Urgent Social Problem.* New York: Basic Books.

Blumstein, Phillip, and Pepper Schwartz. 1983. *American Couples.* New York: William Morrow.

Bordo, Susan. 1993. *Unbearable Weight: Feminism, Western Culture and the Body.* Berkeley: University of California Press.

Boston Women's Health Book Collective. 1992. *Our Bodies, Ourselves.* New York: Simon and Schuster.

Bourdieu, Pierre. 1984. *Distinction: A Social Critique of the Judgement of Taste.* Cambridge, Mass.: Harvard University Press.

Bourdieu, Pierre, and Loïc J. D. Wacquant. 1992. *An Invitation to Reflexive Sociology*. Chicago: University of Chicago Press.

Bozett, Frederick W. 1987a. "Children of Gay Fathers." In *Gay and Lesbian Parents*, edited by F. Bozett, 39–57. New York: Praeger.

Bozett, Frederick W., ed. 1987b. *Gay and Lesbian Parents*. New York: Praeger.

Brady, David, and Kent Tedin. 1976. "Ladies in Pink: Religion and Political Ideology in the Anti-ERA Movement." *Social Science Quarterly* 56:564–75.

Bravemann, Scott. 1996. "Postmodernism and Queer Identities." In *Queer Theory/Sociology*, edited by Steven Seidman, 333–61. Cambridge, England: Blackwell Publishers.

Burawoy, Michael. 1991. Introduction to *Ethnography Unbound: Power and Resistance in the Modern Metropolis*. Berkeley: University of California Press.

Caldwell, M., and L. A. Peplau. 1984. "The Balance of Power in Lesbian Relationships." *Sex Roles* 10:587–99.

California State Department of Finance. 1995. *Financial and Economic Research*. Sacramento: California State Department of Finance.

Cancian, Francesca. 1999. "Gender, Citizenship, and the Work of Caring." *Footnotes*, July/August, 7.

Carothers, Suzanne C. 1990. "Catching Sense: Learning from Our Mothers to Be Black and Female." In *Uncertain Terms: Negotiating Gender in American Culture*, edited by Fay Ginsburg and Anna Lowenhaupt Tsing. Boston: Beacon Press.

Carrington, Christopher. 1995. "Feeding Lesbigay Families." Paper presented at the annual meeting of the Pacific Sociological Association, April, San Francisco.

Castells, Manuel. 1997. *The Power of Identity*. Boston: Blackwell.

Caudill, William. 1952. "Japanese-American Personality and Acculturation." *Genetic Psychology Monographs* 45:3–102.

Chafetz, Janet Saltzman. 1988. "The Gender Division of Labor and the Reproduction of Female Disadvantage: Toward an Integrated Theory." *Journal of Family Issues* 9:108–31.

Chester, Robert. 1985. "The Rise of the Neo-Conventional Family." *New Society* 9 (May): 185–88.

Chicago Tribune. 1996. "Most Disapprove of Gay Marriages, Adoption, Poll Says." August 19, 6N.

Chodorow, Nancy. 1978. *The Reproduction of Mothering*. Berkeley: University of California Press.

———. 1994. *Femininities, Masculinities, Sexualities.* Lexington: University Press of Kentucky.

———. 1995. "Gender as a Personal and Cultural Construction." *Signs* 20, no. 3:501–26.

Clifford, James. 1986. "Introduction: Partial Truths." In *Writing Culture: The Poetics and Politics of Ethnography,* edited by James Clifford and George E. Marcus, 1–26. Berkeley: University of California Press.

Clifford, James, and George E. Marcus, eds. 1986. *Writing Culture: The Poetics and Politics of Ethnography.* Berkeley: University of California Press.

Clunis, M., and G. D. Green. 1988. *Lesbian Couples.* Seattle, Wash.: Seal.

Coleman, Marion Tolbert. 1988. "The Division of Household Labor: Suggestions for Future Empirical Consideration and Theoretical Development." *Journal of Family Issues* 9:132–48.

Collins, Patricia Hill. 1992. "Black Women and Motherhood." In *Rethinking the Family: Some Feminist Questions,* edited by B. Thorne and M. Yalom, 215–45. Boston: Northeastern University Press.

Coltrane, Scott. 1989. "Household Labor and the Routine Production of Gender." *Social Problems* 36: 473–90.

———. 1990. "Birth Timing and the Division of Labor in Dual-Earner Families: Exploratory Findings and Suggestions for Future Research." *Journal of Family Issues* 11:157–81.

———. 1996. *Family Man: Fatherhood, Housework, and Gender Equity.* New York: Oxford University Press.

Connell, R. W. 1987. *Gender and Power.* Stanford, Calif.: Stanford University Press.

———. 1995. *Masculinities.* Berkeley: University of California Press.

Conover, Pamela Johnston, and Virginia Gray. 1983. *Feminism and the New Right: Conflict over the American Family.* New York: Praeger.

Cooley, Charles Horton. [1902] 1964. *Human Nature and the Social Order.* New York: Schocken Books.

Coontz, Stephanie. 1992. *The Way We Never Were: American Families and the Nostalgia Trap.* New York: Basic Books.

Corea, Genoveffa. 1984. "Egg Snatchers." In *Test-Tube Women: What Future for Motherhood?* edited by R. Arditti, R. Duelli Klein, and S. Minden, 37–51. London: Pandora Press.

Cussins, Charis. 1998. "Quit Sniveling Cryo-Baby; We'll Work out Which One's Your Mama." In *Cyborg Babies: From Techno-Sex to Techno-Tots,* edited by Robbie Davis-Floyd and Joseph Dumit. New York: Routledge.

Daniels, Cynthia. 1998. *Lost Fathers.* New York: St. Martin's Press.

Davis-Floyd, Robbie, and Joseph Dumit. 1998. *Cyborg Babies: From Techno-Sex to Techno-Tots.* New York: Routledge.

de Beauvoir, Simone. [1952] 1989. *The Second Sex.* New York: Vintage Books.

de Lauretis, Teresa. 1994. *The Practice of Love: Lesbian Sexuality and Perverse Desire.* Bloomington: Indiana University Press.

D'Emilio, John. 1983. *Sexual Politics, Sexual Communities: The Making of a Homosexual Minority in the United States, 1940–1970.* Chicago: University of Chicago Press.

DiLapi, E. 1989. "Lesbian Mothers and the Motherhood Hierarchy." *Journal of Homosexuality* 18, nos. 1–2:101–21.

Dinnerstein, Dorothy. 1976. *The Mermaid and the Minotaur.* New York: Harper and Row.

Di Stefano, Christine. 1990. "Dilemmas of Difference: Feminism, Modernity and Postmodernism." In *Feminism/Postmodernism,* edited by L. Nicholson, 63–82. New York: Routledge.

Donovan, J. 1992. "Homosexual, Gay and Lesbian: Defining the Words and Sampling the Populations." In *Gay and Lesbian Studies,* edited by H. Minton, 27–47. New York: Haworth Press.

Dornbusch, Sanford M., and Myra H. Strober, eds. 1988. *Feminism, Children and the New Families.* New York: Guilford Press.

Dworkin, Andrea. 1983. *Right-Wing Women.* New York: Coward-McCann.

Ehrensaft, Diane. 1987. *Parenting Together: Men and Women Sharing the Care of Their Children.* New York: Free Press.

Elliot, Faith Robertson. 1996. *Gender, Family and Society.* New York: St. Martin's Press.

Engels, Friedrich. 1972. *The Origin of the Family, Private Property and the State.* New York: International Publishers.

Ettlebrick, Paula L. 1989. "Since When Is Marriage a Path to Liberation?" *Out/Look: National Lesbian and Gay Quarterly,* no. 6 (Fall): 9, 14–17.

Ettore, E. M. 1980. *Lesbians, Women and Society.* Boston: Routledge and Kegan Paul.

Faderman, Lillian. 1991. *Odd Girls and Twilight Lovers.* New York: Penguin Books.

Falk, P. J. 1989. "Lesbian Mothers: Psychosocial Assumptions of Family Law." *American Psychologist* 44:941–47.

Fay, R. E., C. F. Turner, A. D. Klassen, and J. H. Gagnon. 1989. "Prevalence and Patterns of Same-Gender Sexual Contact among Men." *Science* 243:338–48.

Ferguson, Ann. 1982. "Patriarchy, Sexual Identity, and the Sexual Revolution." In *Feminist Theory: A Critique of Ideology*, edited by Nannerl O. Keohane, Michelle Z. Rosaldo, and Barbara C. Gelpi, 147–61. Chicago: University of Chicago Press.

Ferree, Myra Marx. 1991. "The Gender Division of Labor in Two-Earner Marriages: Dimensions of Variability and Change." *Journal of Family Issues* 12:158–80.

Fineman, Martha. 1995. *The Neutered Mother, the Sexual Family, and Other Twentieth Century Tragedies.* New York: Routledge.

Firestone, Shulamith. 1970. *The Dialectic of Sex.* New York: Bantam Books.

Francis, Samuel. 1982. "Message from MARs: The Social Politics of the New Right." In *The New Right Papers*, edited by Robert Whitaker. New York: St. Martin's Press.

Frankenberg, Ruth. 1993. *White Women, Race Matters: The Social Construction of Whiteness.* Minneapolis: University of Minnesota Press.

Franklin, Sarah. 1995. "Postmodern Procreation: A Cultural Account of Assisted Reproduction." In *Conceiving the New World Order*, edited by F. Ginsburg and R. Rapp, 323–45. Berkeley: University of California Press.

———. 1997. *Embodied Progress: A Cultural Account of Assisted Conception.* New York: Routledge.

Freud, Sigmund. [1925] 1961. "Some Psychical Consequences of the Anatomical Distinction between the Sexes." In *The Standard Edition of the Complete Psychological Works of Sigmund Freud*, vol. 19, edited and translated by James Strachey, 243–58. London: Hogarth Press.

Friedan, Betty. 1963. *The Feminine Mystique.* New York: Dell.

Gans, Herbert. 1991. Preface to *America at Century's End*, edited by Alan Wolfe. Berkeley: University of California Press.

Garfinkel, Harold. 1967. *Studies in Ethnomethodology.* Englewood Cliffs, N.J.: Prentice Hall.

Geertz, Clifford. 1973. "Thick Description: Toward an Interpretive Theory of Culture." In *The Interpretation of Cultures.* New York: Basic Books.

Gerson, Kathleen. 1985. *Hard Choices: How Women Decide about Work, Career, and Motherhood.* Berkeley: University of California Press.

Giddens, Anthony. 1990. *The Consequences of Modernity.* Stanford, Calif.: Stanford University Press.

———. 1992. *The Transformation of Intimacy.* Stanford, Calif.: Stanford University Press.

Gillis, John R. 1996. *A World of Their Own Making: Myth, Ritual, and the Quest for Family Values.* New York: Basic Books.

Gilman, Charlotte Perkins. [1898] 1998. *Women and Economics.* Mineola, N.Y.: Dover Publications.

Ginsburg, Faye, and Rayna Rapp, eds. 1998. *Conceiving the New World Order.* Berkeley: University of California Press.

Glaser, B., and A. L. Strauss. 1967. *The Discovery of Grounded Theory: Strategies for Qualitative Research.* Chicago: Aldine.

Glenn, Evelyn Nakano. 1986. *Issei, Nisei, War Bride: Three Generations of Japanese Women in Domestic Service.* Philadelphia: Temple University Press.

Goffman, Erving. 1963. *Stigma.* New York: Simon and Schuster.

Goldberg, Carey. 1999. "M.I.T. Admits Discrimination against Female Professors." *New York Times,* March 23, A1, A16.

Golombok, S., A. Spencer, and M. Rutter. 1983. "Children in Lesbian and Single-Parent Households: Psychosocial and Psychiatric Appraisal." *Journal of Child Psychology and Psychiatry* 24:551–72.

Gonsiorek, John C. 1991. "The Definition and Scope of Sexual Orientation." In *Homosexuality: Research Implications for Public Policy,* edited by John C. Gonsiorek and James Weinrich. Newbury Park, Calif.: Sage.

Gonsiorek, John C., and James D. Weinrich. 1991. "The Definition and Scope of Sexual Orientation." In *Homosexuality: Research Implications for Public Policy,* edited by John C. Gonsiorek and James Weinrich. Newbury Park, Calif.: Sage.

Gordon, Deborah. 1988. "Writing Culture, Writing Feminism: The Poetics and Politics of Experimental Ethnography." *Inscriptions* 3/4:1–7.

Gordon, Linda, and Allen Hunter. 1977. "Sex, Family and the New Right: Anti-Feminism as a Political Force." *Radical America* 11/12 (November 1977–February 1978): 9–25.

Gottman, J. S. 1990. "Children of Gay and Lesbian Parents." In *Homosexuality and Family Relations,* edited by F. W. Bozett and M. B. Sussman, 177–96. New York: Harrington Park.

Gouldner, Alvin. 1970. *The Coming Crisis in Western Sociology.* New York: Basic Books.

Graff, E. J. 1999. "Same Sex Spouses in Canada." *Nation,* July 12, 23–24.

Green, R. 1978. "Sexual Identity of 37 Children Raised by Homosexual or Transsexual Parents." *American Journal of Psychiatry* 135:692–97.

Green, R., J. B. Mandel, M. E. Hotvedt, J. Gray, and L. Smith. 1986. "Lesbian Mothers and Their Children: A Comparison with Solo Parent Heterosexual Mothers and Their Children." *Archives of Sexual Behavior* 15, no. 2:167–83.

Greer, Germaine. 1999. *The Whole Woman.* New York: Anchor Books.

Griffin, Carolyn W., M. Wirth, and A. Wirth, eds. 1986. *Beyond Acceptance: Parents of Lesbians and Gays Talk about Their Experiences.* New York: St. Martin's Press.

Griffin, Kate, and Lisa A. Mulholland, eds. 1997. *Lesbian Motherhood in Europe.* London: Cassell.

Gubrium, Jaber F., and James A. Holstein. 1990. *What Is Family?* Mountain View, Calif.: Mayfield Publishing.

Halle, David. 1993. "Portraits and Family Photographs: From the Promotion to the Submersion of Self." In *Inside Culture,* 87–118. Chicago: University of Chicago Press.

Haraven, Tamara. 1983. "Review Essay: Origins of the Modern Family in the United States." *Journal of Social History* 17:343.

Haraway, Donna. 1985. "A Manifesto for Cyborgs: Science, Technology, and Socialist Feminism in the 1980s." *Socialist Review* 15, no. 80:65–107.

———. 1988. "Situated Knowledges: The Science Question in Feminism and the Privilege of Partial Perspective." *Feminist Studies* 14 (Fall): 575–99.

Harding, Sandra, ed. 1987. *Feminism and Methodology: Social Science Issues.* Bloomington: Indiana University Press.

Harding, Susan. 1981. "Family Reform Movements: Recent Feminism and Its Opposition." *Feminist Studies* 7, no. 1:57–75.

Harlow, Holly J. 1996. "Paternalism without Paternity: Discrimination against Single Women Seeking Artificial Insemination by Donor." *Southern California Review of Law and Women's Studies* 6:173.

Harris, M. B., and P. H. Turner. 1985/1986. "Gay and Lesbian Parents." *Journal of Homosexuality* 12:101–13.

Harry, J. 1983. "Gay Male and Lesbian Relationships." In *Contemporary Families and Alternative Life Styles,* edited by E. D. Macklin and R. H. Rubin, 216–34. Beverly Hills, Calif.: Sage.

Hartmann, Heidi. 1981. "The Family as the Locus of Gender, Class, and Political Struggle: The Example of Housework." *Signs: Journal of Women in Culture and Society* 6:366–94.

Harvard Law Review. 1990. *Sexual Orientation and the Law.* Cambridge, Mass.: Harvard University Press.

Harvey, David. 1989. *The Condition of Postmodernity*. London: Blackwell.

Hayden, Corinne. 1995. "Gender, Genetics and Generation: Reformulating Biology in Lesbian Kinship." *Cultural Anthropology* 10, no. 1:41–63.

Hess, Robert D., and Gerald Handel. 1959. *Family Worlds*. Chicago: University of Chicago Press.

Hiller, D., and W. Philliber. 1986. "The Division of Labor in Contemporary Marriage: Expectations, Perceptions, and Performance." *Social Problems* 33:191–201.

Hirsch, Julia. 1981. *Family Photographs*. New York: Oxford University Press.

Hochschild, Arlie. 1989. *The Second Shift*. New York: Avon.

———. 1997. *The Time Bind: When Work Becomes Home and Home Becomes Work*. New York: Metropolitan Books.

Hoem, Britta A., and Jan M. Hoem. 1988. "The Swedish Family: Aspects of Contemporary Developments." *Journal of Family Issues* 9 (September):397–424.

Holmstrom, L. L. 1972. *The Two-Career Family*. Cambridge, Mass.: Schenkman.

hooks, bell. 1990. *Yearning: Race, Gender and Cultural Politics*. Boston: South End Press.

———. 1994. *Teaching to Transgress*. New York: Routledge.

Hornstein, Francie. 1984. "Children by Donor Insemination: A New Choice for Lesbians." In *Test Tube Women: What Future for Motherhood?* edited by R. Arditti, R. Duelli Klein, and S. Minden, 373–81. London: Pandora Press.

Huber, Joan. 1988. "A Theory of Family, Economy, and Gender." *Journal of Family Issues* 9:9–26.

Huggins, S. 1989. "A Comparative Study of Self-Esteem of Adolescent Children of Divorced Lesbian Mothers and Divorced Heterosexual Mothers." In *Homosexuality and the Family*, ed. F. W. Bozettt, 123–35. New York: Harrington Park Press.

Humphreys, L. 1972. *Out of the Closets: The Sociology of Homosexual Liberation*. Englewood Cliffs, N.J.: Prentice Hall.

Hunter, Nan D. 1991. "Marriage, Law, and Gender: A Feminist Inquiry." *Law and Sexuality* 1, no. 1:9–30.

———. [1991] 1997. "Sexual Dissent and the Family: The Sharon Kowalski Case." In *Reconstructing Gender: A Multicultural Anthology*, edited by E. Disch, 295–99. Mountain View, Calif.: Mayfield Publishing.

Ingraham, Chrys. 1996. "The Heterosexual Imaginary: Feminist Sociology and Theories of Gender." In *Queer Theory/Sociology*, edited by Steven Seidman, 169–93. Cambridge, England: Blackwell Publishers.

Jacobs, Andrew. 1999. "Gay Couples Are Divided by '96 Immigration Laws." *New York Times,* March 23, A25.

Jameson, Fredric. 1984. "Postmodernism, or the Cultural Logic of Late Capitalism." *New Left Review,* no. 146:53–93.

———. 1990. *Postmodernism, or the Cultural Logic of Late Capitalism.* Durham, N.C.: Duke University Press.

Jay, K., and A. Young. 1979. *The Gay Report: Lesbians and Gay Men Speak out about Several Experiences and Lifestyles.* New York: Summit Books.

Joffe, Carole. 1995. *Doctors of Conscience: The Struggle to Provide Abortion before and after* Roe v. Wade. Boston: Beacon Press.

Kamo, Yoshinori. 1988. "Determinants of Household Division of Labor: Resources, Power and Ideology." *Journal of Family Issues* 9:177–200.

Kantrowitz, Barbara. 1996. "Gay Families Come Out." *Newsweek,* November 4, 50.

Kaplan, Morris. 1997. *Sexual Justice: Democratic Citizenship and the Politics of Desire.* New York: Routledge.

Katz, Jonathan. 1976. *Gay American History.* New York: Crowell.

Keating, C. T. 1991. *Legacies: An Exploratory Study of Young Adult Children of Lesbians.* M.A. thesis, Smith College School for Social Work, Northampton, Mass.

Kirkpatrick, M. 1987. "Clinical Implications of Lesbian Mother Studies." *Journal of Homosexuality* 14:201–11.

Kirkpatrick, M., C. Smith, and R. Roy. 1981. "Lesbian Mothers and Their Children: A Comparative Survey." *American Journal of Orthopsychiatry* 5:545–51.

Klatch, Rebecca. 1987. *Women of the New Right.* Philadelphia: Temple University Press.

Klein, Renate Duelli. 1984. "Doing It Ourselves: Self-Insemination." In *Test Tube Women: What Future for Motherhood?* edited by R. Arditti, R. Duelli Klein, and S. Minden, 382–90. London: Pandora Press.

Kurdek, Lawrence. 1993. "The Allocation of Household Labor in Gay, Lesbian, and Heterosexual Married Couples." *Journal of Social Issues* 49:127–39.

Lacquer, Thomas. 1992. "The Facts of Fatherhood." In *Rethinking the Family: Some Feminist Questions,* edited by Barrie Thorne and Marilyn Yalom, 155–75. Boston: Northeastern University Press.

Laing, R. D. 1965. *The Divided Self.* New York: Penguin Books.

Laing, R. D., and Aaron Esterson. 1964. *Sanity, Madness and the Family.* London: Tavistock Publications.

Laird, Joan. 1993. "Lesbian and Gay Families." In *Normal Family Processes,* edited by F. Walsh, 282–328. New York: Guilford.

Lasch, Christopher. 1979. *Haven in a Heartless World.* New York: Basic Books.

Le Guin, Ursula. 1969. *The Left Hand of Darkness.* New York: Ace Books.

Lévi-Strauss, Claude. 1969. *The Elementary Structures of Kinship.* Boston: Beacon Press.

Lewin, Ellen. 1993. *Lesbian Mothers.* Ithaca, N.Y.: Cornell University Press.

———. 1994. "Negotiating Lesbian Motherhood: The Dialectics of Resistance and Accommodation." In *Mothering: Ideology, Experience and Agency,* edited by E. Nakano Glenn, G. Chang, and L. R. Forcey, 333–53. New York: Routledge.

———. 1998. *Recognizing Ourselves.* New York: Columbia University Press.

Lorca, Federico Garcia. [1929] 1998. "Letter to His Parents." Translated by Christopher Maurer. Reprinted in *Doubletake,* Summer, 110–11.

Lorde, Audre. 1992. "Uses of the Erotic: The Erotic as Power." In *Sister Outsider,* 53–59. New York: Quality Paperback Book Club.

Lynch, J., and M. E. Reilly. 1986. "Role Relationships: Lesbian Perspectives." *Journal of Homosexuality,* 12:53–69.

Lyotard, Jean Francois. 1984. *The Postmodern Condition: A Report on Knowledge.* Minneapolis: University of Minnesota Press.

MacKinnon, Catharine A. 1993. *Only Words.* Cambridge: Harvard University Press.

Mainardi, Pat. 1970. "The Politics of Housework." In *Sisterhood Is Powerful,* edited by Robin Morgan, 447–54. New York: Vintage Books.

Mamo, Laura. 2002. "Sexuality, Reproduction, and Biomedical Negotiations: An Analysis of Achieving Pregnancy in the Absence of Heterosexuality." Ph.D. diss., University of California, San Francisco.

Marcuse, Herbert. 1955. *Eros and Civilization.* Boston: Beacon Press.

Marshner, Connaught. 1982. *The New Traditional Woman.* Washington, D.C.: Free Congress Research and Education Foundation.

Martin, April. 1993. *The Lesbian and Gay Parenting Handbook: Creating and Raising Our Families.* New York: HarperCollins.

Mascia-Lees, E. Frances, P. Sharpe, and C. B. Cohen. 1989. "The Postmodernist Turn in Anthropology: Cautions from a Feminist Perspective." *Signs: Journal of Women in Culture and Society* 15, no. 1:7–33.

Mauss, Marcel. 1954. *The Gift: Forms and Functions of Exchange in Archaic Societies.* Translated by Ian Cunnison. London: Cohen and West.

May, Elaine. 1988. *Homeward Bound: American Families in the Cold War Era.* New York: Basic Books.

McClandlish, Barbara M. 1987. "Against All Odds: Lesbian Mother Family Dynamics." In *Gay and Lesbian Parents,* edited by F. W. Bozett, 23–36. New York: Praeger.

Meeker, Martin. 1999. "The Gay and Lesbian Historical Society of Northern California. Archives Review." *Journal of Gay, Lesbian, and Bisexual Identity* 4, no. 2:197–205.

Mendola, Mary. 1980. *The Mendola Report: A New Look at Gay Couples.* New York: Crown.

Miller, D. A. 1988. "Secret Subjects, Open Secrets." In *The Novel and the Police.* Berkeley: University of California Press

Miller, J. B. 1979. "Gay Fathers and Their Children." *Family Coordinator* 28:544–552.

Minow, Martha. 1991. "Redefining Families: Who's In and Who's Out?" *University of Colorado Law Review* 62, no. 2:269–85.

Minter, Shannon. 1996. "United States." In *Unspoken Rules: Sexual Orientation and Women's Human Rights,* edited by Rachel Rosenbloom, 209–22. New York: Cassell.

Mitchell, Juliet. 1971. *Woman's Estate.* New York: Pantheon Books.

———. 1974. *Psychoanalysis and Feminism.* New York: Vintage Books.

Mitchell, Valory. 1996. "Two Moms: Contribution of the Planned Lesbian Family to the Deconstruction of Gendered Parenting." In *Lesbians and Gays in Couples and Families,* edited by J. Laird and R.-J. Green, 343–57. San Francisco: Jossey-Bass Publishers.

Mohr, Richard. 1994. *A More Perfect Union: Why Straight America Must Stand up for Gay Rights.* Boston: Beacon Press.

Muller, Ann. 1987. *Parents Matter: Parents' Relationships with Lesbian Daughters and Gay Sons.* Tallahassee, Fla.: Naiad Press.

Myers, Michael F. 1982. "Counseling the Parents of Young Homosexual Male Patients." *Journal of Homosexuality* 7, no. 2/3:131–43.

National Center for Lesbian Rights. 1997a. *Second Parent Adoptions.* San Francisco.

———. 1997b. *Twentieth Anniversary Album: 1977–1997.* Current Docket: 12–14. San Francisco.

———. 2002. "Fact Sheet: Second Parent Adoption." Retrieved September 2002 from www.nclrights.org.

National Gay and Lesbian Task Force. 2002. "Specific Anti-Same-Sex Marriage Laws in the U.S." Retrieved November 2002 from www.ngltf.org.

Neibuhr, Gustav. 1999. "Methodist Pastor Faces Trial for Uniting 2 Men." *New York Times,* March 25, A18.

New York Times. 1998. "A Pattern of Abuse." August 8.

Nichols, Margaret. 1987. "Lesbian Sexuality: Issues and Developing Theory." In *Lesbian Psychologies,* edited by Boston Lesbian Psychologies Collective, 97–125. Chicago: University of Illinois Press.

Novaes, Simone B. 1989. "Giving, Receiving, and Repaying: Gamete Donors and Donor Policies in Reproductive Medicine." *International Journal of Technology Assessment in Health Care* 5:639–57.

Parsons, Talcott, and Robert F. Bales. 1955. *Family Socialization and Interaction Process.* New York: Free Press.

Patterson, Charlotte. 1991. "Children of the Lesbian Baby Boom: Behavioral Adjustment, Self-Concepts, and Sex-Role Identity." In *Lesbian and Gay Psychology: Theory, Research, and Clinical Applications,* edited by B. Greene and G. M. Herek, 156–75. Thousand Oaks, Calif.: Sage.

———. 1992. "Children of Lesbian and Gay Parents." *Child Development* 63:1025–42.

———. 1995. "Lesbian Mothers, Gay Fathers, and Their Children." In *Lesbian, Gay, and Bisexual Identities over the Lifespan: Psychological Perspectives,* edited by A. R. D'Augelli and L. J. Patterson, 262–90. New York: Oxford University Press.

Paul, J. P. 1986. "Growing up with a Gay, Lesbian or Bisexual Parent: An Exploratory Study of Experiences and Perceptions." Ph.D. diss., University of California, Berkeley.

Petchesky, Rosalind Pollack. 1981. "Antiabortion, Antifeminism and the Rise of the New Right." *Feminist Studies* 7 (Summer): 206–45.

———. 1987. "Foetal Images: The Power of Visual Culture in the Politics of Reproduction." In *Reproductive Technologies: Gender, Motherhood and Medicine,* edited by Michelle Stanworth, 57–80. Oxford, England: Polity Press.

Pirandello, Luigi. [1922] 1978. "Six Characters in Search of an Author." In *Twenty-Three Plays: An Introductory Anthology,* edited by O. Reinert and P. Arnott. Boston: Little, Brown.

Polikoff, Nancy. 1987. "Lesbians Choosing Children: The Personal Is Political." In *Politics of the Heart: A Lesbian Parenting Anthology,* edited by Sandra Pollack and Jeanne Vaughn, 47–65. Ithaca, N.Y.: Firebrand Books.

———. 1990. "This Child Does Have Two Mothers: Redefining Parenthood to

Meet the Needs of Children in Lesbian-Mother and Other Nontraditional Families." *Georgetown Law Journal* 78:459–575.

———. 1993. "We Will Get What We Ask For: Why Legalizing Gay and Lesbian Marriage Will Not 'Dismantle the Legal Structure of Gender in Every Marriage.' " *Virginia Law Review* 79:1535–50.

———. 1996. "The Deliberate Construction of Families without Fathers: Is It an Option for Lesbian and Heterosexual Mothers?" *Santa Clara Law Review* 36:375–94.

Pollack, Sandra, and Jeanne Vaughn, eds. 1987. *Politics of the Heart: A Lesbian Parenting Anthology.* Ithaca, NY: Firebrand Books.

Popenoe, David. 1996. *Life without Father.* New York: Martin Kessler Books.

Rabinow, Paul. 1986. "Representations Are Social Facts: Modernity and Post-Modernity in Anthropology." In *Writing Culture,* edited by James Clifford and George E. Marcus, 234–61. Berkeley: University of California Press.

Radin, Norma. 1988. "Primary Caregiving Fathers of Long Duration." In *Fatherhood Today: Men's Changing Role in the Family,* edited by Phyllis Bronstein and Carolyn Pape Cowan. New York: Wiley.

Rafkin, Louise. 1987. *Different Daughters: A Book by Mothers of Lesbians.* Pittsburgh, Pa.: Cleis Press.

Rapp, Rayna. 1990. "Constructing Amniocentesis: Maternal and Medical Discourses." In *Uncertain Terms: Negotiating Gender in American Culture,* edited by Faye Ginsburg and Anna Lowenhaupt Tsing, 28–42. Boston: Beacon Press.

Raymond, Janice. 1993. *Women as Wombs: Reproductive Technologies and the Battle over Women's Freedom.* New York: HarperCollins.

Rees, R. L. 1979. "A Comparison of Children of Lesbian and Single Heterosexual Mothers on Three Measures of Socialization." Ph.D. diss., California School of Professional Psychology, Berkeley.

Reimann, Renate. 1998. "Shared Parenting in a Changing World of Work: Lesbian Couples' Transition to Parenthood and Their Division of Labor." Ph.D. diss., Department of Sociology, CUNY Graduate School, New York.

Remafedi, Gary. 1994. *Death by Denial.* Boston: Alyson Publications.

Rich, Adrienne. 1980. "Compulsory Heterosexuality and Lesbian Existence." In *Powers of Desire,* edited by Ann Snitow, Christine Stansell, and Sharon Thompson, 177–205. New York: Monthly Review Press.

Riley, Denise. 1988. *Am I That Name? Feminism and the Category of "Women" in History.* New York: Macmillan.

Risman, Barbara, and D. Johnson-Sumerford. 1998. "Doing It Fairly: A Study of Postgender Marriages." *Journal of Marriage and the Family* 60:23–40.

Rivers, Daniel. 1998. "Radical Relations: Herbert Marcuse and the Historical Emergence of Gay/Lesbian Families in the United States." Paper presented at the conference "Legacies of Herbert Marcuse," November 6–7, University of California, Berkeley.

Robson, Ruthann. 1994. "Repositioning Lesbians in Legal Theory." *Signs: Journal of Women in Culture and Society* 19:975–96.

Rohrbach, J. B. 1992. "Lesbian Families: Clinical Issues and Theoretical Implications." *Professional Psychology: Research and Practice* 23:467–73.

Rothman, Barbara Katz. 1989. "Women as Fathers: Motherhood and Child Care under a Modified Patriarchy." *Gender and Society* 3 (March): 89–104.

Rubin, Gayle. 1975. "The Traffic in Women: Notes on the 'Political Economy' of Sex." In *Toward an Anthropology of Women,* edited by Rayna R. Reiter, 157–210. New York: Monthly Review Press.

Rubin, Lillian. 1976. *Worlds of Pain.* New York: Basic Books.

Ruddick, Sarah S. 1989. *Maternal Thinking.* Boston: Beacon Press.

Rupp, Leila J. 1980. "Imagine My Surprise: Women's Relationships in Historical Perspective." *Frontiers* 5 (Fall): 63–64.

Scanzoni, J., K. Polonko, J. Teachman, and L. Thompson. 1989. *The Sexual Bond: Rethinking Families and Close Relationships.* Newbury Park, Calif.: Sage.

Schlafly, Phyllis. 1977. *The Power of the Positive Woman.* New Rochelle, N.Y.: Arlington House.

Schneider, David M. 1968. *American Kinship: A Cultural Account.* Englewood Cliffs, N.J.: Prentice Hall.

———. 1984. *A Critique of the Study of Kinship.* Ann Arbor: University of Michigan Press.

Schulenberg, J. 1985. *Gay Parenting.* New York: Doubleday.

Schwartz, Pepper. 1995. *Peer Marriage: How Love between Equals Really Works.* New York: Free Press.

Scott, Joan W. 1990. "Deconstructing Equality-Versus-Difference." In *Conflicts in Feminism,* edited by Marianne Hirsch and Evelyn Fox Keller, 134–48. New York: Routledge.

Sedgwick, Eve Kosofsky. 1988. "Privilege of Unknowing." *Genders,* no. 1 (Spring): 102–24.

———. 1990. *Epistemology of the Closet.* Berkeley: University of California Press.

Seelye, Katharine. 1998. "House Votes Another Antigay Measure." *New York Times,* August 9, A11.

Segal, Lynne, ed. 1983. *What Is to Be Done about the Family?* Harmondsworth, England: Penguin Books.

Seidman, Steven, ed. 1996. Introduction to *Queer Theory/Sociology,* Cambridge, Mass.: Blackwell Publishers.

Sherman, Suzanne, ed. 1992. *Lesbian and Gay Marriage.* Philadelphia: Temple University Press.

Slater, Courtenay M., and George E. Hall, eds. 1994. *County and City Extra: Annual Metro, City and County Data Book.* Lanham, Md.: Berman Press.

Smith, Dorothy. 1987. "Women's Perspective as a Radical Critique of Sociology." In *Feminism and Methodology: Social Science Issues,* edited by S. Harding, 84–96. Bloomington: Indiana University Press.

———. 1993. "The Standard North American Family: SNAF as an Ideological Code." *Journal of Family Issues* 14:52–72.

Stacey, Judith. 1988. "Can There Be a Feminist Ethnography?" *Women's Studies International Forum* 11, no. 1:21–27.

———. 1990. *Brave New Families.* New York: Basic Books.

———. 1991. "Backward toward the Postmodern Family: Reflections on Gender, Kinship, and Class in the Silicon Valley." In *America at Century's End,* edited by Alan Wolfe. Berkeley: University of California Press.

———. 1996. *In the Name of the Family.* Boston: Beacon Press.

———. 1998. "Dada-ism in the 1990s: Getting Past Baby Talk about Fatherlessness." In *Lost Fathers,* edited by Cynthia Daniels. New York: St. Martin's Press.

Stack, Carol. 1974. *All Our Kin.* New York: Harper and Row.

Stack, Carol, and Linda M. Burton. 1993. "Kinscripts." *Journal of Comparative Family Studies* 24, no. 2:157–70.

Steckel, Ailsa. 1985. "Separation-Individuation in Children of Lesbian and Heterosexual Couples." Ph.D. diss., Wright Institute Graduate School, Berkeley, Calif.

Stein, Arlene. 1997. *Sex and Sensibility: Stories of a Lesbian Generation.* Berkeley: University of California Press.

Strathern, Marilyn. 1988. *The Gender of the Gift.* Berkeley: University of California Press.

———. 1995. "Displacing Knowledge: Technology and the Consequences for Kinship." In *Conceiving the New World Order,* edited by F. Ginsburg and R. Rapp, 346–64. Berkeley: University of California Press.

Strauss, A., and J. Corbin. 1990. *Basics of Qualitative Research: Grounded Theory Procedures and Techniques.* Newbury Park, Calif.: Sage.

Strong, C. 1984. "The Single Woman and Artificial Insemination by Donor." *Journal of Reproductive Medicine* 29:293–99.

Stryker, Susan, and James Van Buskirk. 1996. *Gay by the Bay: A History of Queer Culture in the San Francisco Bay Area.* San Francisco: Chronicle Books.

Stychin, Carl, and Didi Herman. 1995. Introduction to *Legal Inversions: Lesbians, Gay Men, and the Politics of Law,* edited by D. Herman and C. Stychin, ix–xv. Philadelphia: Temple University Press.

Sullivan, Andrew. 1998. "Going Down Screaming." *New York Times Magazine,* October 11, 46–51, 88–91.

———, ed. 1997. *Same-Sex Marriage: Pro and Con, a Reader.* New York: Vintage Books.

Takagi, Dana. 1994. "Japanese American Families." In *Minority Families in the United States: A Multicultural Perspective,* edited by R. Taylor, 146–63. Englewood Cliff, N.J.: Prentice Hall.

Tasker, Fiona, and Susan Golombok. 1995. "Adults Raised as Children in Lesbian Families." *American Journal of Orthopsychiatry* 65:203–15.

Taylor, Charles. 1994. "The Politics of Recognition." In *Multiculturalism: Examining the Politics of Recognition,* edited by Amy Gutman, 25–73. Princeton, N.J.: Princeton University Press.

Taylor, Janelle S. 1998. "Image of Contradiction: Obstetrical Ultrasound in American Culture." In *Reproducing Reproduction: Kinship, Power and Technological Innovation,* edited by Sarah Franklin and Helena Ragone, 15–45. Philadelphia: Temple University Press.

Thorne, Barrie. 1992. "Feminism and the Family: Two Decades of Thought." In *Rethinking the Family: Some Feminist Questions,* edited by Barrie Thorne and Marilyn Yalom, 3–30. Boston: Northeastern University Press.

Thorne, Barrie, and Marilyn Yalom, eds. 1992. *Rethinking the Family.* Boston: Northeastern University Press.

Tilly, Louise, and Joan W. Scott. 1975. Women's Work in Nineteenth Century Europe. *Comparative Studies in Society and History* 17:36–64.

U.S. Bureau of the Census. 1992. "Money Income of Households, Families, and Persons in the United States: 1991." *Current Population Reports,* Series P-60, No. 180.

U.S. Congress, Office of Technology Assessment. 1988. *Artificial Insemination: Practice in the United States: Summary of a 1987 Survey-Background Paper.* Washington, D.C.: Government Printing Office.

Visweswaran, Kamala. 1994. *Fictions of Feminist Ethnography.* Minneapolis: University of Minnesota Press.

Voeller, B. 1990. "Some Uses and Abuses of the Kinsey Scale." In *Homosexuality/Heterosexuality,* edited by Daniel P. McWhirter, Stephanie A. Sanders, and June M. Reinisch, 32–38. New York: Oxford University Press.

Wardle, Lynn D. 1997. "The Potential Impact of Homosexual Parenting on Children." *University of Illinois Law Review* 3:833–920.

Weeks, Jeffrey. 1977. *Coming Out: Homosexual Politics in Britain, from the Nineteenth Century to the Present.* London: Quartet Books.

———. 1986. *Sexuality.* London: Tavistock.

———. 1989. *Sex, Politics and Society: The Regulation of Sexuality Since 1800.* 2d ed. London: Longman.

Weiner, Annette. 1976. *Women of Value, Men of Renown: New Perspectives in Trobriand Exchange.* Austin: University of Texas Press.

Weitzman, Lenore J. 1985. *The Divorce Revolution.* New York: Free Press.

West, Candace, and Sarah Fenstermaker. 1993. "Power, Inequality, and the Accomplishment of Gender: An Ethnomethodological View." In *Theory on Gender/Feminism on Theory,* edited by Paula England, 151–73. New York: Aldine.

———. 1995. Doing Difference. *Gender and Society* 9:8–37.

West, Candace, and Don Zimmerman. 1987. "Doing Gender." *Gender and Society* 1:125–51.

Weston, Kath. 1991. *Families We Choose.* New York: Columbia University Press.

White, Deborah Gray. 1985. *Ar'n't I a Woman?* New York: Norton.

Wikler, Daniel, and Norma J. Wikler. 1991. "Turkey-Baster Babies: The Demedicalization of Artificial Insemination." *Milbank Quarterly* 69, no. 1:5–40.

Williams, Patricia J. 1998. "What's Love Got to Do with It?" *Nation,* November 23, 10.

Winch, Peter. 1958. *The Idea of Social Science.* London: Routledge and Kegan Paul.

Wittig, Monique. 1982 (1992). *The Straight Mind and Other Essays.* New York: Harvester Wheatsheaf.

Wolf, Diane, ed. 1996. *Feminist Dilemmas in Fieldwork.* Boulder, Colo.: Westview Press.

Wolfe, Alan. 1991. *America at Century's End.* Berkeley: University of California Press.

Wolfson, Evan. 1994–95. "Crossing the Threshold: Equal Marriage Rights for Lesbians and Gay Men and the Intra-Community Critique." *New York University Review of Law and Social Change* 21:567–615.

Yanagisako, Sylvia J. 1987. "Mixed Metaphors: Native and Anthropological Models of Gender and Kinship Domains." In *Gender and Kinship: Essays towards a Unified Analysis,* edited by Jane Collier and Sylvia J. Yanagisako, 86–118. Stanford, Calif.: Stanford University Press.

Yanagisako, Sylvia J., and Jane Collier. 1987. "Toward a Unified Analysis of Gender and Kinship." In *Gender and Kinship Theory,* edited by Jane Collier and Sylvia J. Yanagisako, 14–52. Stanford, Calif.: Stanford University Press.

Yeatman, Anna. 1994. "Postmodern Epistemological Politics and Social Science." In *Knowing the Difference: Feminist Perspectives in Epistemology,* edited by Kathleen Lennon and Margaret Whitford, 187–202. New York: Routledge.

Young, Iris Marion. 1990. "The Ideal of Community and the Politics of Difference." In *Feminism/Postmodernism,* edited by L. Nicholson, 300–323. New York: Routledge.

Young, Michael, and Peter Willmott. 1973. *The Symmetrical Family.* New York: Pantheon Books.

INDEX

abortion, 256n59

adoption, 64, 122, 128, 158, 243; biogenetic relatedness versus, 43–46; by gay male couples, 234, 235; open, 47; *see also* second-parent adoption

advocacy, 137–38

African Americans, 2, 5, 11, 274n10, 278n19; family values ideology on, 19; kinship ties of, 65; under slavery, 274n10

Agigian, Amy, 33, 211, 213–14, 254n45, 255n49

AIDS, *see* HIV/AIDS

Alaska, 35–36

Alcoholics Anonymous (A.A.), 90

alternative procreative service organizations, 33–34

Altman, Dennis, 26

Alton, Sarah (pseudonym), 60–61, 99–100, 173

American College of Obstetricians and Gynecologists, 201, 275n3

American Psychological Association, 281n6

amniocentesis, 222

anonymous donors, 53–54, 259n10, 260n11; agreement to release identity of, 193–94; availability of, 192–93; extended relations with, 200–205, 207–10, 224; gay men as, 276n4

Anti-Social Family, The (Barrett and McIntosh), 173

antisodomy laws, 1, 26–27, 255n50

artificial insemination by donor (AID), *see* donor insemination

assimilation, resistance versus, 28–30, 122

assisted-reproduction technologies, 3, 10–11, 16, 42, 213, 277n19, 279n21; availability of, 241; cost of, 242; kinship and, 276n14; legal implications of, 37, 214; social implications of, 220–29; *see also* donor insemination

attachment, relations of, 8–9, 64

Atwood, Margaret, 10

Australia, 36, 261n6

authority, distribution of, 8–9

Avedon, Tori (pseudonym), 187–88

Baby M. surrogacy case, 37, 268n12

Baehr v. Lewin (1993), 29

Barrett, Michelle, 173–74

Bartlett, Katherine, 35

Basics of Qualitative Research (Strauss and Corbin), 282n12

Beauvoir, Simone de, 3

Belgium, 36

Benjamin, Jessica, 65

Berk, Sarah, 98, 101

Beyond Acceptance (Griffin, Wirth, and Wirth), 152

biogenetic relatedness, 43–46, 228, 268n12, 270n3, 276n15; compensation for, in shared primary caregiving, 67, 75, 78; with donors,

biogenetic relatedness *(continued)*
195–98, 200, 202–5, 208, 210, 224; with family of origin, 125, 128, 131, 133–35, 137, 138, 146, 156; kinship and, 224–26, 279n28; legal privileging of, 216; names and, 117–18; sociofamilial identity and, 159–60
birthing classes, 183
bisexuality, 25, 231, 232
blacks, *see* African Americans
Blumstein, Philip, 267n9
Bottoms, Sharon, 257n61
Bowen, Angeline (pseudonym), 58–59, 181
Bowers v. Hardwick (1986), 26–27
Bozett, Frederick, 27
Brazil, 36
breastfeeding, 68–72, 74–76, 262n8, 263n10; sociofamilial identity and, 165, 183–85
Bryant, Anita, 19
Burawoy, Michael, 235, 236

Caldwell, M., 267n9
California, second-parent adoptions in, 37–38
Callahan, Marcy (pseudonym), 147, 149
Cameron, Paul, 281n6
Canada, 1, 36, 256n56
caretaking relationships, definition of family based on, 215, 216, 219–20
Carlton, Sharon (pseudonym), 67–68, 101–3, 107, 148
Carrington, Christopher, 267n9
Castells, Manuel, 20–23
cathexis, 9, 64–65, 86, 266n1; socioaffective, 158
Catholics, 127, 136
Cavner, Shannon (pseudonym), 54–57, 120–23, 187
Chaucer, Diane (pseudonym), 46, 48, 133–35
Chester, Robert, 22
child-care arrangements, 101, 102, 105, 106, 121
Chinese Americans, 105, 202–3
Chodorow, Nancy, 7, 65–66, 78, 80, 82, 84, 87–89, 262n7, 265n32
Choosing Children (film), 31
chosen families, 30–32, 253n41, 270n3, 274n10
Christians, fundamentalist, 132, 143
Cipolini, Penny (pseudonym), 129–31, 135–38, 163–64, 183–85, 271n12, 272n19
class background, 131, 137; allocation of labor and, 102–11; caregiving activities and, 76–77; family values rhetoric and, 123; upward mobility from, 136

Clifford, James, 245, 283n22
Clinton, Bill, 29
Clunis, M., 267n9
Cohen, Eliza (pseudonym), 42, 177, 195–96, 200
Collins, Jill (pseudonym), 47, 57, 83, 90, 106–11
Collins, Patricia Hill, 274n10
Coming Crisis of Western Sociology, The (Gouldner), 244
coming out, 131, 153; of grandparents to extended family and friends, 147–49, 151, 152, 154; to family of origin, 125–26, 139, 145, 155, 272n15; in workplace, 186–88
Connell, R. W., 4, 7, 8, 10, 26, 27, 65, 249n11, 266n1
consanguinity, 209; inadvertent, 201; *see also* biogenetic relatedness
conscious kinship, 229–30
contraceptives, 221
convenience sampling, 237–38, 240–41
conversions, postbaby, 129–38
Cooley, Charles Horton, 153, 156
Corbin, J., 282n12
Covington, Bobbie and Mindy (pseudonym), 93–95, 97–98
culture wars, 17
Cussins, Charis, 210, 259n6
custody, 278n19; gender-neutral policy on, 216–17; kinship and, 38, 257n61
Czech Republic, 36

Dalton, Natalie (pseudonym), 73–75, 198–200, 267n9
Damon, Linda (pseudonym), 167, 171, 178–79
day care, 101, 102, 121, 123; familism in, 175–77; on-site, 108
Defense of Marriage Act (DOMA; 1996), 29, 34, 36–37
deindustrialization, 41
de Lauretis, Teresa, 248n8, 276n9
"Deliberate Construction of Families without Fathers, The" (Polikoff), 215
D'Emilio, John, 24–25
Democratic Party, 18
Denmark, 36
descriptive practice, 157
designer children, 228–29
Dialectic of Sex, The (Firestone), 3
Digital Queers, 41
Dinnerstein, Dorothy, 65

disclosure strategies, comother, 164–73, 182; full, 165–68; partial, 168–71; passing as birth mother, 171–73

"Displacing Knowledge" (Strathern), 222

divorce, 21, 266n3; custody policy and, 216

DNA, shared, *see* biogenic relatedness

doctor appointments: familism and, 177–78; shared responsibility for, 103–4

Doctors of Conscience (Joffe), 256n59

donor insemination, 10, 18, 32, 42–45, 113, 133, 137, 221, 232, 243, 255n49; cost of, 242; designer children through, 228–29; family of origin and, 146; fertility industry standards for, 201, 221–22, 275n3, 279n21; HIV and, 276nn4, 5; kinship networks and, 15–16, 190–210; paternity claims and, 38; selection of donors, 47–49, 254n46 (*see also* anonymous donors; known donors); sperm management in, 54–59; woman-controlled, 32–34, 254nn45, 47, 280n35

Donovan, J., 231

dual-income families, 241; equitable allocation of labor in, 97–111; heterosexual, 96–97

Duncan, Nora (pseudonym), 47, 57, 106–11

educational attainment, 242

Ehrensaft, Diane, 264n13

Elementary Structures of Kinship, The (Lévi-Strauss), 205

Elliott, Faith, 247n5

empathic regard, 152

endogamy, 209–10

Engels, Dana (pseudonym), 58–59, 181

Engels, Friedrich, 96, 208–9, 266n2

England, *see* United Kingdom

England, Molly (pseudonym), 76–78, 263n9

Epistemology of the Closet (Sedgwick), 260n12

Equal Rights Amendment (ERA), 19

Eros and Civilization (Marcuse), 27

ethnicity, invocation of, 140, 142

exogamy, 206, 207, 209–10

extended families, 146; coming out by grandparents to, 147–49, 151, 152, 154; disavowal by, 138; of donors, 198, 200, 202

Faderman, Lillian, 25

families of origin, 14–15, 124–56, 229, 272n22, 273n28; denunciation by, 138–44; of donors, 192, 194, 197–99, 224; postbaby conversions of, 129–38, 142; redefinition of, 145–52; rejec-tion by, 28, 125–27; response to arrival of grandchildren of, 127–29; shame in, 151–56

Families We Choose (Weston), 30

familism, 173–89; in group settings, 183–85; in institutional settings, 175–81; in public space, 181–82; in workplace, 185–88

family law, 34–39, 213–20

family values, politics of, 18–20, 23, 174, 251; adoption of, by "Rozzie and Harriet" couples, 121–23

Family World (Hess and Handel), 191

Feminine Mystique, The (Friedan), 111

feminism, 2–5, 26, 233, 267n9; jurisprudence and, 213–20; lesbian separatist, 131; Marxist, 96; object relations theory and, 64–65, 87–88; procreative services and, 32–33; research techniques and, 236; right-wing mobilization against, 18, 19, 173–74

Feminist Self-Insemination Group, 32

fictive kin, 274n10

Fierer, Marlene (pseudonym), 90

Filipino Americans, 240

financial management, responsibility for, 106, 116

Fineman, Martha, 215–20, 256n57, 278nn18, 19

Finland, 36

Firestone, Shulamith, 3

flexibly defined fatherhood, 195–99

food-mother/fun-mother distinction, 70–77

France, 36

Frank, Resa (pseudonym), 51–52, 160, 177, 196–200

Frankenberg, Ruth, 243

Franklin, Sarah, 229, 259n5

Frantz, Kristen (pseudonym), 90, 150–51

Freud, Sigmund, 6, 8, 64–65, 89, 206–7, 245

Friedan, Betty, 111

functional definition of family, 214, 215, 256n57

functionalist theory, gender in, 112

fundamentalism, 132, 143

Garfinkel, Harold, 243, 246

Gay and Lesbian Historical Society of Northern California, 40–41, 258n1

gay identity, emergence of, 24–28

gay men, 231, 237, 267n9; caretaking relationships of, legal protection for, 219; cofather families of, 232–34, 249, 250; as donors, 198–200, 276n4; families of origin of, 124, 126–27; reproductive technologies and, 221; "species difference" attributed to, 140; suicides of, 275n13

gender identity, 11, 14, 91–92; familial mechanisms in, 64–66; labor allocation and, 99–100, 110
genealogical grid, 270n3
genetic incest, 201
genetic screening and counseling, 179–80, 222
Georgia, antisodomy law in, 26
Germany, 36
Gerson, Kathleen, 97
Giddens, Anthony, 218, 278n15
Gillis, John, 174
Gilman, Charlotte Perkins, 3, 4
globalization, 17, 278n15
Goffman, Irving, 161–62, 172, 179
Goldstein, Melissa (pseudonym), 166–67, 171–72, 178–79
Gonsiorek, John C., 281n6
Gorman, Sally (pseudonym), 187
Gould-Whitmer, Marian (pseudonym), 54–57, 120–23
Gouldner, Alvin, 244–45, 283n22
grandparents, *see* families of origin
Green, G. D., 267n9
Greenland, 36
Griffin, Carolyn W., 272n22
Griswold v. Connecticut (1965), 26
group settings, familism in, 183–85
Gubrium, Jaber, 157, 162, 173, 180, 186

Habermas, Jurgen, 222
Handel, Gerald, 191
Haraway, Donna, 280n36
Hart, Clarice (pseudonym), 150
Hartmann, Heidi, 266n2
Hawaii, 35–36; Supreme Court of, 29, 252n36
Hay, Harry, 41, 258n2
Hayden, Corrine, 228
Hemings, Sally, 224–25, 276n28
Hess, Robert D., 191
heteronormativity, 161; familism and, 174, 180, 188–89; resistance to versus assimilation into, 28–30, 122
heterosexism, sociocultural structure of, 145, 146, 149–50; internalized shame of, 152–56
heterosexual-parent families, 18, 235, 238, 260n1; division of labor in, 94–99, 105, 110–12, 119, 267n8; family values ideology and, 19, 20, 123, 174; gender relations in, 3–8, 11–12, 14, 64, 79, 233–34; ideology of, 212; legal privileges of, 34, 38, 217, 258n63; lesbians and gays in, 25–27, 73, 232, 235,

265n31; neoconventional, 22; object relations in, 263n11; oedipal crisis in, 87–91; pre-oedipal period in, 80–86; primary caregiving in, 65–68, 261n6, 264n13, 265n32; reproductive function of, 24–25; reproductive technologies and, 221, 254n45, 255n47, 277n19; woman-headed; *see also* heteronormativity; patriarchal family; single-mother families
Hitachi, Jocelyn (pseudonym), 154–56, 165–66, 169–70, 185
HIV/AIDS, 33, 127, 173, 219, 242, 260n12, 276nn4, 5, 281n6
Hochschild, Arlie, 97, 105, 119, 186
Holmes, Marsha (pseudonym), 68, 179–80, 182
Holnick, Becky (pseudonym), 177
Holstein, James, 157, 162, 173, 180, 186
housework: equitable allocation of, 103–4, 109–10; marketization of, 101–3, 106, 109
Human Nature and the Social Order (Cooley), 153
Hungary, 36
Hunter, Nan, 30, 34–35

Iceland, 36
ignorance, social power of, 53, 163–64, 260n12
immigration, 36
incest: inadvertent, 201; universal prohibition of, 206, 209
infertility, 11, 221, 254n45, 279n21
insemination, *see* donor insemination
institutional settings, familism in, 175–81
interracial marriage, 149, 210, 252n36
interview techniques, 238–40, 243–46, 269n13
In the Name of the Family (Stacey), 145, 251n6
intimacy, expansion of, 91–92
intrauterine insemination, 279n21
in vitro fertilization, 259n5, 279n21
Israel, 36, 261n6, 265n32
Italian Americans, 136

Jacobson, Brenda (pseudonym), 58, 76, 116–20, 122–23, 151, 152, 156, 167, 174, 193, 270n21
Japanese Americans, 154–55, 165, 240, 273n28
Jefferson, Thomas, 224–25, 279n28
Jews, 105, 141–42, 193, 240
Joffe, Carole, 256n59
Johnson, Carrie (pseudonym), 58, 132–33, 151, 152, 175–77
Johnson, Megan (pseudonym), 129–31, 135–38, 164, 183–85, 272n19
Johnson-Sumerford, D., 267n8

Journal of Reproductive Medicine, 255n49
jurisprudence, *see* legal system
Justice Department, U.S., 260n12

Kaplan, Morris, 30
Keating, Pat (pseudonym), 57, 60–61, 99–100, 173
Kennedy, Rosanne, 35
kinship relations, 10, 14, 15, 22, 271n3, 276n14; of African American families, 65, 274n10; anthropological analysis of, 205–7; biogenic relatedness and, 223–26; conscious, 229–30; custody claims and, 38; with donors, 190–205, 207–10; *see also* extended families; families of origin
known donors, 48–52, 259n10; availability of, 192; extended relations with, 194–200, 224
Kronenberg, Kelly (pseudonym), 46, 48, 50, 133–35
Kurdek, Lawrence, 267n9
Kyle, Jane (pseudonym), 80

labor, division of, 236, 238; equitable allocation versus, 97–111, 234, 267nn8, 9, 268n12; "Rozzie and Harriet" pattern of, 100–101, 111–23; sexual, 8–9, 14, 18, 78–79, 93–97, 233–34, 247n5, 250n3, 282n13
Lanier, Lee (pseudonym), 72–73, 86–87, 131–32, 143–44
laparoscopy, 279n21
Lasch, Christopher, 186
Latinas, 175, 240
Lawrence decision (2003), 12
Left Hand of Darkness (Le Guin), 4
legal system; biogenetic relatedness and, 228; feminist theories of change in, 213–20; implications for reproductive technologies of, 37; privileges of heterosexual families in, 34
Le Guin, Ursula, 3–4
Lesbian and Gay Parenting Handbook, The (Martin), 48
Lévi-Strauss, Claude, 205–10
Levi-Strauss & Company, 41
Lewin, Ellen, 27–28
Life magazine, 40
looking-glass self, 153
Lorca, Federico Garcia, 154, 156
Lorde, Audre, 27
Lotti, Cathy (pseudonym), 43–48, 50, 57, 60, 68–70, 127–29, 188

Lovadas, Madeline (pseudonym), 57, 112–15, 269n20
Loving v. Virginia (1967), 252n36
Lukács, George, 230
Lynch, J., 242, 267n9
Lyon-Martin organization, 31
Lyotard, Jean-François, 20

Mamo, Laura, 279n21, 280n35
Marcus, James E., 283n22
Marcuse, Herbert, 27
marketization of domestic labor, 101–3, 106, 109
marriage, 253n39; elimination of legal status of, 217–18; heterosexual, reconstruction of, 21–22; interracial, 149, 210, 252n36; *see also* same-sex marriage
Marshner, Connie, 19
Martin, April, 48–49
Marxism, 41, 96
masculinity, 91; paternal, 89–90
Massachusetts Institute of Technology (MIT), 277n2
Maternal Thinking (Ruddick), 220
Mattachine Society, 41
Mauss, Marcel, 206
McIntosh, Mary, 173–74
Melanesians, 222, 226
Mesner, Sophie (pseudonym), 62–64, 138–40, 204–5, 210
middle-class families, allocation of labor in, 101–6
Miller, D. A., 159
Million Man March, 19
Minow, Martha, 214
Mitchell, Juliet, 65, 266n1
Mitchell, Valory, 82, 268n9
Mohr, Richard, 30, 253n39
Mueller, Clara (pseudonym), 57, 112–15, 269n20
multiparenting arrangements, 198–200

names, significance of, 59, 93, 117–18, 270n21
National Center for Lesbian Rights (NCLR), 257nn60, 61
Nature (journal), 224
Netherlands, 36
Neutered Mother, The Sexual Family, and Other Twentieth Century Tragedies, The (Finemann), 216
"New Home Economic" analysis, 98

New Jersey, 36
New Right, 19, 173
New York Times, The, 225, 277n2
New Zealand, 36
Norway, 36, 248n7

object choice, sexual, 7
object relations theory, feminist, 64–66, 87–88, 263n11
oedipal period, 79, 80, 83–84, 87–92, 248n8
omnipotent mother, 80, 82, 87
Origin of the Family, Private Property and the State, The (Friedrich), 96
Oryx and Crake (Atwood), 10
"othering," sexual, 83–85
othermothers, 274n10

Pacific Reproductive Services, 254n45
Paltz, Eleanor (pseudonym), 103–4, 140–42, 168, 169, 171, 172, 182
parenting classes, 183
Parents and Friends of Lesbians and Gays (PFLAG), 152, 271n12, 272n22
patriarchal family, 20–23, 211–12, 219, 230, 258n63; feminist and gay critiques of, 26; resistance-assimilation problem and, 28, 29; sexual division of labor in, 233; state sponsorship of, 218
Peplau, L. A., 267n9
Peterson, Kathleen (pseudonym), 67–68, 101–3, 107, 147–49
phallus, representational meanings of, 83
Piercy, Marge, 3
Pirandello, Luigi, 157
"plastic sexuality," 218
playgroups, 183, 185
pleasure principle, 86
Polikoff, Nancy, 29, 122, 215–16
Porzak, Olena (pseudonym), 51–52, 177–78, 196–200
potlatch, 206, 207
poverty, feminization of, 2
pregnancy, 45–47; acclimation of family of origin during, 178; involvement of nonbirth mother during, 59–61; out-of-wedlock, 121–22; working during, 108
premature birth, 138–39
preoedipal period, 79–87
primary caregiving: in heterosexual-parent families, 65–66; in "Rozzie and Harriet" families, 111–12; shared, 66–82

primitive societies, kinship in, 205–6
professional status, 242
Promise Keepers, 19
psychoanalytic theory, 7, 14, 18, 64, 266n33; feminist object-relational revisions of, 64–66; oedipal situation in, 79, 87–92; pre-oedipal situation in, 79–87
public space, familism in, 181–82

"quarter-shift" system, 104–6

racism, 12, 149, 243; institutionalized, 5
Radin, Norma, 261n6, 265n32
Rainbow Flag Health Services, 254n45
Raley, Naomi (pseudonym), 97–98, 101
Rawlins, Marjorie (pseudonym), 62–64, 138–40, 142, 204–5, 210
Reagan, Ronald, 173
reality principle, 85–86
reciprocity, systems of, 206–7, 209
Reilly, M. E., 242, 267n9
Reimann, Renate, 241, 262n7, 268n9
Reproduction of Mothering (Chodorow), 65–66
reproductive technologies, *see* assisted-reproduction technologies; donor insemination
Republican Party, 174
resistance, assimilation versus, 28–30, 122
Resnick, Alana (pseudonym), 103–4, 141–42, 168, 172, 182
Reynolds, Kim, 159
Rich, Adrienne, 26, 65
Richardson, Kim (pseudonym), 73–75, 198–200, 267n9
Risman, Barbara, 267n8
Rivers, Daniel, 8
Roe v. Wade (1973), 19, 256n59
Roesner, Arlene (pseudonym), 105–6, 116, 202–4
role models, male, 90, 91, 265n31
Rothman, Barbara Katz, 276n15
"Rozzie and Harriet" families, 100, 104, 111–23
Rubin, Gayle, 7, 8, 206–8, 212
Ruddick, Sara, 220, 262n7
Ruiz, Jamie (pseudonym), 68, 179–80

same-sex marriage, 11, 29–30, 35–38, 148, 214, 257n59, 282n15; countries recognizing, 1, 36; legalization of, 240, 255n50; prohibition against, 11, 35–36, 210, 231, 252n36
San Francisco General Strike (1934), 41
Scanzoni, John, 22

Schlafly, Phyllis, 19
Schnieder, David, 188
schools, familism in, 178–79
Schwartz, Pepper, 267n9
second-parent adoption, 11, 59, 93, 136, 196, 240, 270n21, 274n10; anonymous donors and, 53; custody challenges to, 258n61; families of origin and, 148–50; home visits required for, 238; legal system and, 37–39
"second shift," 105
Sedgwick, Eve, 168–69, 172, 173, 254n43, 260n12
selection criteria, 234–35, 240
self-insemination, 33
separation-individuation process, 81, 84, 263n11
Seventh Day Adventists, 148
Sex and Sensibility (Stein), 159
sexuality, separation from procreation of, 24, 26, 220–22
sexual orientation, 7
Sexual Politics, Sexual Communities (D'Emilio), 24
sexuo-economic relation, 3, 4
shame, social, 151–52; in Japanese culture, 154–56; rejection of, 153
Shaw, Karen (pseudonym), 105–6, 116, 202–4
Silicon Valley, 41
Simonds, Caitlin (pseudonym), 56–57, 70, 203–4
single-mother families, 9, 248n6, 251n16, 264n31; family values ideology on, 19–20, 174, 251n6; legal issues for, 213, 215, 219; reproductive technologies and, 221
slavery, 274n10
Smith, Katrina (pseudonym), 43–48, 60, 68–70, 127
socialization, 6, 84, 234
social parenthood, 198–200, 274n10, 276n15
sociofamilial identity, 157–89; disclosure strategies for, 164–73; familism and, 173–88; legitimization of birth mothers and, 159–60, 184; public educational role in, 158–59, 161
South Africa, 36
Spain, 36
"species difference," attribution of, 140, 271n13
Sperm Bank of Oakland, 254n45
sperm banks, 53–54, 113
sperm donation, see donor insemination
Stacey, Judith, 145, 251n6
Stack, Carol, 274n10
STDs, 242, 276n5; see also HIV/AIDS

Steckel, Ailsa, 81–85, 87, 263n11
Stein, Arlene, 159, 160
Stein, Gertrude, 41
Stonewall Riot (1969), 19
Strathern, Marilyn, 190, 222–30, 280n36
Strauss, A., 282n12
Stryker, Susan, 259n3
study sample: educational attainment of, 242; income level of, 241–42; lack of racial-ethnic diversity in, 240–41; professional status of, 242; selection criteria for, 234–35; self-selection of, 237–38
suicide, 275n13
Sullivan, Andrew, 122
superovulation, 279n21
Supreme Court, U.S., 1, 12, 26–27, 255n50
Sweden, 261n6, 248n7
symbolic fatherhood, 50–52, 194, 195, 199

Takata, Amy (pseudonym), 154–56, 165–66, 169–71, 185
Taringetti, Nina (pseudonym), 43, 70–72, 262n8
Tarpin, Belinda (pseudonym), 56–57, 70, 186–87, 203–4
Texas, antisodomy law in, 1
Thatcher, Margaret, 173
Time Bind, The (Hochschild), 105, 186
Toklas, Alice B., 41
"Traffic in Women, The" (Rubin), 206
Transformation of Intimacy, The (Giddens), 278n15
transgender movements, 259n3
Trindall, Emily (pseudonym), 43, 70–72, 75, 262n8
Tyson, Jolene (pseudonym), 76–78, 263n9

ultrasound, 222
Unitarians, 136
United Kingdom, 2, 11, 19, 36, 259n5
United Methodist Church, 257n59
United Parcel Service, 99
urbanization, 25
"Uses of the Erotic: Erotic as Power" (Lorde), 27
utopianism, 10; feminist, 3–4

Van Buskirk, James, 259n3
Vermont, 36
Virginia, Supreme Court of, 257n61
Virginia Law Review, 29

Walby, Serena (pseudonym), 58, 132–33, 140, 151, 175–77

Walton, Danielle (pseudonym), 72–73, 86–87, 131–32, 143–44

Wardle, Lynn, 281n6

Weeks, Jeffrey, 22–23

Weiner, Annette, 208

Weinrich, James D., 281n6

Weiss, Marilyn (pseudonym), 58, 76, 116–20, 122–23, 151, 152, 156, 270n21

Weitzman, Lenore J., 266n3

welfare recipients, 251n16

Wellstone, Paul, 252n16

Weston, Kath, 30–32, 124–28, 138, 142, 145–46, 150, 152, 153, 253n41, 270n3, 271nn13, 15, 274n10

What Is Family? (Gubrium and Holstein), 157

Winch, Peter, 236

Wirth, A., 272n22

Wirth, M., 272n22

Wittig, Monique, 3, 4

Wolfson, Evan, 30

working-class families: allocation of labor in, 106–11; of origin, 131

workplace: familism in, 185–88; passing as birth mother in, 171

Writing Culture (Clifford and Marcus) 245, 283n22

Zindosa, Gretchen (pseudonym), 42, 177, 195–96, 200

Compositor: Binghamton Valley Composition, LLC
Indexer: Ruth Elwell
Text: 11/14 Adobe Garamond
Display: Adobe Garamond/Gill Sans Book